1001 IDEAS FOR TRIMWORK

1001 IDEAS FOR TRIMWORK

Wayne Kalyn

CREATIVE HOMEOWNER®, Upper Saddle River, New Jersey

CREATIVE HOMEOWNER®

A Division of Federal Marketing Corp.
Upper Saddle River, NJ

1001 Ideas for Trimwork
Managing Editor: Fran J. Donegan
Layout: David Geer
Editorial Assistants: Evan Lambert (proofreading); Robyn Poplasky, Lauren Manoy (photo research)
Indexer: Schroeder Indexing Services
Front Cover Photography: Brian Vanden Brink, architect: Tom Catalano; insets *top to bottom* illustration: Robert LaPointe; Jessie Walker; illustration: Robert LaPointe; www.davidlivingston.com
Back Cover Photography: *top right* www.carolynbates.com; *bottom right* Brian Vanden Brink
Back Cover Illustrations: *left all* Mario Ferro; *center both* Robert LaPointe

Creative Homeowner
VP/Publisher: Brian Toolan
VP/Editorial Director: Timothy O. Bakke
Production Manager: Kimberly H. Vivas
Art Director: David Geer
Managing Editor: Fran J. Donegan

1001 Ideas for Trimwork, First Edition
Library of Congress Catalog Card Number: 2005924461
ISBN-10: 1-58011-260-9
ISBN-13: 978-1-58011-260-4

Manufactured in the United States of America

Current Printing (last digit)
10 9 8 7 6 5 4 3 2

CREATIVE HOMEOWNER®
A Division of Federal Marketing Corp.
24 Park Way
Upper Saddle River, NJ 07458
www.creativehomeowner.com

Metric Equivalents

Length

1 inch	25.4 mm
1 foot	0.3048 m
1 yard	0.9144 m
1 mile	1.61 km

Area

1 square inch	645 mm^2
1 square foot	0.0929 m^2
1 square yard	0.8361 m^2
1 acre	4046.86 m^2
1 square mile	2.59 km^2

Volume

1 cubic inch	16.3870 cm^3
1 cubic foot	0.03 m^3
1 cubic yard	0.77 m^3

Common Lumber Equivalents

Sizes: Metric cross sections are so close to their U.S. sizes, as noted below, that for most purposes they may be considered equivalents.

Dimensional lumber	1 × 2	19 × 38 mm
	1 × 4	19 × 89 mm
	2 × 2	38 × 38 mm
	2 × 4	38 × 89 mm
	2 × 6	38 × 140 mm
	2 × 8	38 × 184 mm
	2 × 10	38 × 235 mm
	2 × 12	38 × 286 mm
Sheet sizes	4 × 8 ft.	1200 × 2400 mm
	4 × 10 ft.	1200 × 3000 mm
Sheet thicknesses	¼ in.	6 mm
	⅜ in.	9 mm
	½ in.	12 mm
	¾ in.	19 mm
Stud/joist spacing	16 in. o.c.	400 mm o.c.
	24 in. o.c.	600 mm o.c.

Capacity

1 fluid ounce	29.57 mL
1 pint	473.18 mL
1 quart	1.14 L
1 gallon	3.79 L

Weight

1 ounce	28.35g
1 pound	0.45kg

Temperature

Fahrenheit = Celsius × 1.8 + 32
Celsius = Fahrenheit – 32 × 5⁄9

Nail Size & Length

Penny Size	Nail Length
2d	1"
3d	1¼"
4d	1½"
5d	1¾"
6d	2"
7d	2¼"
8d	2½"
9d	2¾"
10d	3"
12d	3¼"
16d	3½"

Acknowledgments

The author and publisher would like to thank the following companies for their assistance in preparing this book: Forester Moulding & Lumber, Inc., Bendix Mouldings, Inc., and Ornamental Mouldings.

Contents

Introduction

Adding trimwork is a decorating technique that can dramatically change the look of your home. Whether you are building a new house or remodeling an existing home, including trimwork and molding in your plans adds character and a level of detail that other decorating techniques cannot match. Use *1001 Ideas for Trimwork* to select molding for your home.

The molding and trimwork found in older homes helps identify the architectural style of the house and adds a look that is not possible with other decorating techniques.

At its most basic level, trimwork serves to hide gaps between walls and floors, around doors and windows, and where walls meet ceilings. But if you have ever visited a home that contains distinctive trimwork, you have no doubt noticed that the molding, columns, ceiling medallions, and fireplace mantels add a richness and texture to the room that cannot be accomplished with paint, wallpaper, and furniture alone.

In the past, most homes contained decorative trimwork. Builders of even modest buildings included trimwork and molding details that reflected the decorating style of the day. All of the housing styles that we think of as being American contained distinctive trimwork designs. In fact, distinguishing one style of house from another is often based on the types of molding and trimwork found in each.

Things began to change in home construction during the postwar building boom of the 1950s. Builders reduced the amount of trimwork they incorporated into the houses they built, which cut costs and allowed the builders to build more houses faster. This left a generation of housing stock that lacks the distinctive look of houses built earlier.

If you live in one of these houses, you have the opportunity to enhance your home by replacing or installing new trimwork. *1001 Ideas for Trimwork* contains the ideas you can use in your own home.

Above Simple head treatments over the door and bed alcove add distinction.

Below Decorative pillars are becoming more common in today's homes.

Trimwork Choices

When selecting trimwork for your home, you will make a number of decisions—what rooms will get a new molding treatment, what types of trimwork are available, and what styles and designs will work best in your home.

1001 Ideas for Trimwork helps you answer all of those questions. The book is divided into three main sections: "The Basics of Trimwork," "Trimwork from the Bottom Up," and "Trimwork in Today's Home."

The "Basics of Trimwork," beginning on page 11, will get you started on selecting trimwork and molding. Divided into three chapters, the section begins by showing how to select trimwork to fit the design of your home. The second chapter, "Trimwork Options," beginning on page 48, introduces the different types of molding available. The last

Right Decorative molding helps set the mood around this inviting window seat.

Below right Trimwork makes a grand design statement on this staircase.

chapter in the section, "Tools and Techniques," beginning on page 78, shows the tools used to install trimwork if you plan on doing the work yourself.

Section 2 "Trimwork from the Bottom Up," beginning on page 90, covers trimwork and molding types in more detail. In this section, you will find ideas for baseboards; wall treatments such as wainscoting, chair rails, and wall frames; columns and pilasters; stairs; and ceiling treatments, including cornice and crown moldings, decorative beams, and ceiling medallions. Each chapter covers dozens of design ideas, a look at scores of molding designs, or profiles, and tips you can use on your own project.

The last section, "Trimwork in Today's Home," beginning on page 222, takes you on a tour throughout the home, showing how trimwork and molding can work in every room of your home.

Part 1

The Basics of Trimwork

Chapter 1

Designing with Trimwork

Choosing the right trimwork dramatically contributes to the overall design scheme of a room. It can also add character to a space without the need to change its basic structure. Trim comes in a wide range of profiles and sizes that can enhance the look of doors, ceilings, walls, and floors. Selecting the right style will make all the difference in your home.

In the past, homes were built with a wealth of architectural ornamentation that lent character, beauty, and substance to their interiors. Today the prevalent style is much simpler, and few new houses display the kind of detail that was once standard. But trimwork can have an almost magical effect on the look and character of your home.

The architectural style of your home and your personal taste will play large parts in selecting trim, but there are other considerations that should guide your decision. Above all, the size and scale of the trim should be appropriate for the room. Low ceilings (8 feet or less) have a harder time supporting large or elaborate ceiling molding (called cornice). Plain, slender molding disappears in a large room. The scale of a molding relates to its profile as well as its size. Deep and heavy detailing creates bold shadow lines and has greater visual presence than a subtle profile.

Coordinating the various moldings with one another and with other room elements lends a sense of balance and unity that brings together any design scheme.

Arched ceiling and window casing open up this large bank of windows. Note the strip lighting installed behind the crown molding.

1 Decorative corner jams add architectural flourish to a door casing.

2 A pilaster enhances the stair railing while an extended cornice lengthens the hallway.

3 The arched trim crowning the door casing creates a formal, dramatic tone.

Trimwork as a Design Element

Trim and molding not only hide gaps and dress up corners but also set the tone of a room's design. Molding used to trim doors, windows, and other openings is called casing. It is commonly used for chair rails, cabinet trim, and other decorative purposes. Cornices create a decorative transition between walls and ceilings and work especially well in rooms with high ceilings. They are often combined with other moldings to form decorative mantels and frames.

Baseboard molding protects the bottom of a wall from wear and tear and hides irregularities where the wall and floor meet. Depending on the choice, it can also reinforce the design elements in the room. Wall frames stick out from the wall, creating a striking three-dimensional appearance. Wainscoting can impart a country look to kitchens and bathrooms or a more formal appearance to living or dining rooms. Pillars and pilasters are architectural elements that can add a memorably classical look.

3

1

Design Tip **Mixing Styles**

Today's homes tend to be eclectic, giving a homeowner the freedom to mix trimwork styles. The size and proportion of a room, as well as the furnishings in it, are important when selecting architectural details. Rely on existing styles in your home to determine which details work best.

1 Arched trimwork in the entryway provides a counterpoint to the rectangular table and windows. A coffered ceiling defines its lines.

2 Traditional window casing and shutters echo and reinforce the furnishings' formal tone.

Popular Profiles

Greek and Roman details are a part of so many decorating styles that it's hard to find ornamental trim without some kind of classical design. The ogee shape, for instance, appears on everything from interior trimwork to exterior cornices to milled table edges. Here are some of the basic molding shapes and motifs that have withstood the test of time.

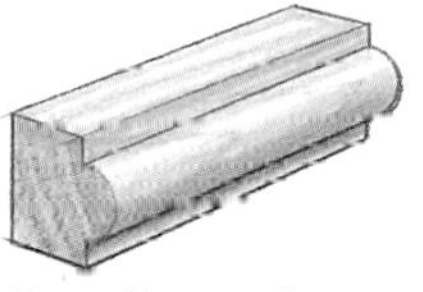

Torus/Astragal

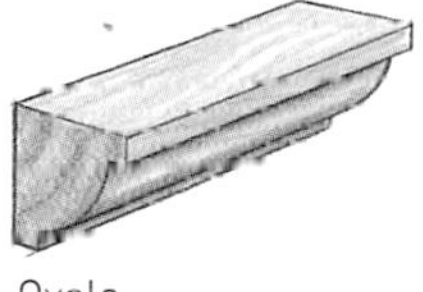

Ovolo

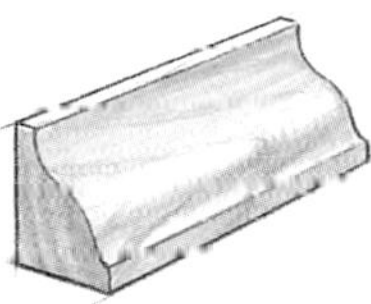

Wall Molding

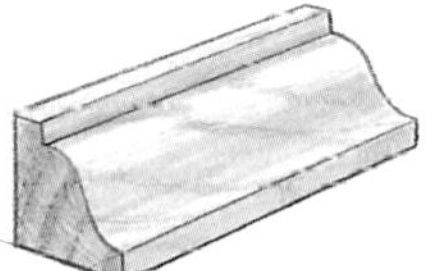

Ogee

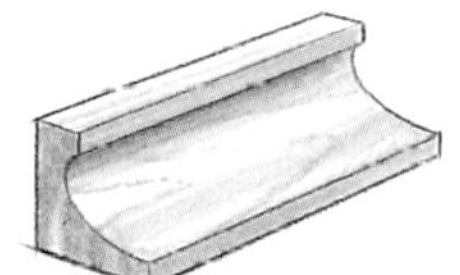

Scotia

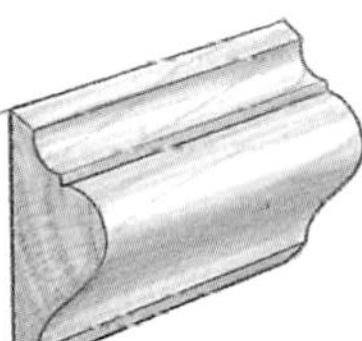

Panel Molding

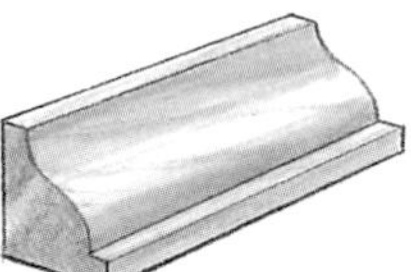

Reverse Ogee

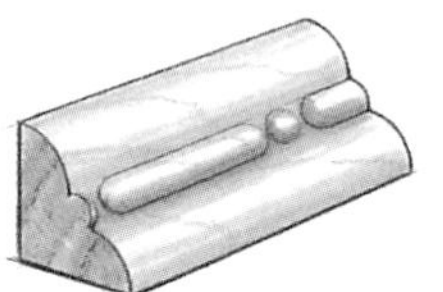

Bead-and-Reel

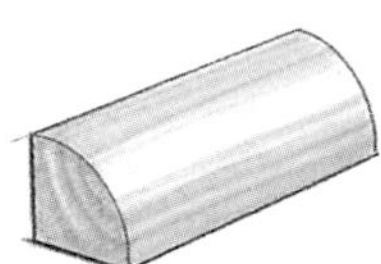

Quarter-Round

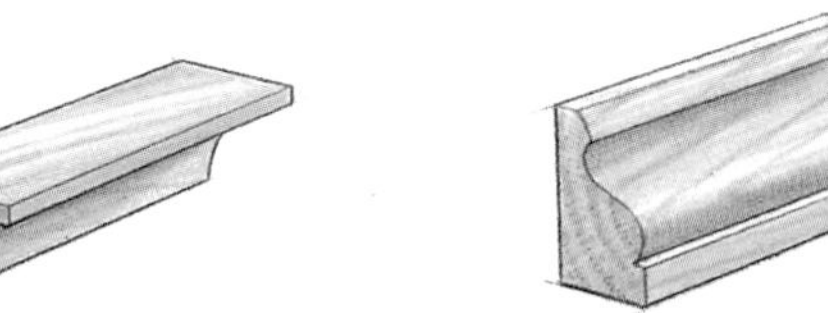

Cavetto

Band Molding

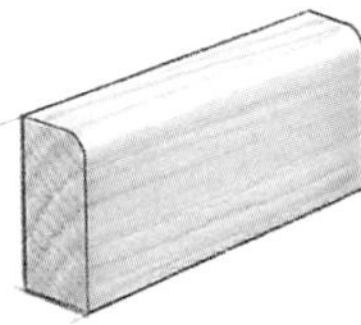

Bullnose

Fret

Egg-and-Dart

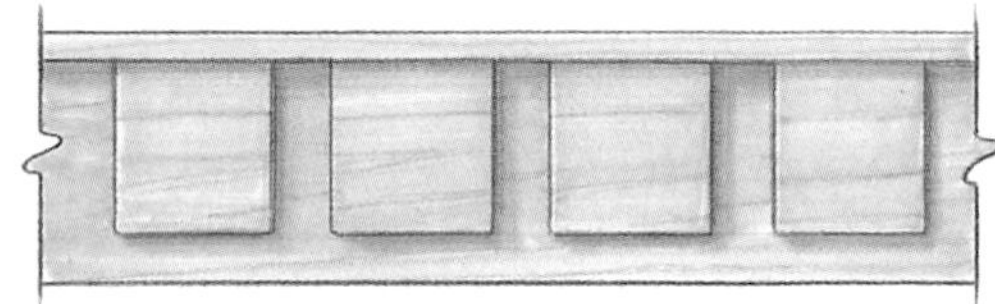

Dentil

Using the Color Wheel

The color wheel is the designer's most useful tool for combining colors. Basically, it presents the spectrum of pigment hues as a circle. The primary colors (yellow, blue, and red) are combined to form the remaining hues (orange, green, and purple). The following are the most often used configurations for creating color schemes using two, three, or four colors.

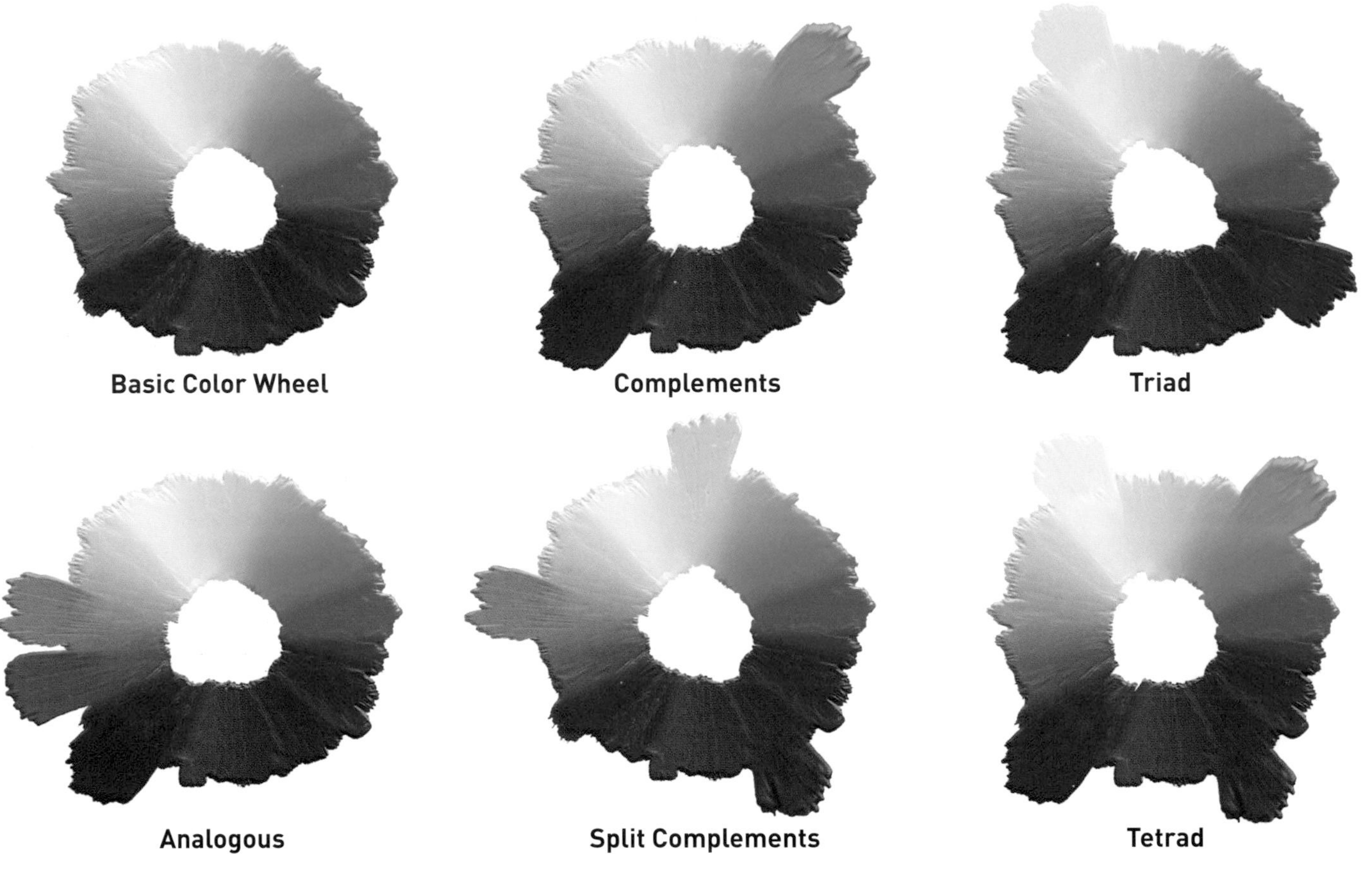

Basic Color Wheel **Complements** **Triad**

Analogous **Split Complements** **Tetrad**

Trimwork and Wall Color

Use color, pattern, and print to play up the visual tension between trimwork and the "filling wall," the area between chair rail, cornice, and crown molding. Because warm colors seem to advance, you can use them to make a large room cozy or to draw attention to an interesting element such as trimwork. Use cool colors, on the other hand, to downplay an element.

Paint for walls, ceilings, and trimwork comes in a variety of finishes—high gloss, semigloss, eggshell, or flat (matte). Use semigloss finish on trimwork to make it stand out against a flat finish wall. Remember, trimwork should not be the focus of the room, but rather a subtle but pleasing detail.

1. The olive green window and door casing and shelves are a striking contrast to the amber walls.
2. The heavy ceiling cornice is painted a complementary color, adding warmth and a grand feel to this space.
3. For the sake of design harmony, it's important to coordinate colors in adjoining rooms.

1

2

3

Classic Paint Schemes

The three most popular paint schemes are traditional, monochromatic, and neoclassic. Traditional involves two colors, usually off-white for trim and a moderate to darker harmonious or contrasting color for the walls. Monochromatic uses different values of the same hue—one on trim and another on the wall to create either a subtle or dramatic contrast. Neoclassic uses just one color, one value. The paint scheme you choose will depend on the style of the room and the look you hope to achieve.

1

2

1 The monochromatic paint scheme creates a dreamlike effect between entryway and the adjoining room.

2 The traditional scheme contrasts an ivory cornice, casing, and wall frames with earth-toned walls.

1

2

1 The red brick walls and portico supported by columns are from the Federal period.

2 Trompe l'oeil on the walls and a heavy ceiling cornice are representative of the Georgian period.

3 Gingerbread fretwork lining the roof's gables are unmistakably Victorian.

4 The Georgian style depended on bold classic ornamentation from the Greeks and Romans.

Trimwork and Period Homes

Today's most popular decorating styles lean toward traditional features. Few people stick strictly to one look, instead preferring to combine elements of more than one related style. Formal traditional-style decorating may include elements from the eighteenth century's English Georgian period or American Federal periods, as well as elements from the formal Victorian style of the nineteenth century. Informal interiors may include a combination of Country styles (typically American, English, and French), informal Victorian, and Arts and Crafts (including Mission- and Stickley-style designs).

4

3

Period Pieces

The following architectural styles—from the Georgian period to Colonial Revival—inspired the creation or popular adaptation of many of the architectural details available to homeowners today:

Georgian style was marked by stout columns, bold cornices and arches, and other classical features, such as doorways trimmed with pilasters and pediments or entablatures. Fireplaces were adorned with classical details as well.

Federal style used slender columns or pilasters supporting graceful elliptical arches, and wall friezes that were patterned on botanical themes. Ceilings often held medallions.

Greek Revival walls were adorned with a large baseboard and cornice molding. Tall walls were trimmed with fairly plain reeded or fluted molding.

Victorian rooms were full of ornament, using dark-stained woods like oak and mahogany. Ceilings were often bordered by a bold cornice. Tripartite arrangements, in which a baseboard, chair rail, and picture rail created three distinct areas, were common.

The **Craftsman** period preferred simplicity and harmony over excessive ornamentation. Craftsman interiors were open-plan yet extremely cozy, with rooms in main living areas being divided by beautiful wood columns. Wainscoting was often used.

Colonial Revival had minimal woodwork—simple baseboards and crown moldings, perhaps a chair rail, and plain door and window trim.

1

2

Trimwork and Period Homes

1 Using many styles of trimwork, right down to the pickets on the fence, creates the character of a home.

2 The country design of this dining room is reinforced by the post-and-beam ceiling.

3 This Federal style mantel incorporates a florid frieze and graceful columns into its design.

4 This Arts & Crafts beauty uses trim to produce balance and symmetry on the exterior as well as the interior.

1

1 The baseboard pairs well with the window casing and completes the tall rectangular wall frames.

2 The striking window and door casings help tie in all the trimwork in this country kitchen.

3 A richly decorated overmantel, capped by a wide mirror, makes an elegant design statement.

4 Think of base trim as a support for what is above it, as is the case with this wainscoting.

Baseboard Styles

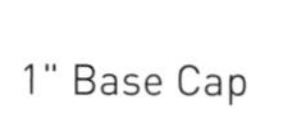

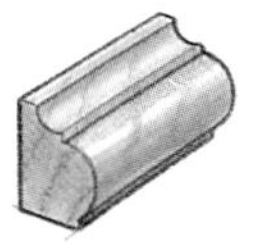

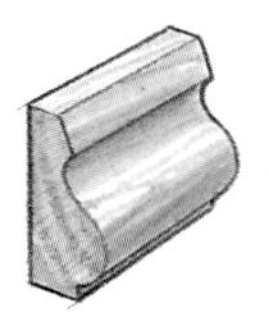

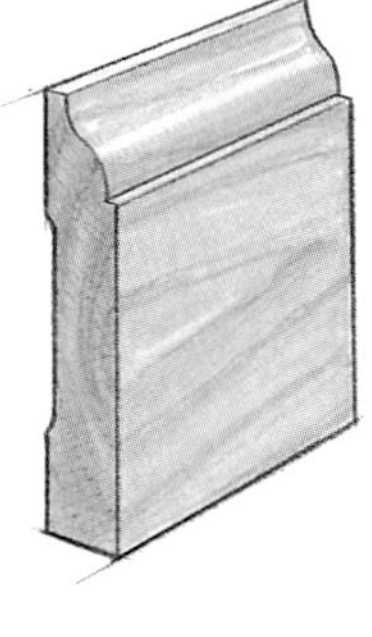

3-Piece Base

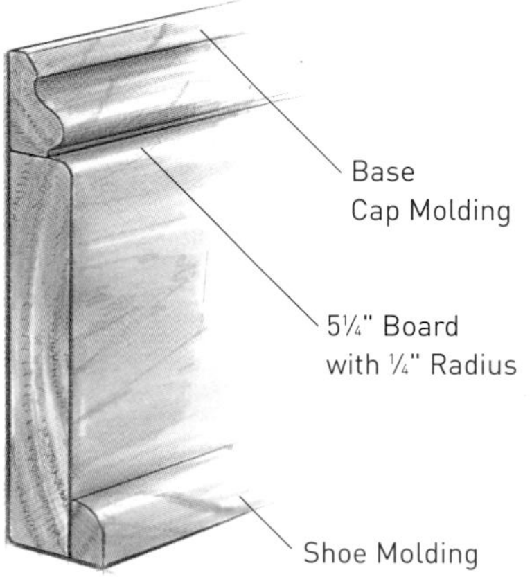

3-Piece Base

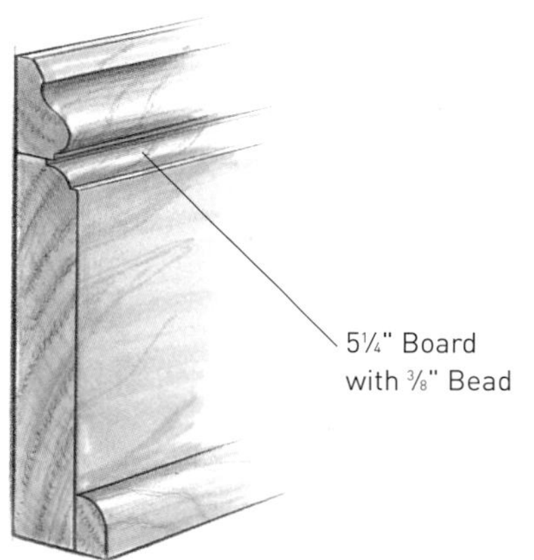

4-Piece Base

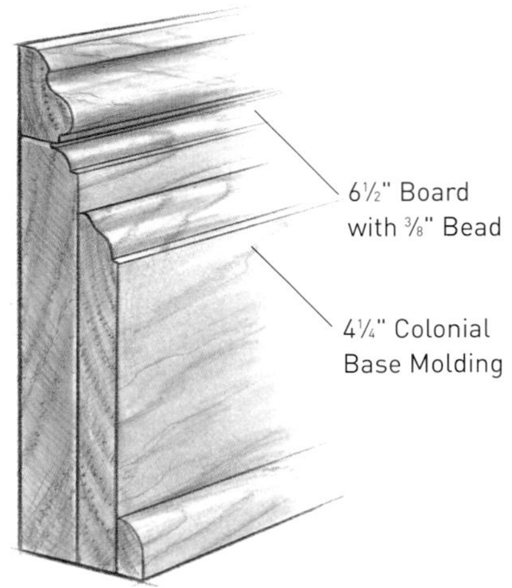

2

3

4

1

2

1 Wainscoting and picture railing can be dressed up with wide shelves.

2 A coffered ceiling and a mantel shelf allow a charming display of possessions.

3 Run wainscoting higher than chair-rail height to add detail to a small room.

4 A picture rail and cornice echo the elegant furnishings and lavish ceiling details.

3

4

Styles of Chair Rail, Picture Rail, and Frieze Molding

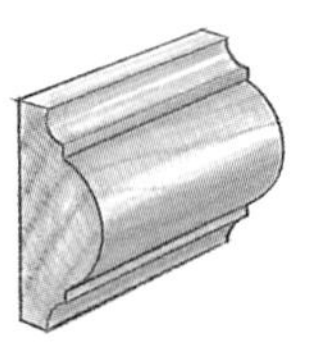

2" Chair Rail

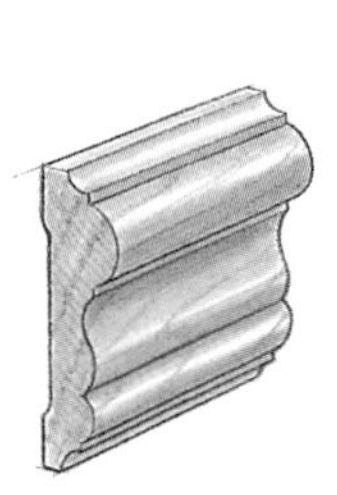

2¾" Chair Rail

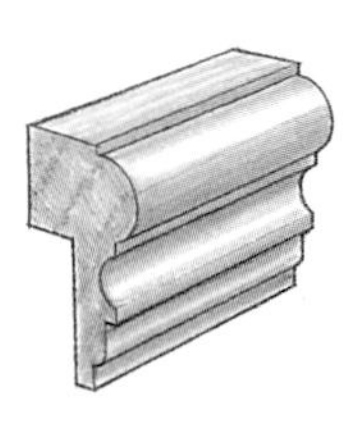

2¼" Wainscot Cap

3-Piece Chair Rail

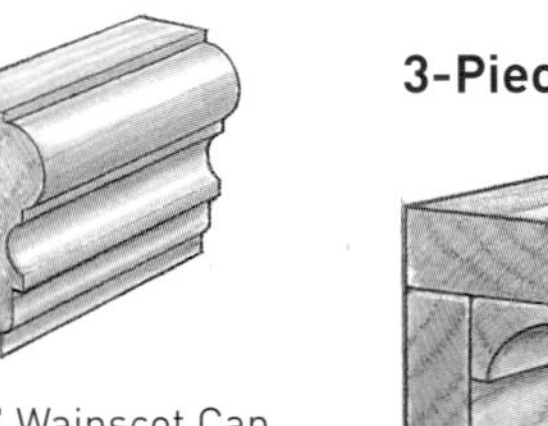

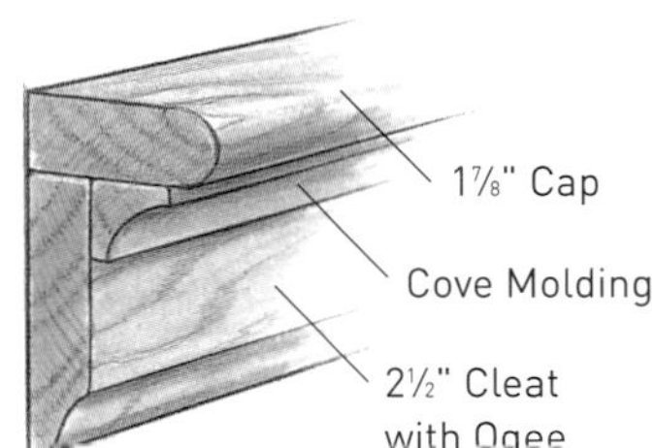

2-Piece Chair Rail

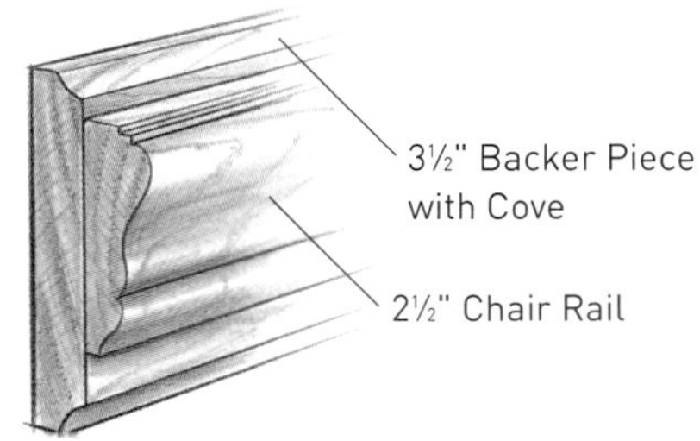

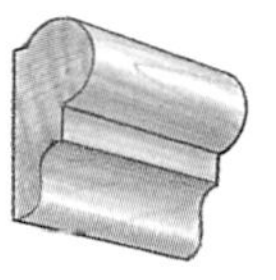

1¾" Picture Rail

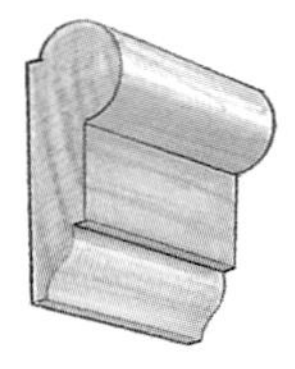

2½" Picture Rail

Frieze

Frieze

1

2

3

1 Wall and cornice molding make this large room more intimate.

2 A plate rail can provide visual relief in a room heavy with trimwork.

3 A plate rail sitting atop wainscoting provides an eye-catching focal point.

Plate-Rail Shelf with Bracket

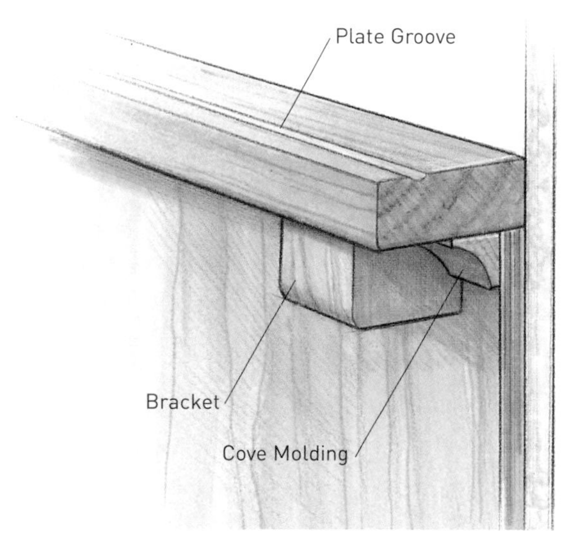

Plate-Rail Shelf with Cove

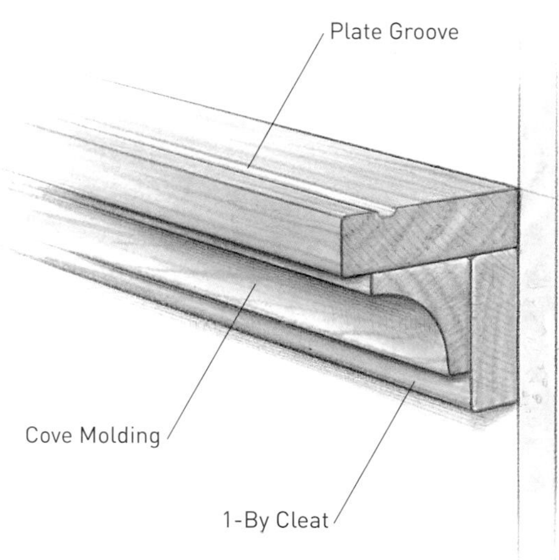

Design Tip **Dressing Up Clamshell Casings**

Most modern homes have ranch or clamshell molding, designed to have a plain, streamlined profile. If you don't want to replace it with more architecturally ornate molding, you can add visual interest to basic molding by contrasting its color from the walls. If you've used a flat paint on the wall, use a high gloss on the molding to provide visual interest. Special paint treatments, like sponging or marbleizing, can also give clamshell character.

1 An arched passageway creates a counterpoint to the linear wall frames.

2 Pilaster style door casing adds a special feel to this doorway.

3 Building up trimwork turns a double-hung window into a focal point.

4 Arching grill work and angular casing dress up this ornate window even more.

1

2

3

4

Components of Door and Window Surrounds

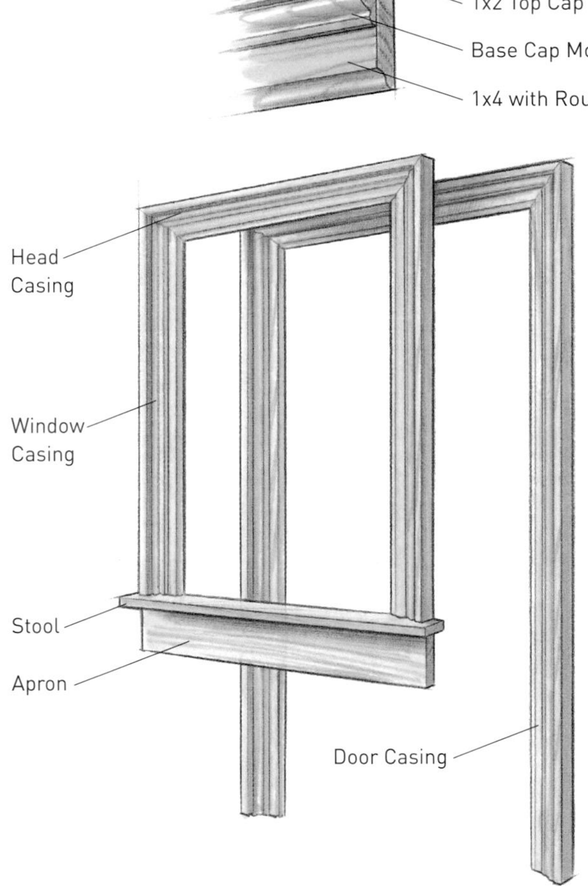

Three-Piece Victorian-Style Mitered Casing

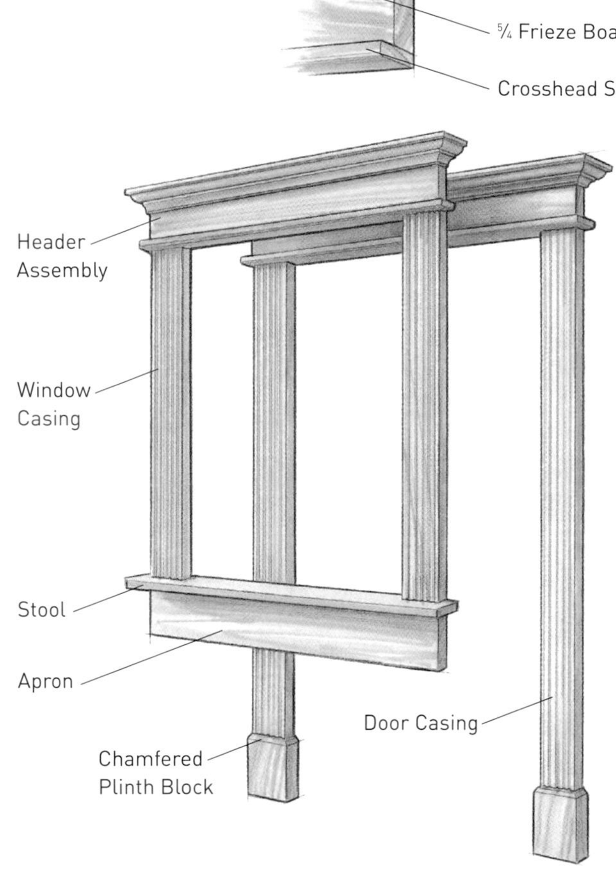

Fluted Casings with Decorative Head

1

1 Combining casing styles creates an elegant frame for these large, prominent windows.

2 The kitchen window seat and casing pick up the curvilinear theme of the wood steps.

3 The interior window and passageway create a seamless transition to the adjoining room.

4 Create eye appeal with a deft display of geometric and linear shapes.

2

3

4

Classical Column Styles

Ionic Column with Entablature

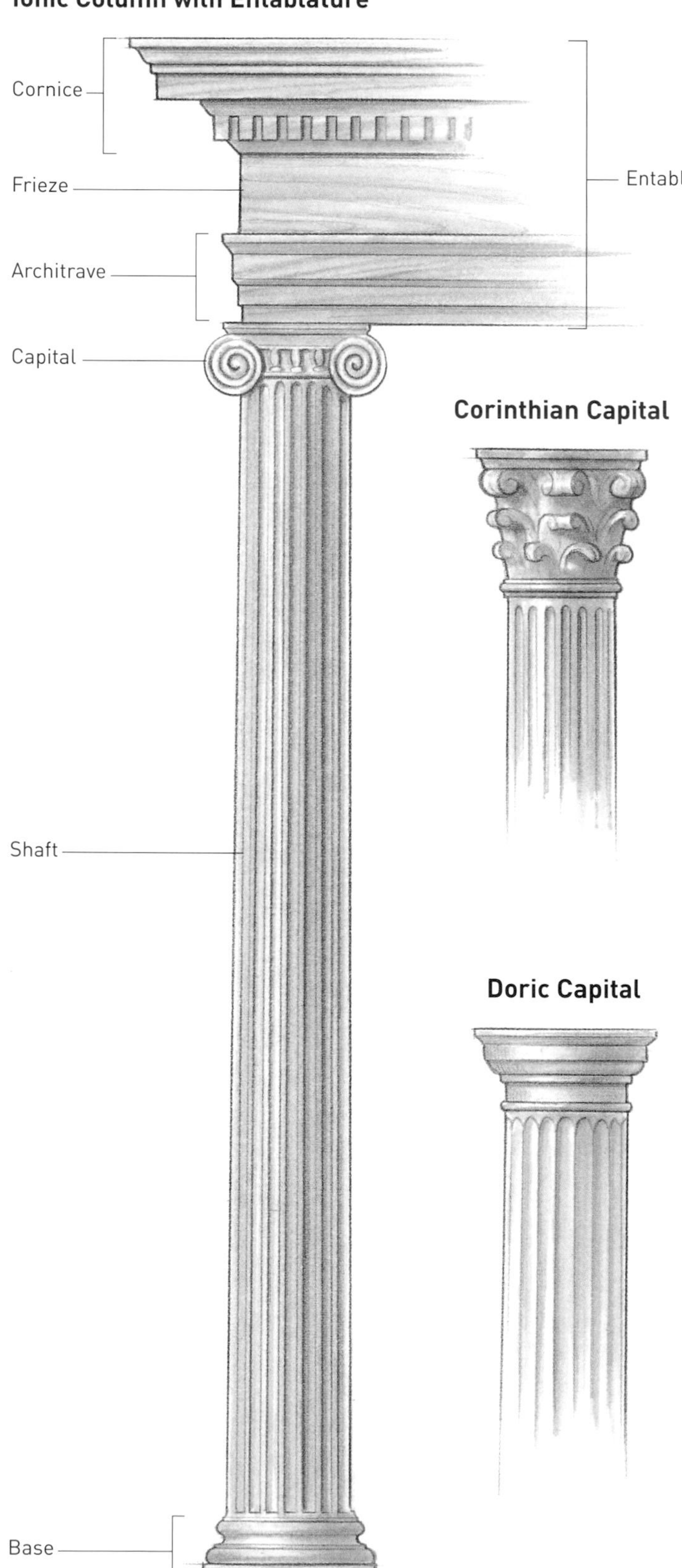

1 The mantel's graceful fluted column punctuates the lines of the traditional wainscoting.

2 Doric columns create a grand, memorable passageway into a large sitting room.

3 Pilasters, a close cousin of the column, and curving grill work dramatize this arching window.

3

1

2

Parts of Stairs

There is more to a staircase than the steps you tread on. Here is a quick course in its other parts:

Stringers. The boards on both sides of the step that support it from below or from the ends.

Treads and risers. The tread is the horizontal part of the step that you walk on and the riser is the vertical part between the treads.

Skirtboard. Where the step runs along a wall. It serves the same purpose as a baseboard.

Balustrades. All the parts belonging to the staircase railing are collectively known as balustrades, which consist of newels (the primary supports for the railing), balusters, and the railing.

3

1 A grand staircase is often the first thing that meets people when they enter the home.

2 The geometric wall frame treatments invite a visitor to climb the stairs.

3 A simple Arts and Crafts-inspired staircase evokes period charm.

Design Tip **Crown Molding and Ceiling Height**

You might be concerned that extensive trimwork will make small rooms feel even smaller. In fact, the opposite occurs. Through a phenomenon called "geometric illusion," trimwork often makes a room appear larger and wider. Long horizontal lines, for example, can cause an observer to feel that a room is longer or wider than it really is. Likewise, long vertical lines can make a low ceiling appear higher than it actually is.

2

1

4

1 An elaborate cornice and mirrored mantel accentuate the drama of this high-ceilinged living room.

2 Crown molding makes a strong design statement above the arched window and door.

3 The cornice serves as a handsome break between the wallpaper and the painted ceiling.

4 A playful mix of curved and linear trimwork liven up this hallway.

Crown & Cornice Styles

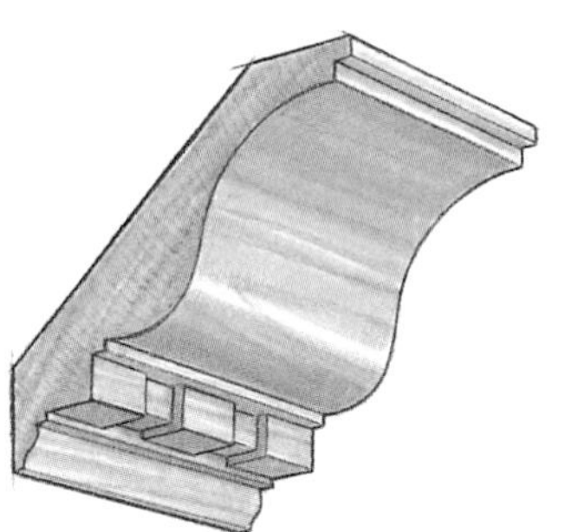
4½" Cornice with Dentil

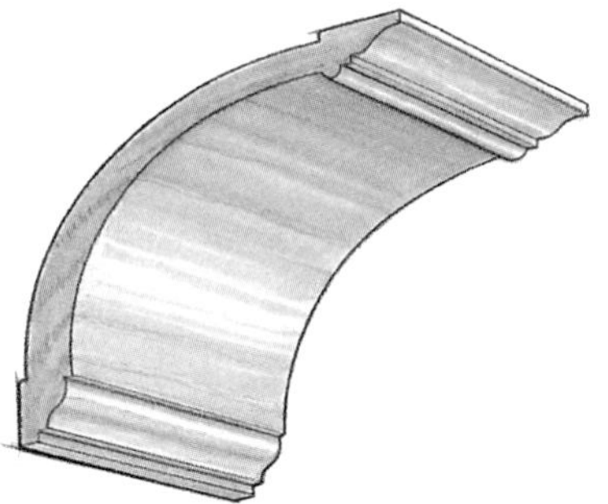
5" Cornice with Cove

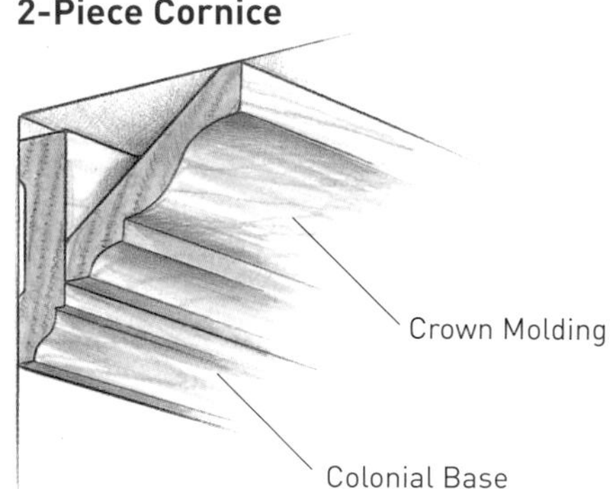

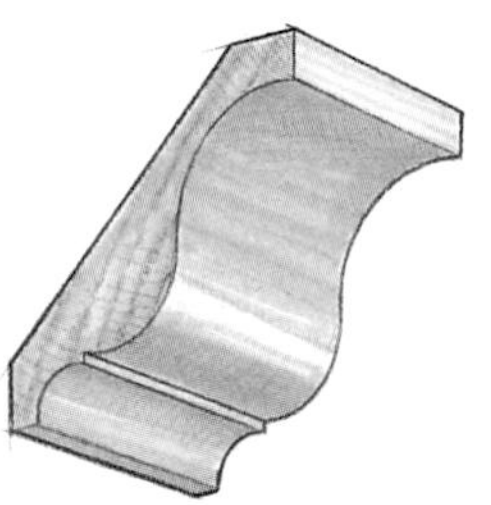
3$^{11}/_{16}$" Crown Molding

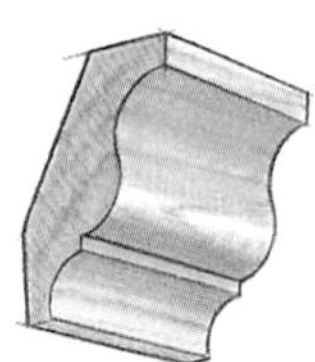
2" Crown Molding

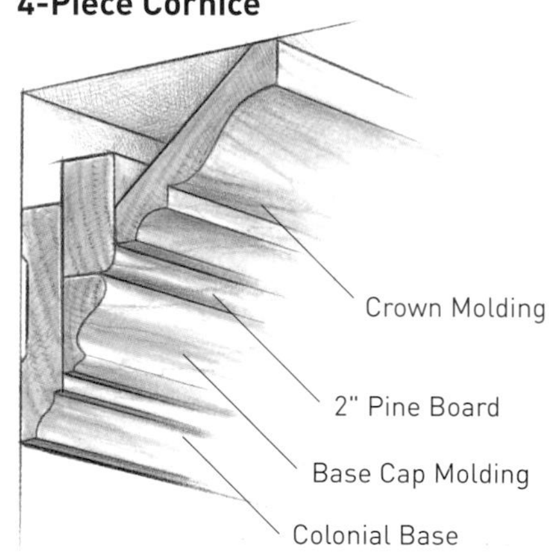

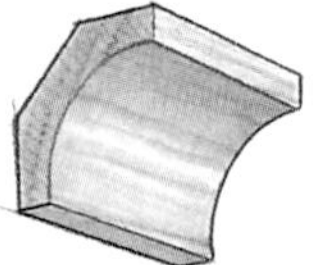
Cove Molding

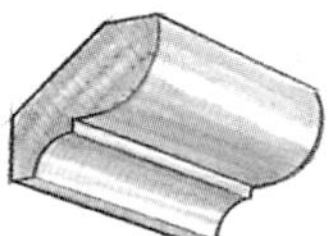
Bed Molding

1 Simple crown molding completes this cozy space and echoes the chair rail.

2 Highlighting the detail of this cornice with light paint provides a graceful transition between ceiling and wall.

2

1

2

3

1 The parquet-like ceiling sets the tone for the trimwork.

2 The detailed ceiling draws the eye to the dramatic window view.

3 The shelves create a strong horizontal and vertical element.

4 A detailed ceiling medallion reflects the ornate design of the chandelier.

5 The carved fretwork adds delicate drama to this passageway.

6 A graceful niche transforms a plain wall into an eye-catching space.

Chapter 2

Trimwork Options

Learning to decorate with trimwork requires a basic understanding of the principles of design and how to apply them. All of the components in a room must relate to one another—and to the space itself—to achieve good design. For some people, this understanding comes naturally. Luckily for the rest of us, the fundamentals are not difficult to learn.

The architectural style of your home and your personal taste will play large parts in selecting trim, but there are other considerations that should guide your decision. Above all, the size and scale of the trim should be appropriate for the room. Low ceilings (8 feet or less) have a harder time supporting large cornices than 10- or 12-foot ceilings.

Just as a plain, slender molding tends to disappear in a large room, a small room can become overwhelmed by large, elaborate trimwork. The scale of a molding relates to its profile as well as its size. Deep and heavy detailing creates bold shadow lines and has greater visual presence than a subtle profile. This can greatly impact the appearance of your room.

Coordinating the various moldings of a room with one another and with other room elements lends an important sense of balance and unity to a design scheme. Walls with multiple moldings, such as baseboard, chair rail, and crown, will look best if their sizes and scales are proportionate and decorative aspects complementary.

Trimwork should be the right size for the room and have both the correct scale and proportion in relation to other design elements. Attention to this detail will ensure design harmony.

Door casings can be built up with molding, including an outer strip of backband molding that creates multiple reveals.

Trimwork Materials

When choosing wood trim, the way you plan to finish the material can help you decide the best materials to use. If you plan to paint, use a paint-grade softwood such as pine, poplar, or aspen. Even less expensive is finger-joined stock, which is trim made up of small pieces of wood forced together with finger-like joinery. Profiles made of medium-density fiberboard (MDF) also accept a painted finish.

If you prefer to retain the natural beauty of the wood grain with a stain or clear finish, choose wood made from knot-free softwood or a hardwood such as oak, maple, or cherry. For a rustic look, you might consider trim made from knotty pine and finished clear or with a diluted whitewash.

An additional option for painted or stained trim is synthetic polymer molding. Made of various urethane materials, the lightweight trimwork is easy to cut and install and can be painted or stained with nonpenetrating stain or gel. Some manufacturers offer flexible polymer molding for trimming around curves.

1

1 Molding is available in thousands of profiles and dozens of wood species.

2 Because the owners opted for a classic white finish, the designer specified paint-grade softwood.

3 This beautiful frieze, crown, and picture rail dissolve into each other as if they were one piece of trim.

1

Smart Tip **Where to Buy Trimwork**

Most standard moldings are available in home centers and lumberyards. But when your trim needs to go beyond the standard selection, you might have difficulty finding what you need. If this is the case, try a custom-millwork shop, mail-order outlet, or Internet site that caters to woodworkers. These sources can often help you design a custom profile or can match a sample of old trim that you provide.

2

1 The wall frame and plate rail make this dining area special.

2 Urethane moldings can consist of elaborate details.

3 Trimwork with a clear finish imparts a simple beauty to a room.

4 Combining trim profiles provides architectural drama to a doorway.

3

4

1

Finishing Options

Because walls are the largest surfaces in a room, they influence the style and mood of an interior. For dramatic effect, use color, pattern, and paint to play up the visual tension between the trimwork and "filling wall," the area between a chair rail and the cornice and crown moldings.

The options are many in terms of how you finish off the molding and the wall. Prime the trimwork first and then use a contrasting color to make paint-grade trim stand out from a wall with a flat finish. There is a full range of paint finishes you can use on the trimwork to create spectacular effects—such as eggshell, satin, semigloss, and high gloss. Using a dark stain on hardwood molding can accomplish the same goal.

Decorative paint techniques such as sponging or rag rolling can lend memorable grace notes to a plain wall. Use wall panels to frame the decorative finish.

The power of wallpaper lies in its capacity to grace walls with highly stylized vignettes of color, texture, and pattern. Classical and historical motifs and faux silk patterns such as moiré or damask look particularly at home in traditional settings that include trimwork.

4

1 Cream-colored molding contributes to the warm colors in this living room.

2 Contrasting-colored trimwork and a wall-paper border lighten the mood.

3 The charm of naturally finished trimwork and furniture opens up the space.

4 Use light and dark stains to create drama between trimwork and furnishings.

1

2

3

4

1 The four types of paint finish—flat, eggshell, semigloss, and gloss range from matte to shiny.

2 Using one color wall and trim creates a seamless look that opens up a room.

3 Using color to highlight architectural detail provides a room with plenty of eye appeal.

4 Crisp off-white casing with light green walls tie together the palettes of the different rooms.

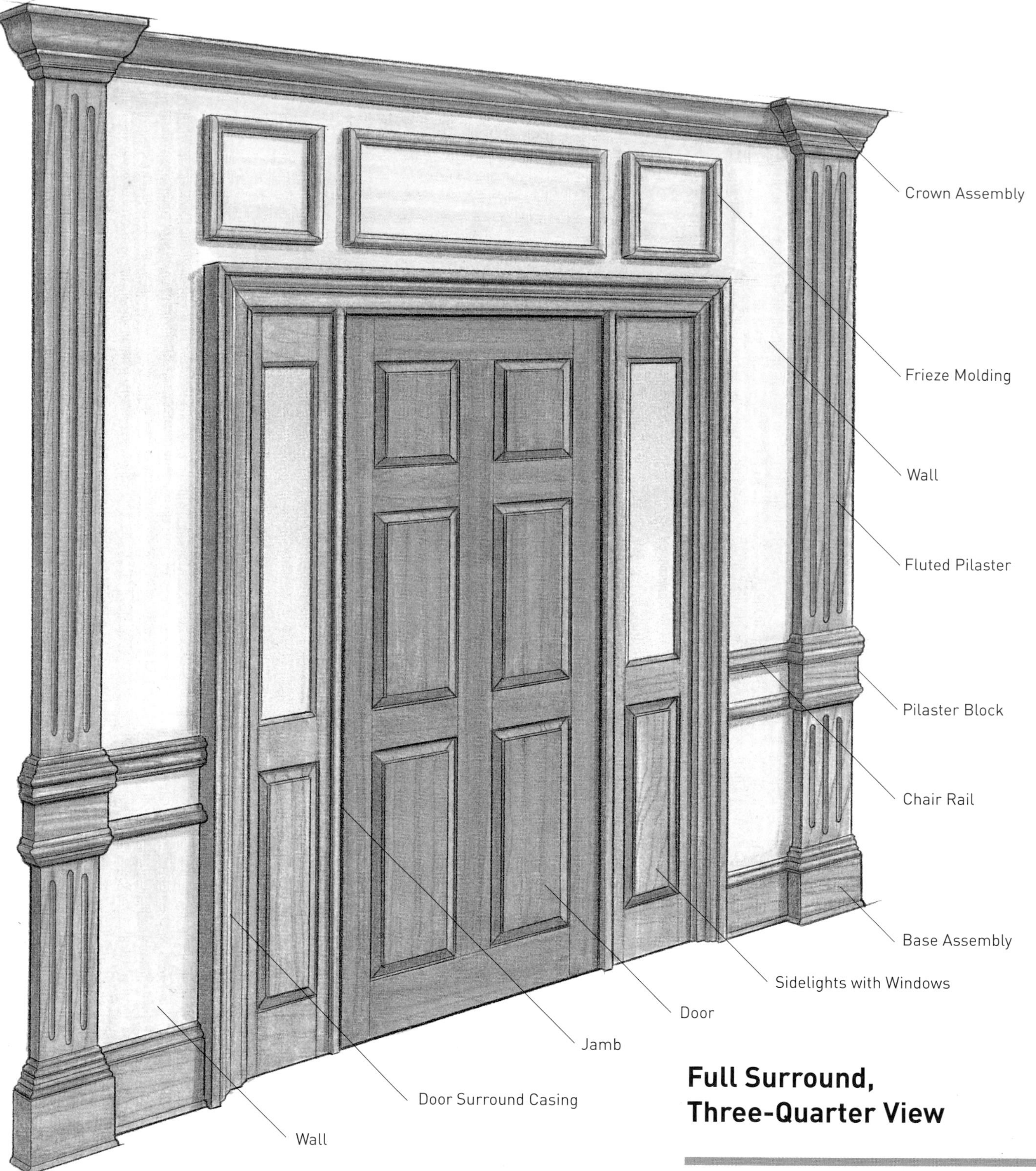

Full Surround, Three-Quarter View

Molding Profiles

Most molding is made of wood, though profiles made from MDF or urethane are available. A single style of molding can be used in a room, or it can be built up with other complementary trimwork styles or dressed up with decorative architectural elements. Combining single-piece moldings with custom-milled profiles is an easy way to create attractive multipiece profiles, and it is a good way to obtain a unique trimwork design. Obtaining custom-milled profiles is less costly than most people believe.

Crown Detail

Ceiling
Crown Molding
1 x 3 with Ogee
Drywall

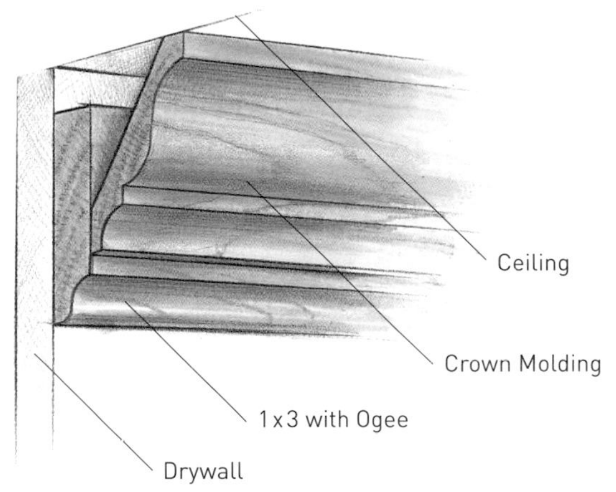

Pilaster Block Detail

1 x 4 with Cove
Chair Rail
1 x 10
Panel Molding
Routed Edge

Base Detail

Upper Base Cap
1 x 4 with Roundover
Base Cap
Baseboard
Shoe Molding
Nailer

Alternative Pilaster and Cap

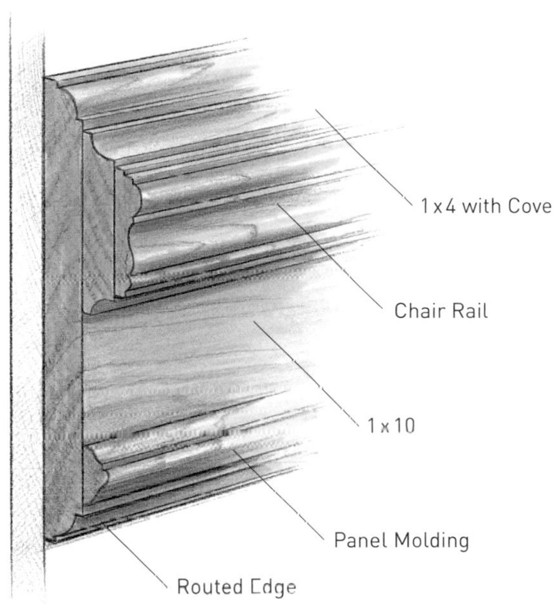

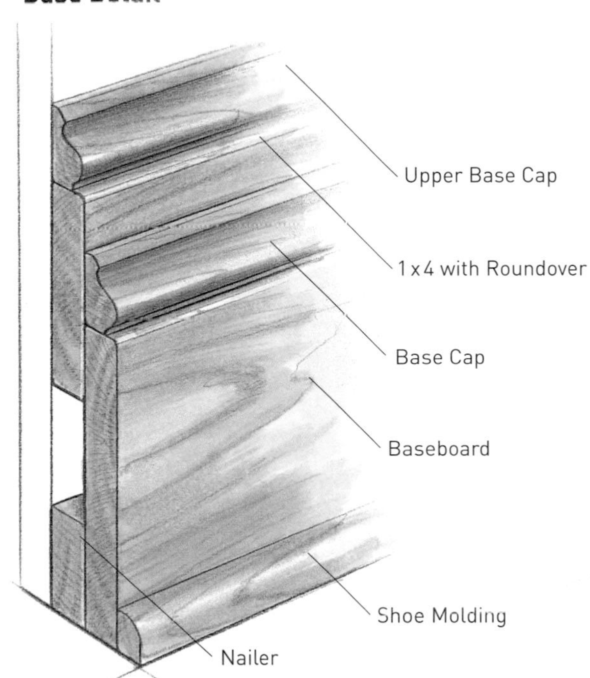

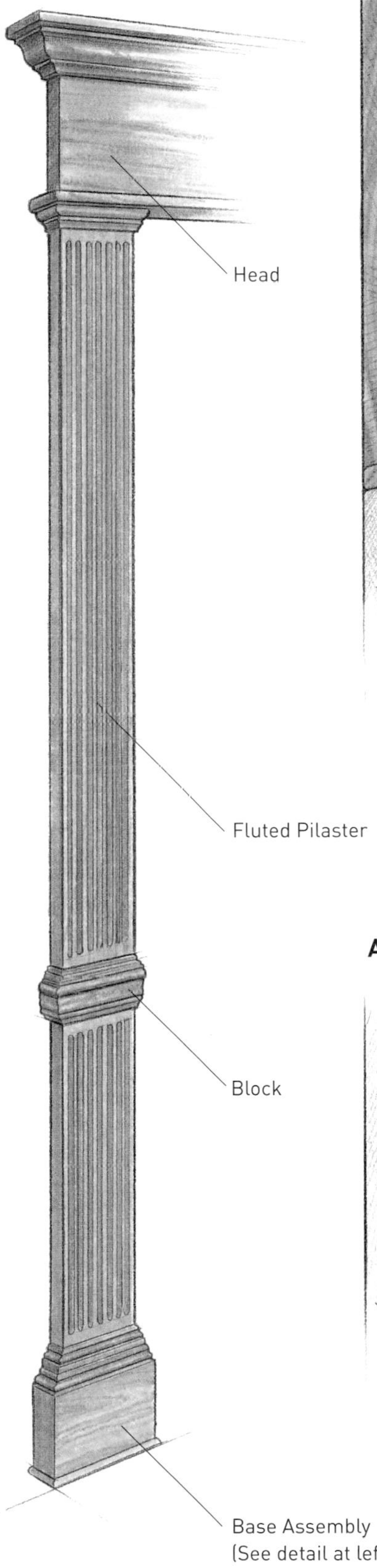

Head
Fluted Pilaster
Block
Base Assembly
(See detail at left.)

Alternative Head Detail

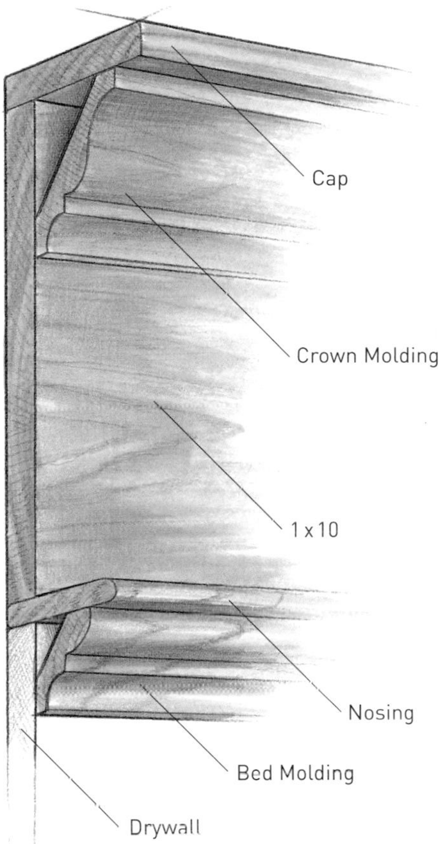

Cap
Crown Molding
1 x 10
Nosing
Bed Molding
Drywall

Alternative Pilaster Block Detail

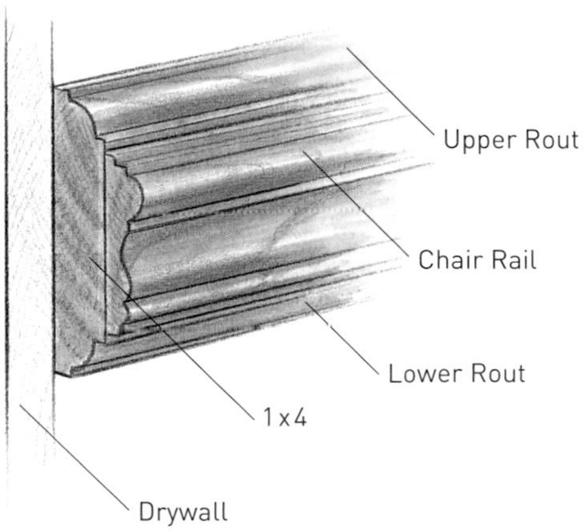

Upper Rout
Chair Rail
Lower Rout
1 x 4
Drywall

Base Molding

Baseboard provides a foundation to a wall, giving the eye a starting point as it absorbs a room's decoration. When choosing baseboard molding, it's important to make sure that it pairs with the door and window casing. Hold a piece of baseboard against the casing's edge in the manner that it will be installed to make sure the two pieces match up nicely. This is an easy way to make sure you choose the correct baseboard for your room.

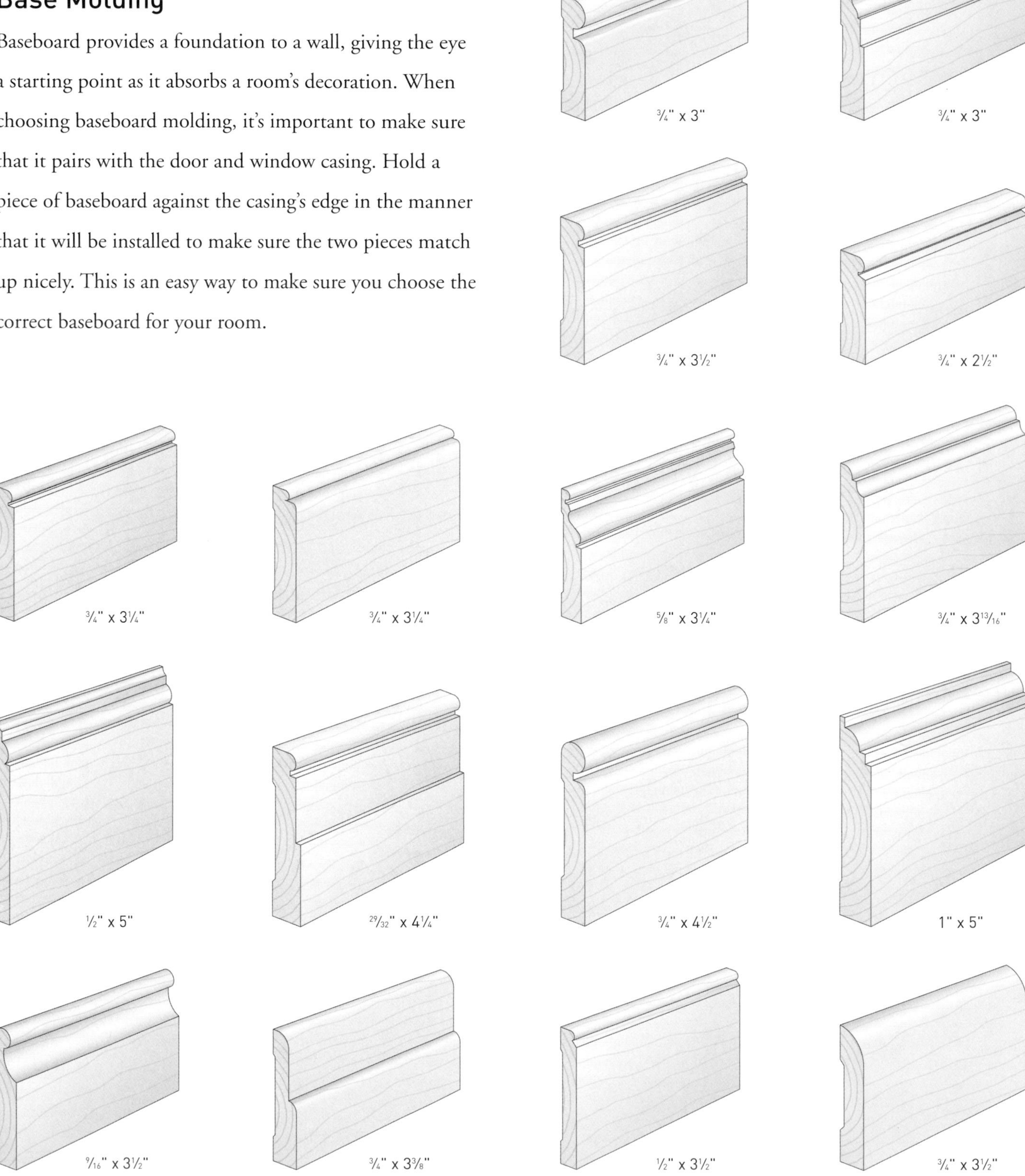

Base Cap Molding

Cap molding makes a nice finishing detail along the base. Make sure the cap molding matches the surrounding trim style. Because base cap molding has a fragile profile, it can easily splinter when attaching it to the wall. Install with care to avoid costly mistakes.

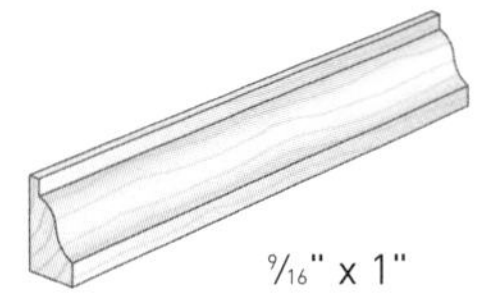
9/16" x 1"

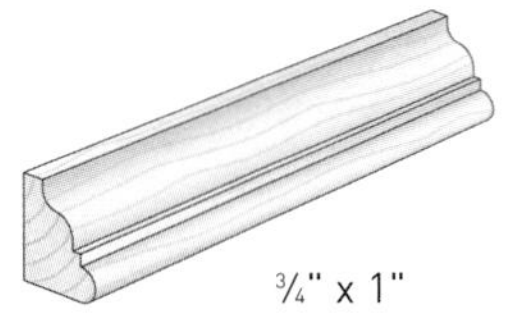
3/4" x 1"

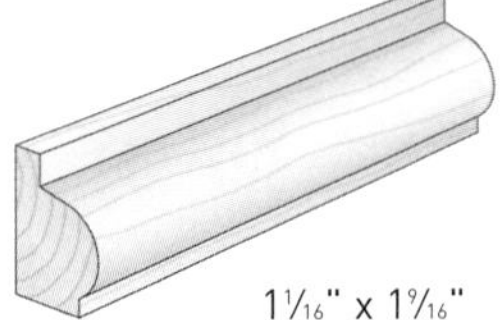
1 1/16" x 1 9/16"

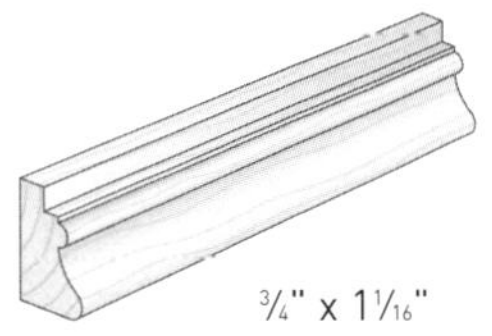
3/4" x 1 1/16"

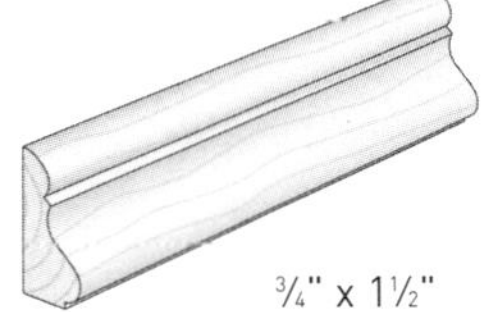
3/4" x 1 1/2"

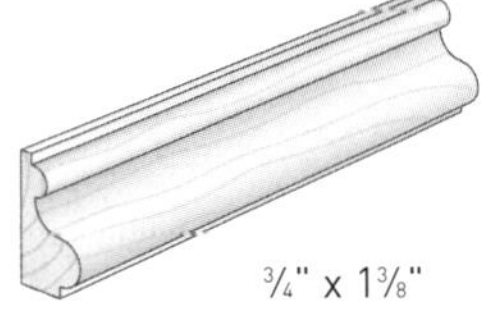
3/4" x 1 3/8"

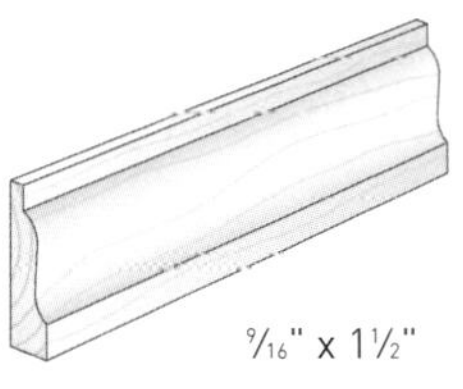
9/16" x 1 1/2"

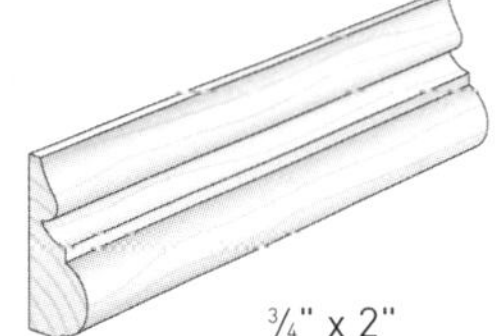
3/4" x 2"

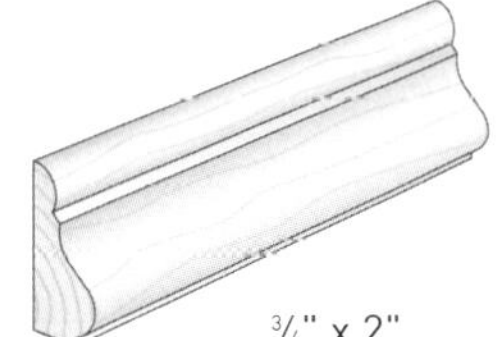
3/4" x 2"

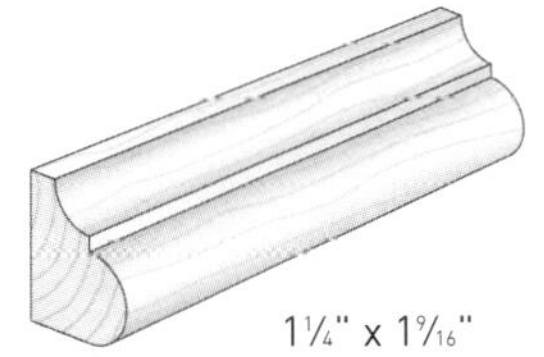
1 1/4" x 1 9/16"

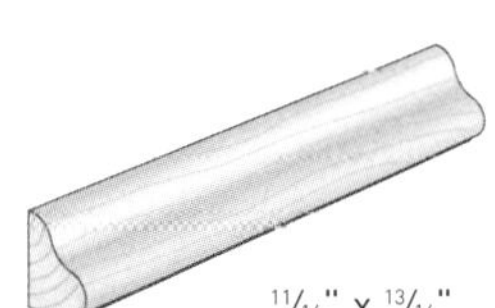
11/16" x 13/16"

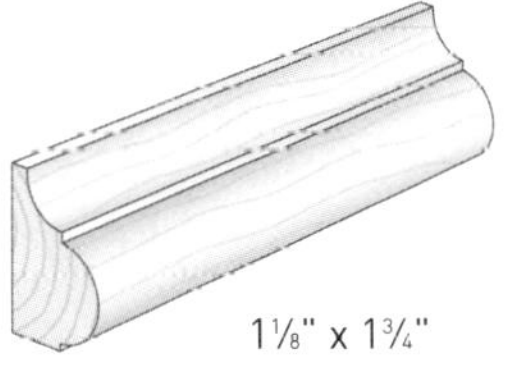
1 1/8" x 1 3/4"

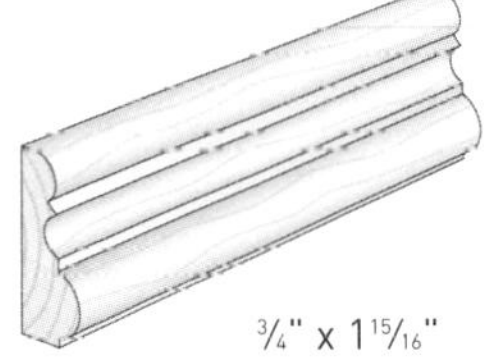
3/4" x 1 15/16"

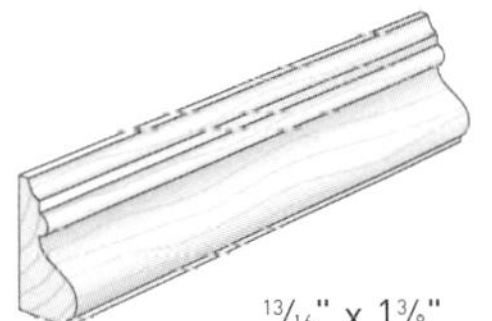
13/16" x 1 3/8"

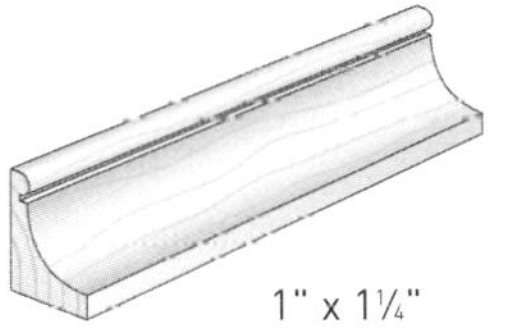
1" x 1 1/4"

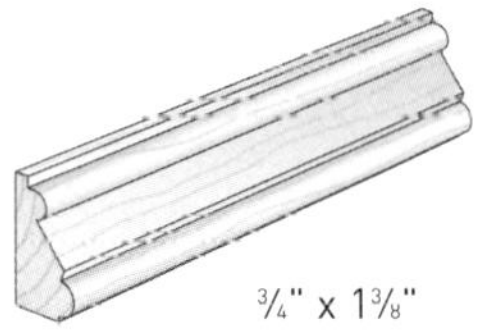
3/4" x 1 3/8"

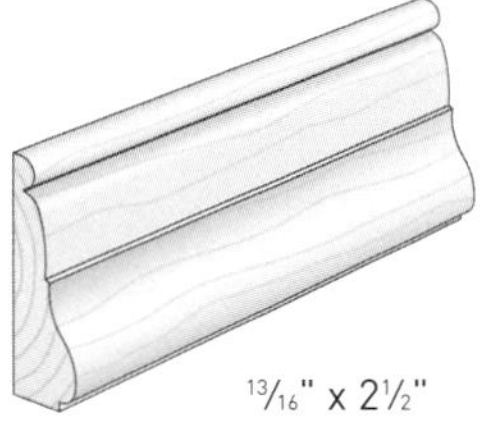
13/16" x 2 1/2"

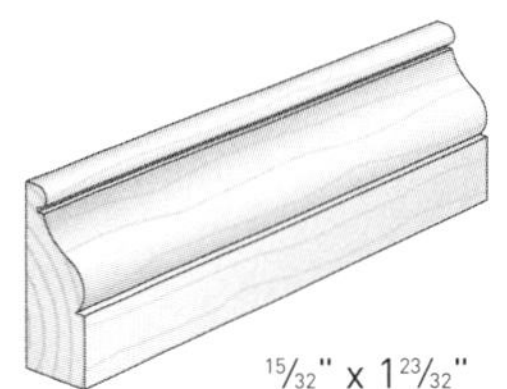
15/32" x 1 23/32"

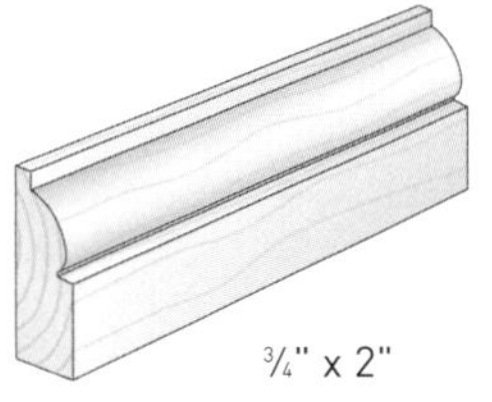
3/4" x 2"

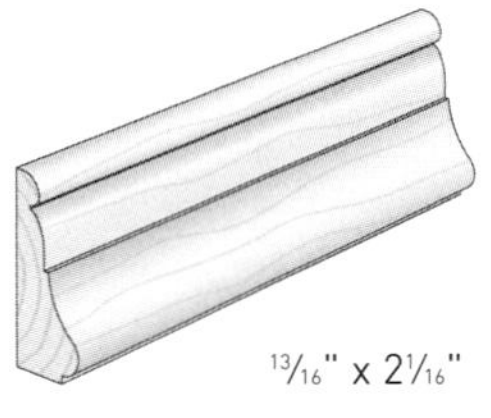
13/16" x 2 1/16"

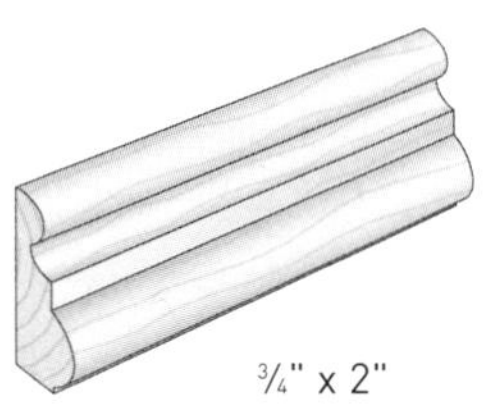
3/4" x 2"

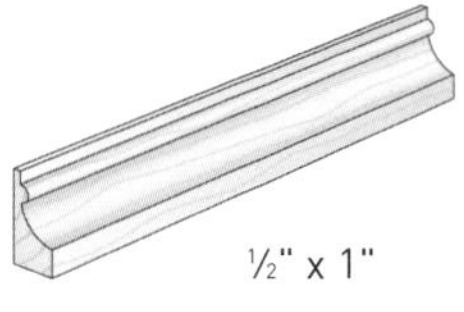
1/2" x 1"

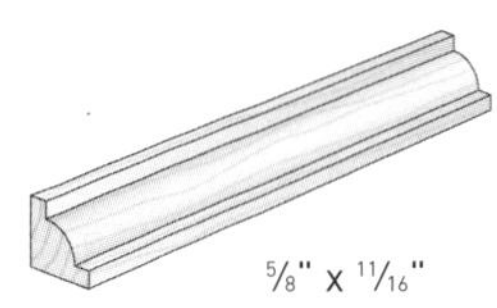
5/8" x 11/16"

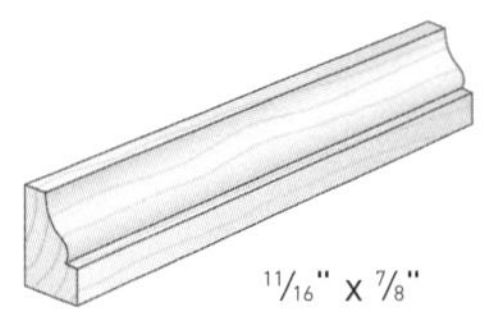
11/16" x 7/8"

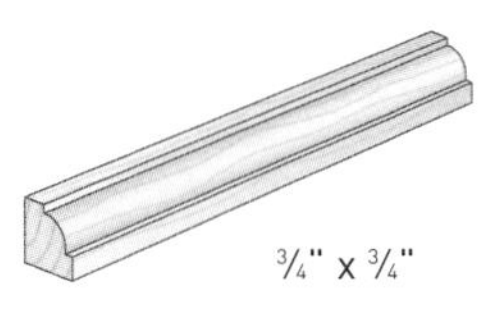
3/4" x 3/4"

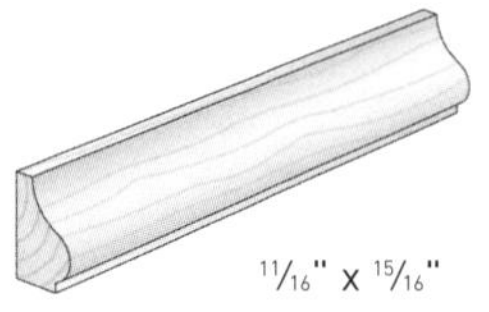
11/16" x 15/16"

Door and Window Casings

Decorative trimwork adds definition and detail around windows, doors, and entryways; makes walls more elegant; and ties together different sizes and types of openings. You can add scale to special places, like a front door, with plinth blocks and decorative headers.

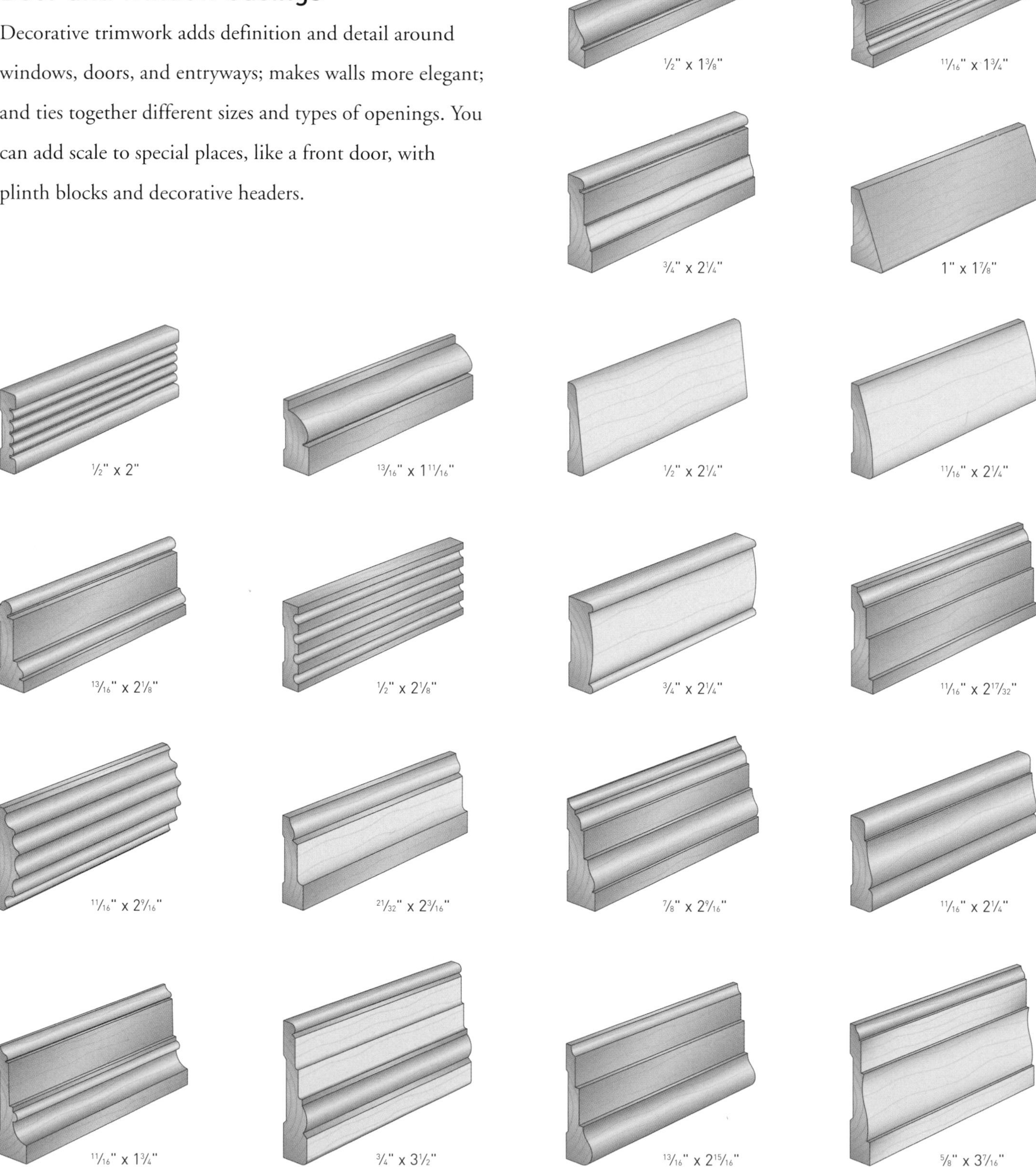

1 5/16" x 3 15/16"

1" x 4"

1 1/16" x 4"

13/16" x 3 7/8"

3/4" x 4"

3/4" x 4"

3/4" x 4"

1" x 4"

13/16" x 4 1/2"

1" x 4 1/8"

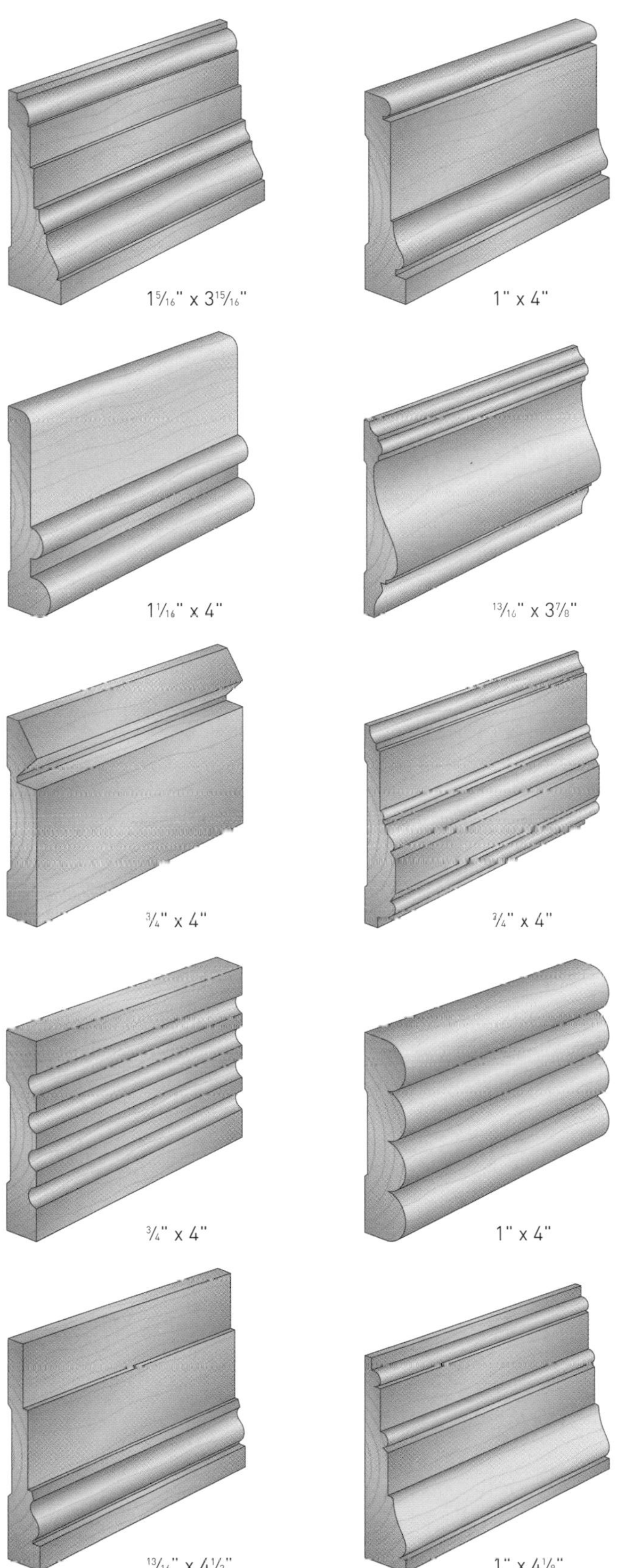

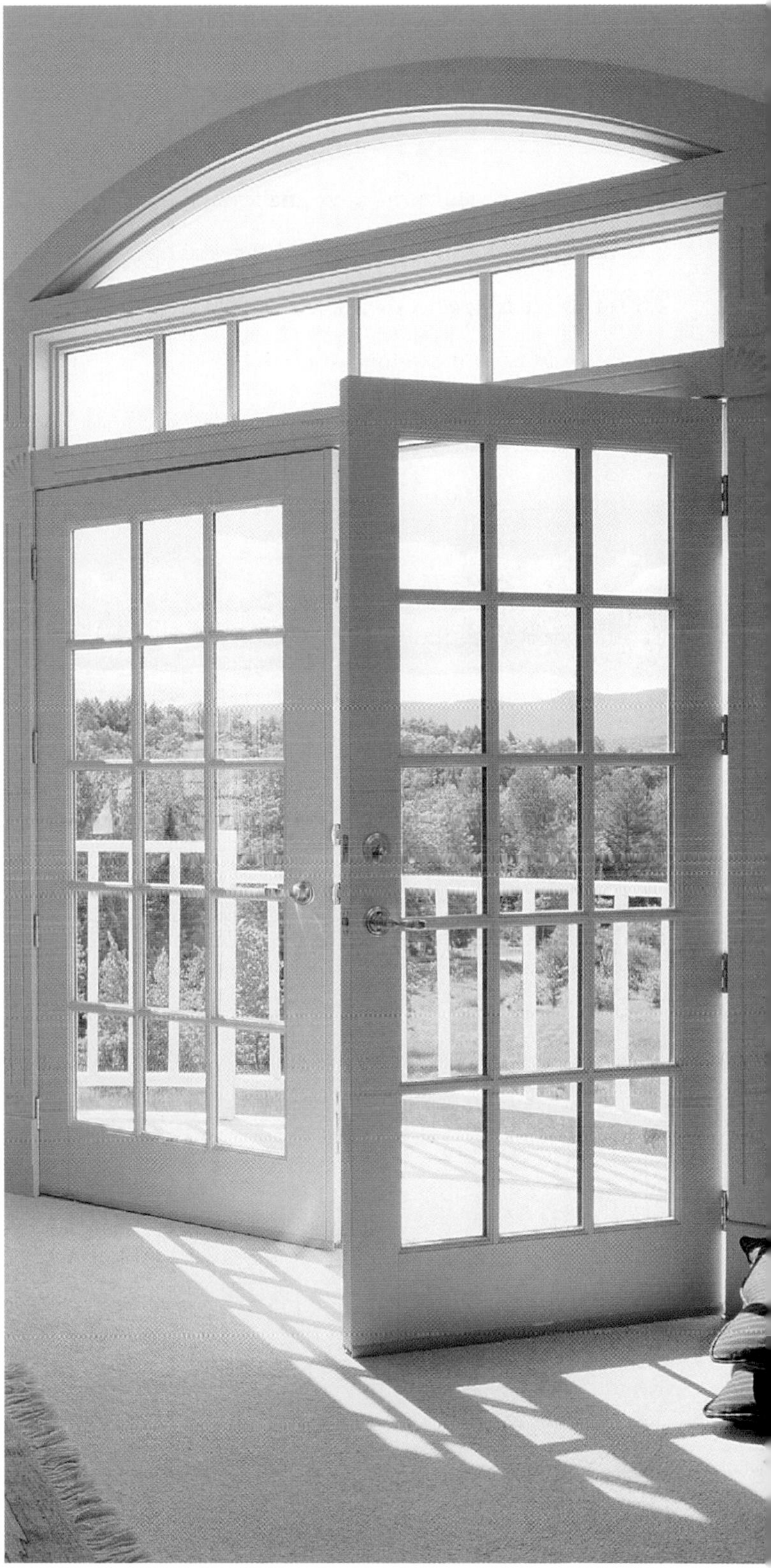

Above The eyebrow window and trim add flowing grace notes to double doors, transforming this into a grand entryway.

Rosettes

These decorative corner blocks, used to dress up door and window trimwork, are usually combined with Victorian bellyband casing. Using rosettes eliminates the need for complicated miter cuts.

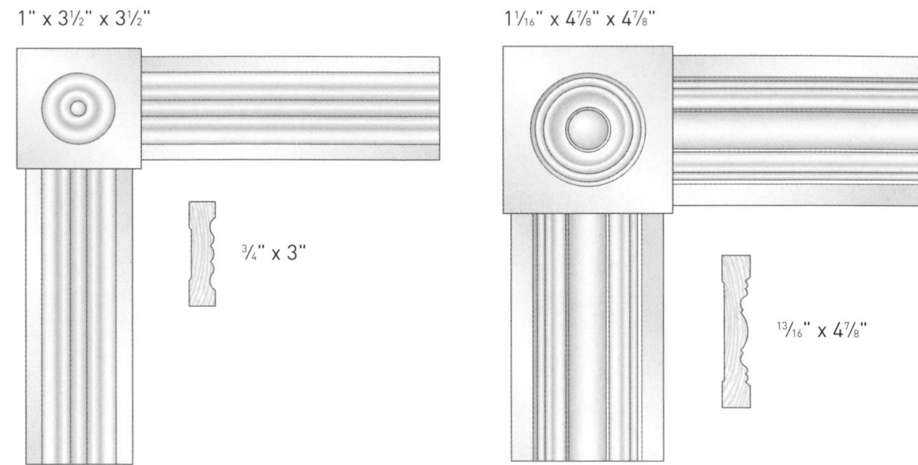

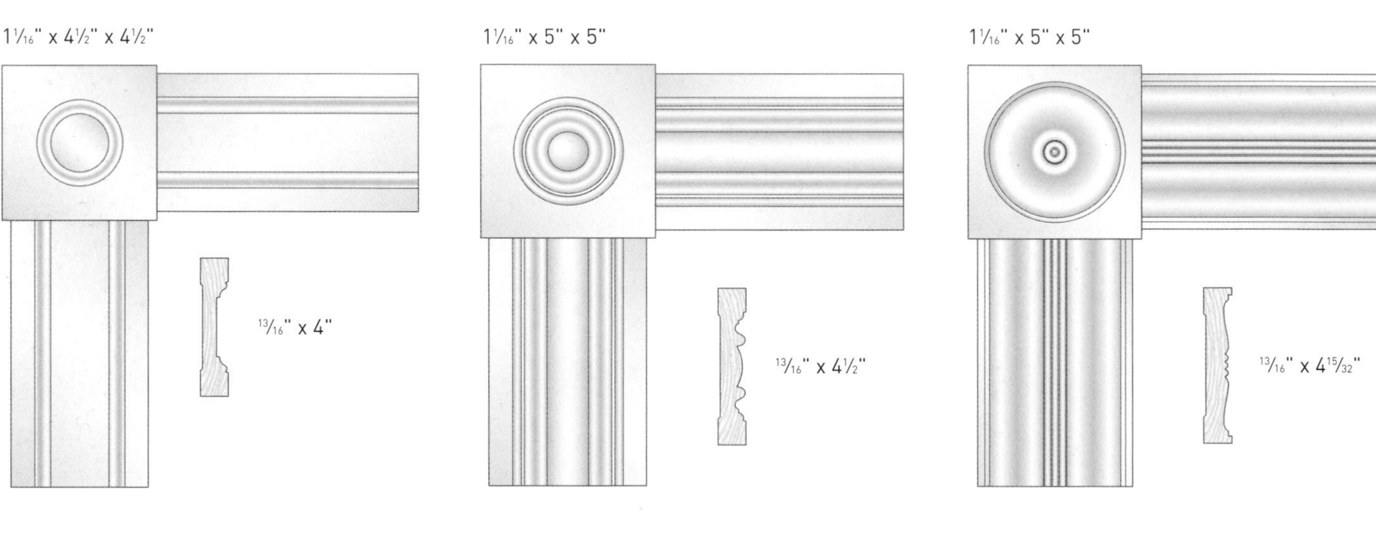

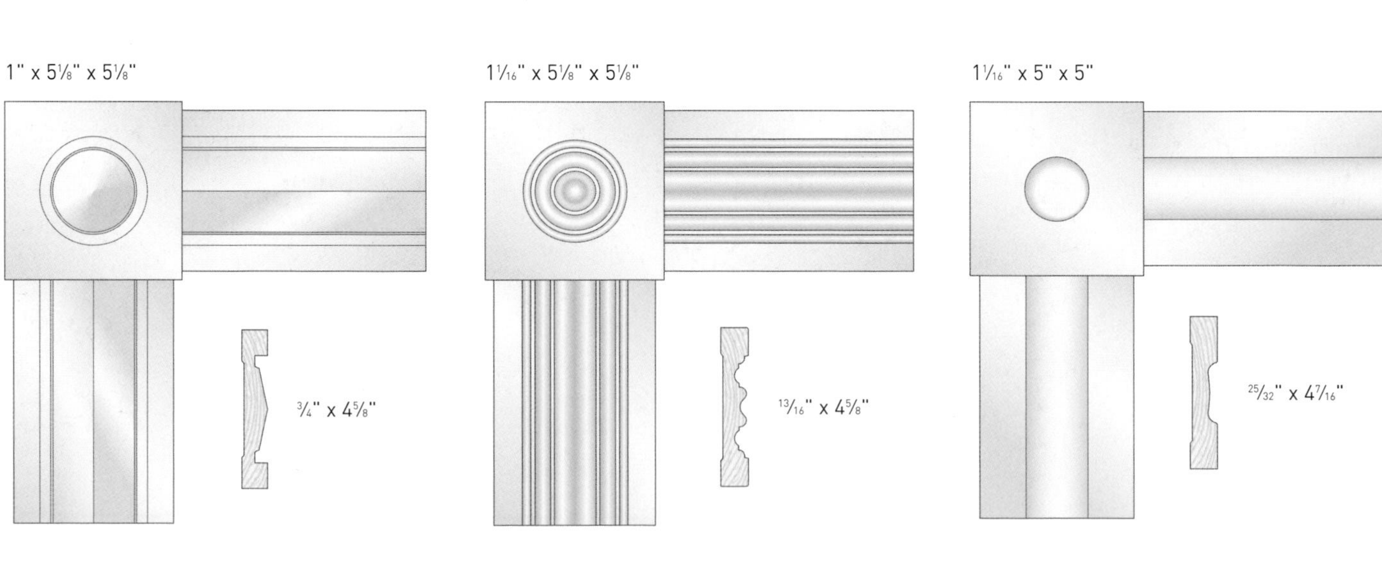

Victorian Casings

Victorian-style casings can add decoration and detail to any room. Finished with a clear sealer, it may be a little heavy in modest-size rooms with standard 8-foot ceilings. If finished with paint, it complements the wall color, adding character to any space.

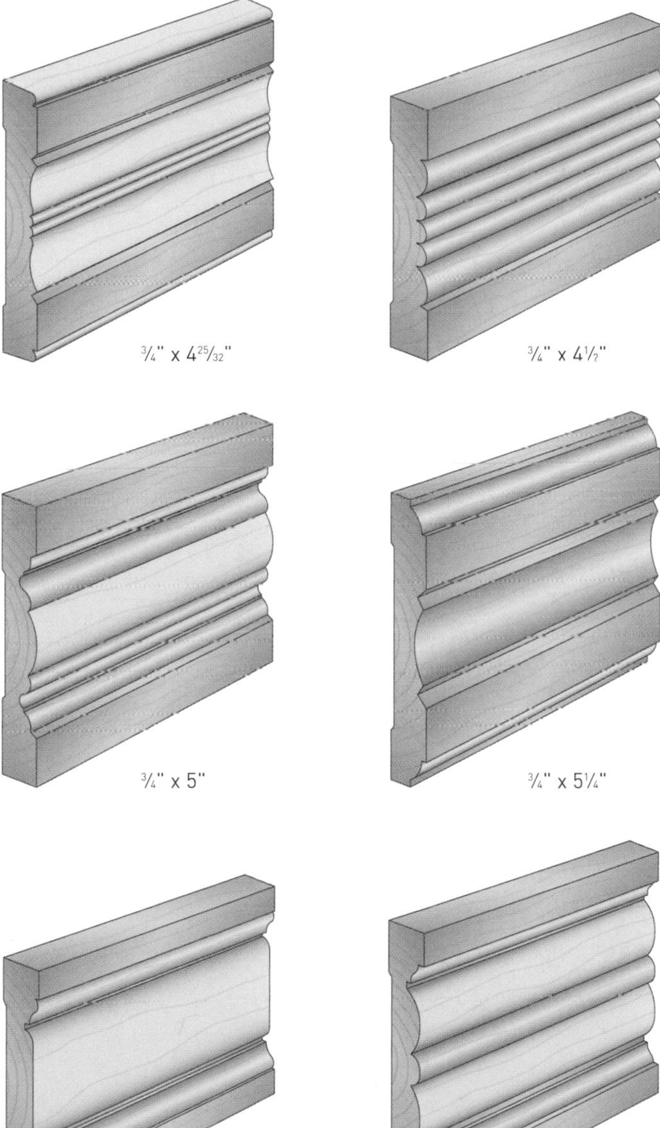

Smart Tip **Casing Reveals**

Typically, the door side of the casing covers most but not all of the jamb, leaving a narrow edge called a reveal. This adds definition to the molding and avoids an unsightly seam where the edge of one board lines up directly over another. A typical reveal creates a handsome transition at cased openings.

Above Victorian-style doorway casing is painted white to accent the floral wallpaper and to blend in with the wainscoting.

Wall Treatments

Chair rails, picture and plate rails, and frieze moldings can transfer plain modern rooms into memorable spaces with period character. Chair rails provide a focal point and help unify the various trim details. Friezes are typically flat moldings with a decorative relief carving or a classical profile. Picture rails are installed one half to one quarter of the way down the wall from the ceiling. Combining these moldings can bring harmony and create architectural interest in any room.

Embossed Moldings

Rosettes 3/8" x 1 7/8"

Floral Pattern 1/4" x 1 1/4"

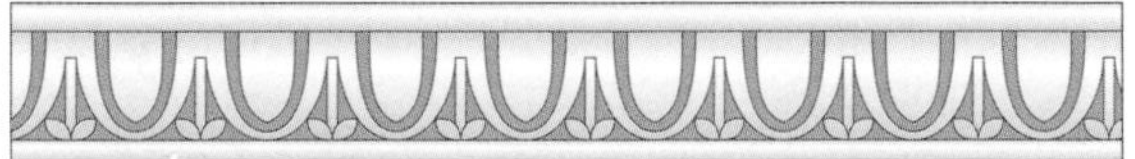

Egg and Dart 5/16" x 5/8"

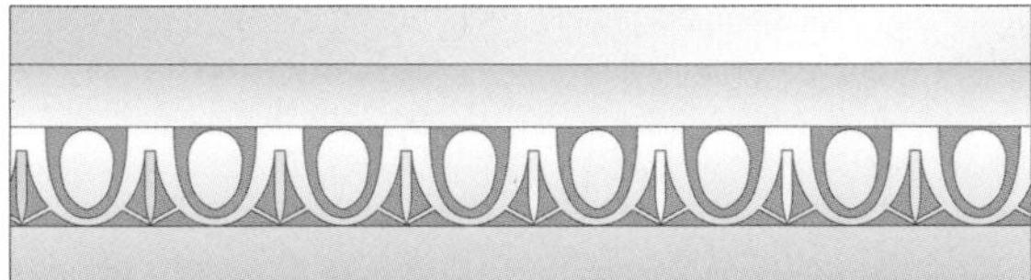

Egg and Dart 5/8" x 1 1/4"

Elongated Ovals 5/16" x 1 3/4"

Floral with Vine 3/8" x 1 7/8"

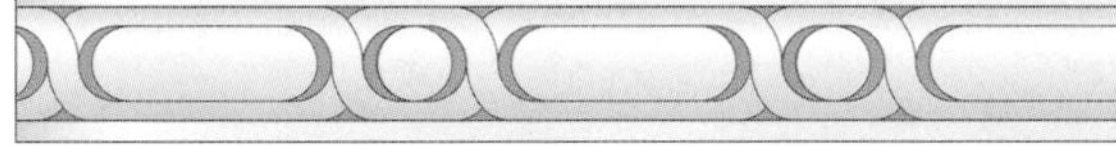

Bead and Billet 5/16" x 5/8"

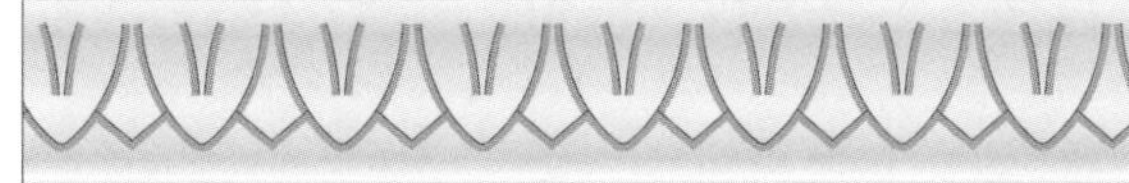

Leaf Pattern 3/8" x 3/4"

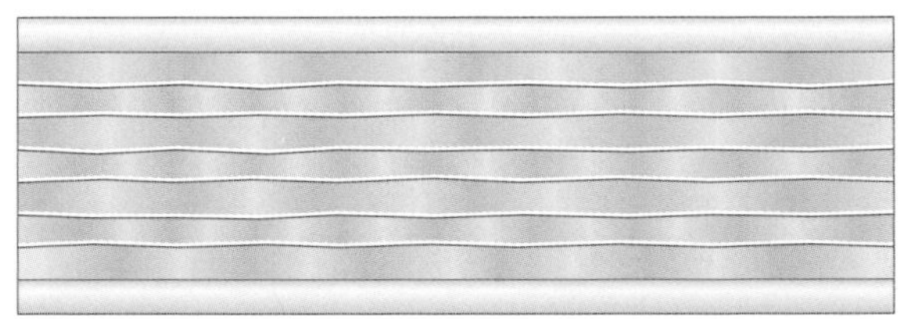

Flat Reeds 1/4" x 1 1/2"

Vertical Pattern 1/4" x 1 3/4"

Left Displaying decorative plates on a plate rail in a dining room is a charming and unique alternative to hanging paintings or photographs on the wall.

Chair Rails

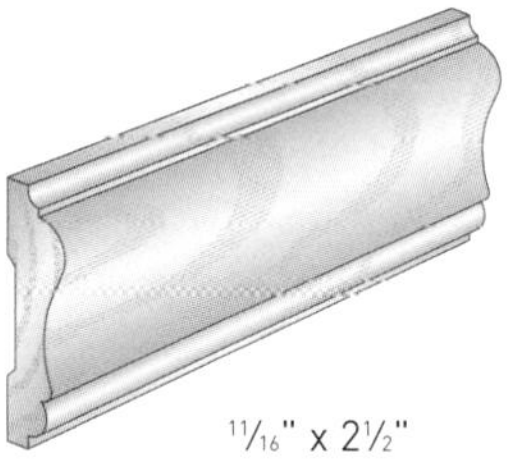

11/16" x 2 1/2"

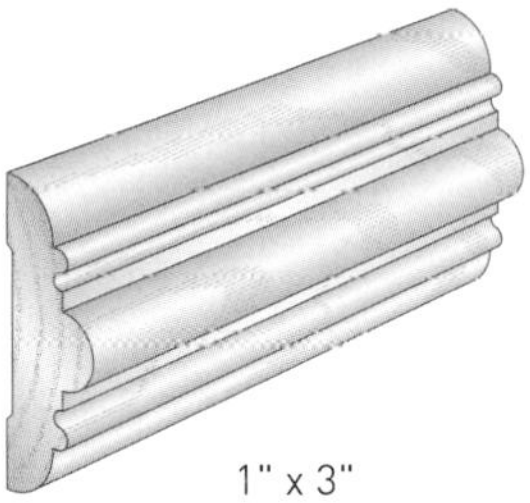

1" x 3"

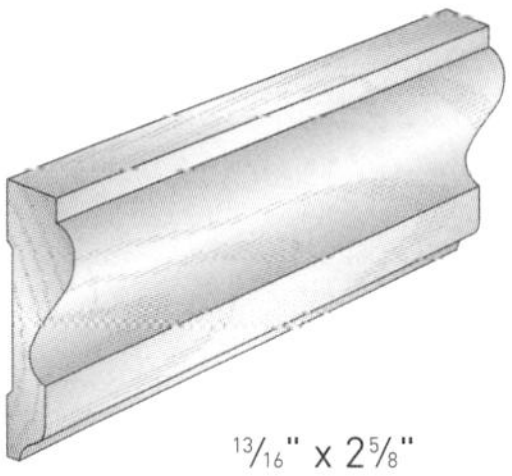

13/16" x 2 5/8"

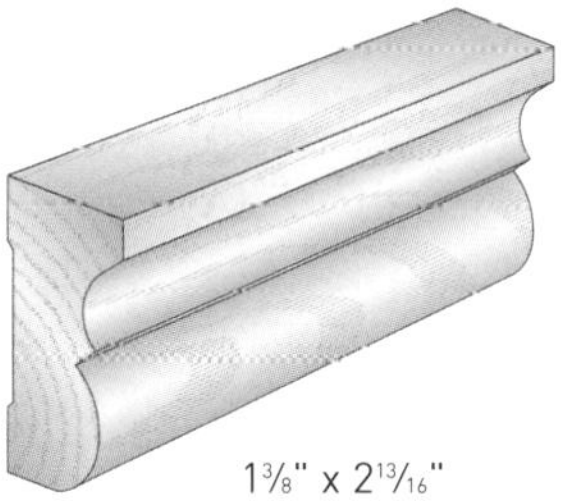

1 3/8" x 2 13/16"

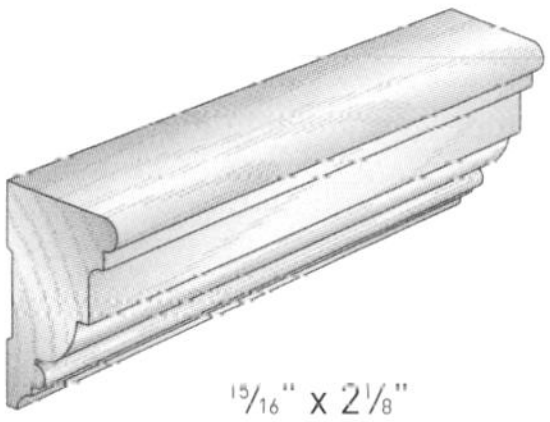

15/16" x 2 1/8"

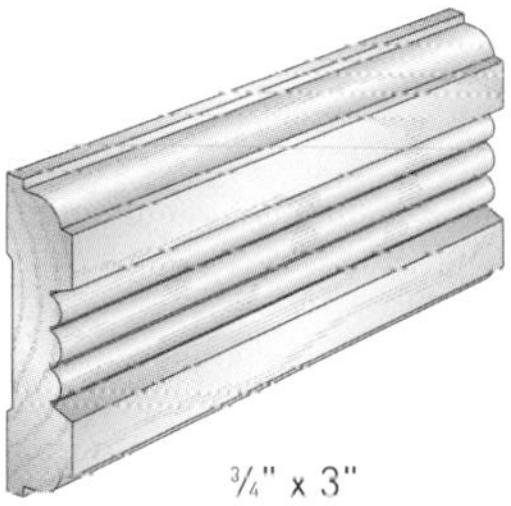

3/4" x 3"

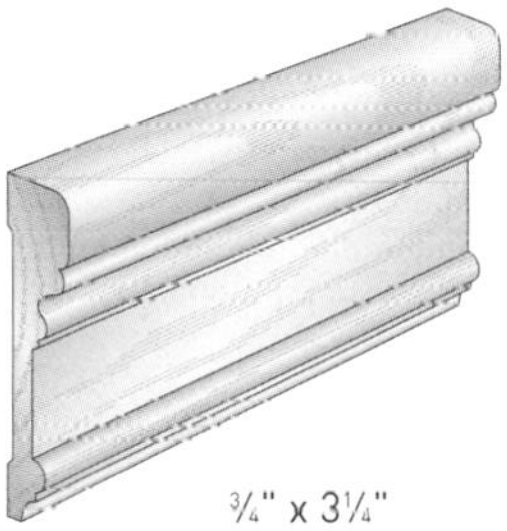

3/4" x 3 1/4"

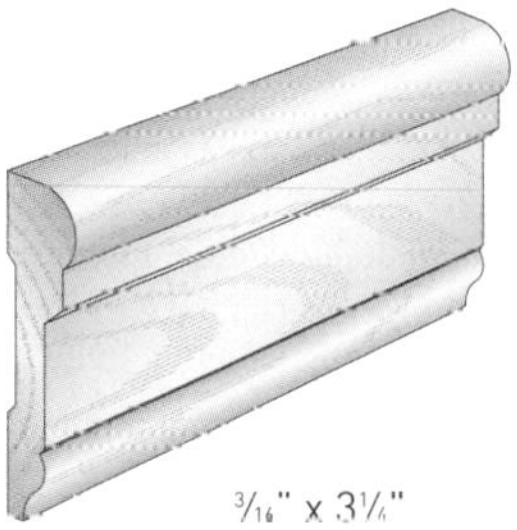

3/16" x 3 1/4"

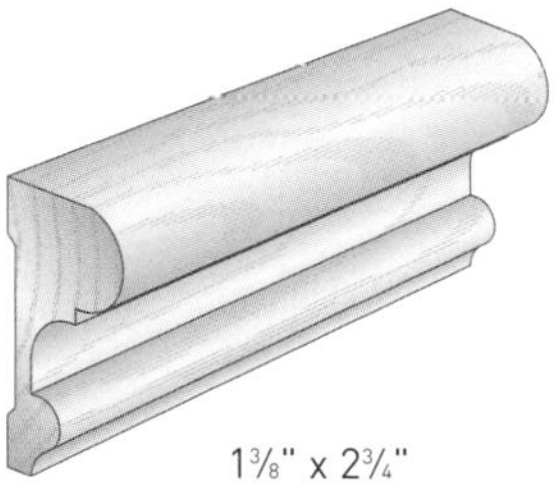

1 3/8" x 2 3/4"

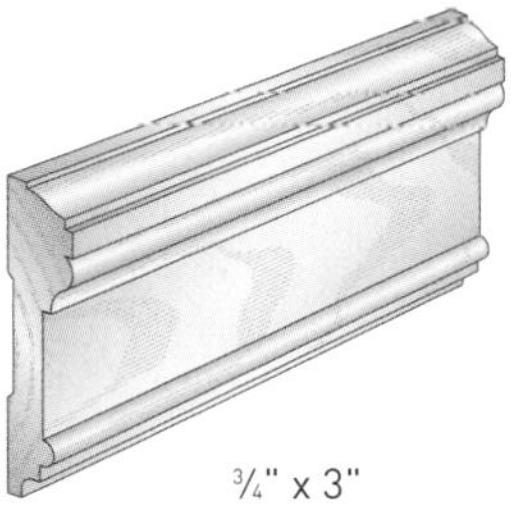

3/4" x 3"

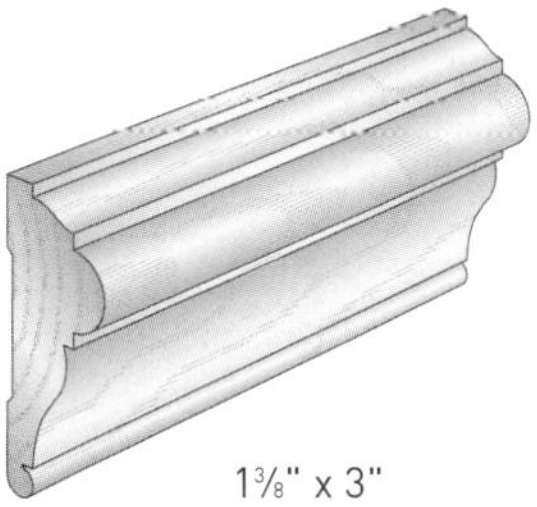

1 3/8" x 3"

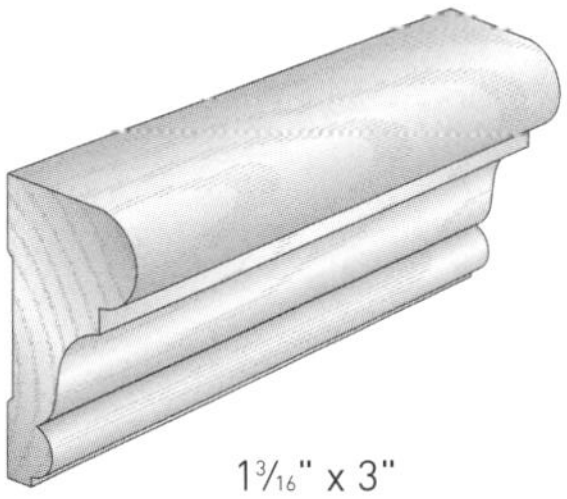

1 3/16" x 3"

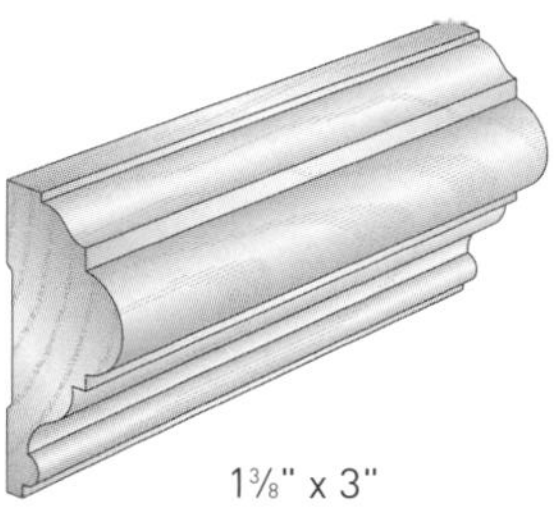

1 3/8" x 3"

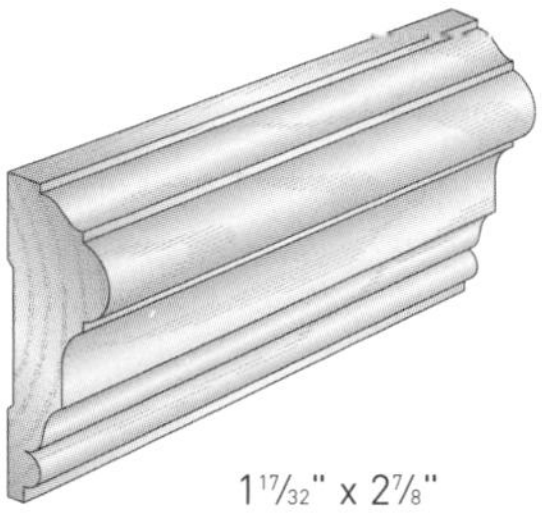

1 17/32" x 2 7/8"

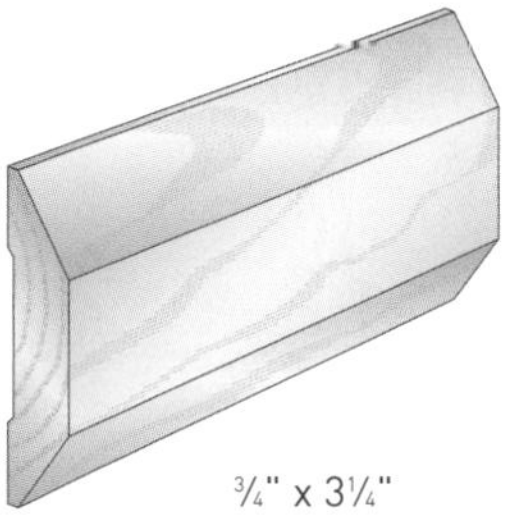

3/4" x 3 1/4"

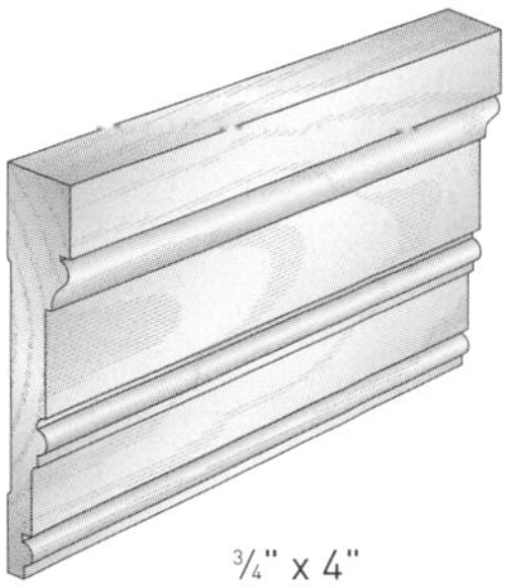

3/4" x 4"

Pillars and Pilasters

Pilasters are made up of a combination of trim elements attached to a wall or other flat surface. Columns and pillars are vertical supports installed under a horizontal beam. They provide a sense of style and stateliness to a room.

Pilaster Construction

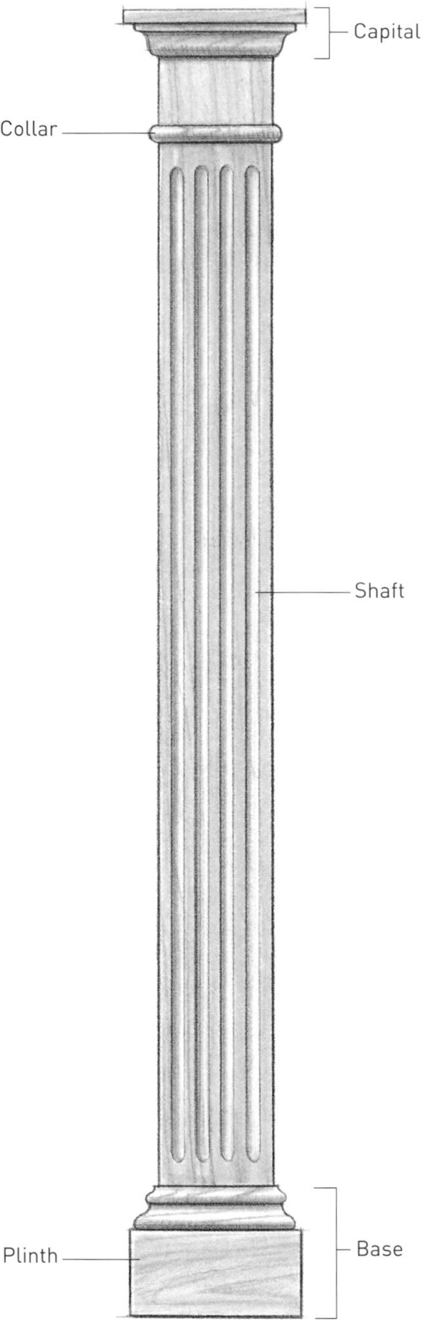

Left The plain natural-finished columns are a welcome counterpoint to the ornate trimwork.

Opposite A trio of marbleized columns delineates entry areas while adding a classical touch.

Trimwork for Stairs

Newels are the primary supports for the railing, and balusters (below) provide secondary support. Using ornate newels and balusters in a modern home can add eye appeal and help create a memorable staircase.

Opposite The simple and naturally finished Craftsman-inspired staircase provides distinctive period charm to this home.

Newels and Balusters

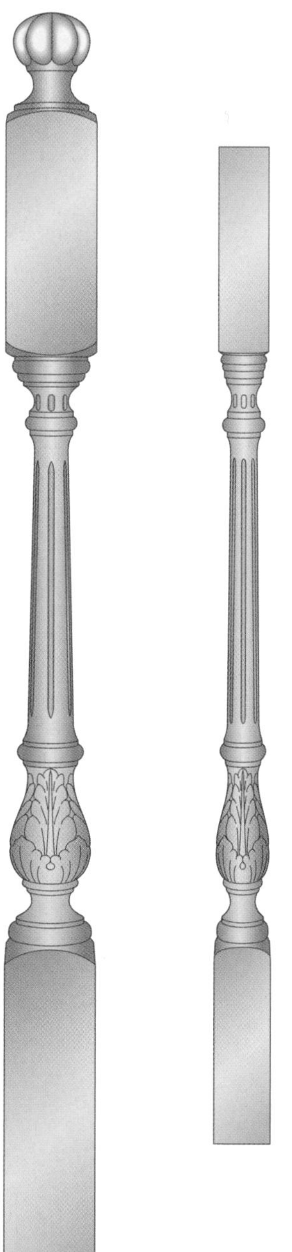

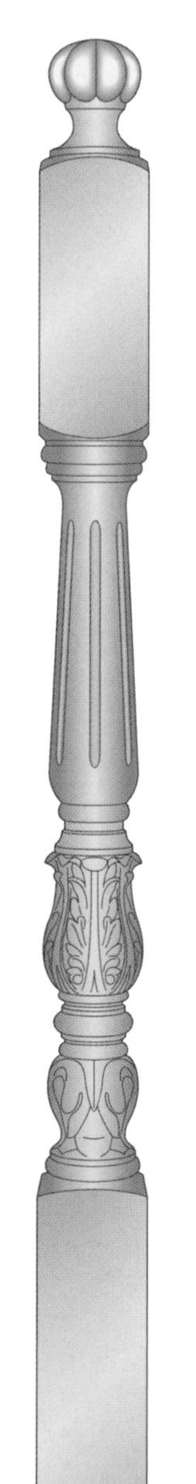

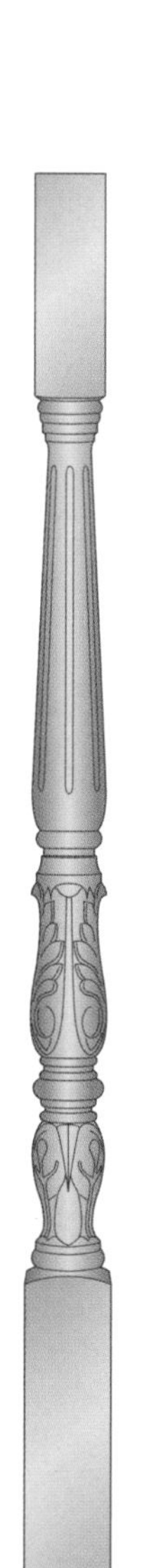

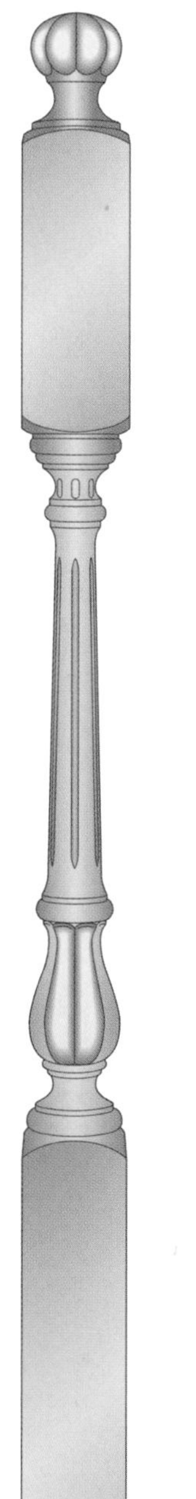

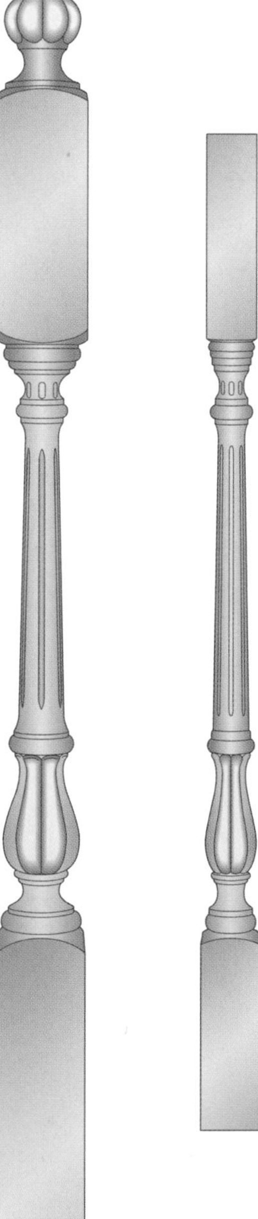

Cornice Molding

The term "cornice" describes large, one-piece molding installed along the top of a wall or above a window, or the same treatment made from multiple pieces of trim, also called a built-up cornice. Traditionally, cornices and crown molding (a type of cornice) reflected the intended use of rooms they decorated. Reception rooms and bedrooms had ornate cornices; kitchens had plainer detailing.

Opposite The crisp white cornice stands out from the neutral-colored walls but reflects the formality of the mantel.

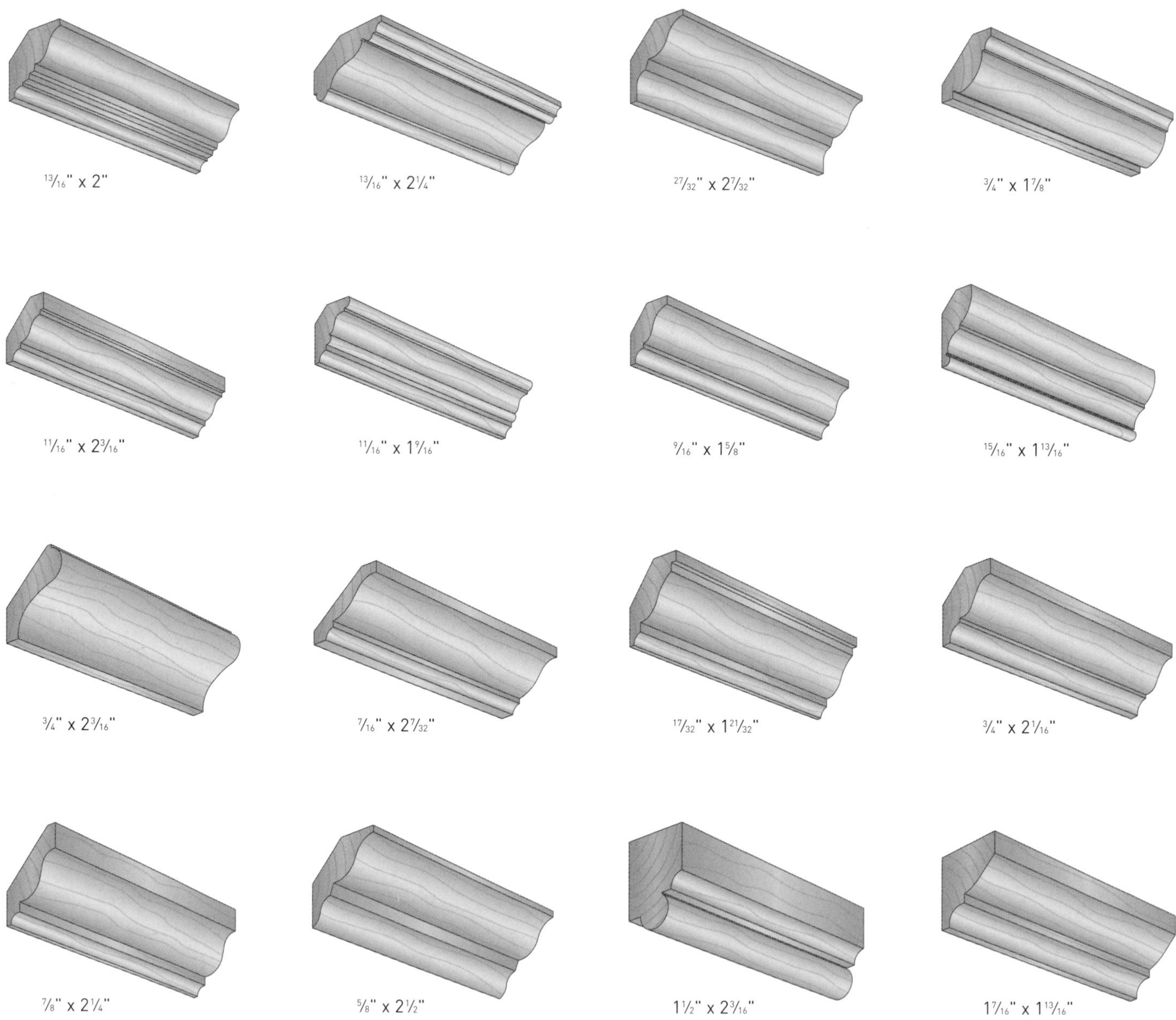

JOHN LE CARRÉ | OUR GAME

Smart Tip **Buying Molding at Home Centers**

Your local home center is a good place to find many standard types of trim. They typically carry pine and poplar for paint-grade work and oak for stain finishes. The material usually comes in 8- or 16-ft. lengths. It is sold by the linear foot, so you can cut larger pieces down to the size you need.

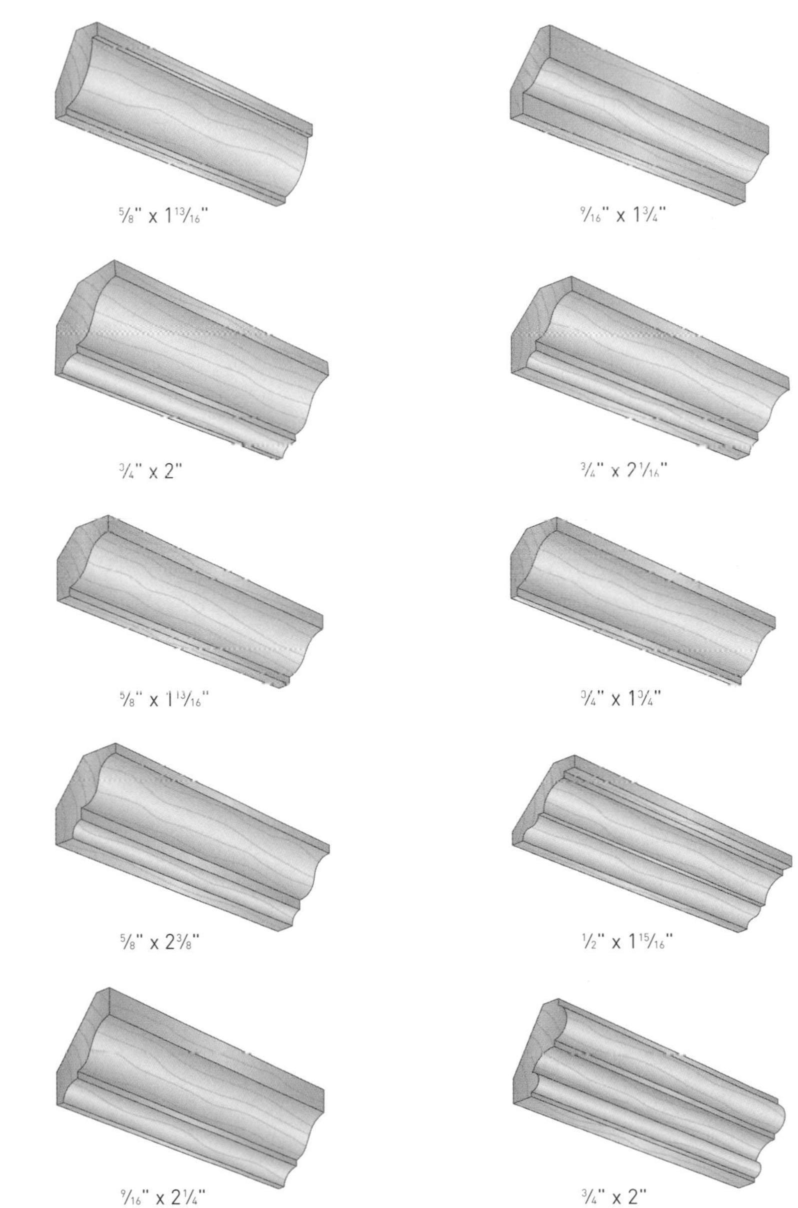

Left This living room's deep cornice draws a contrast to the light-colored walls and is a handsome delineation between the stone wall and ceiling.

Corbels and Ornaments

Corbels, also called brackets, can be used as stand-alone shelves or as supporting brackets for a shelf top. They are often used to dress up and add architectural interest to an elaborate cornice or other trimwork. Using ornamental details above doorways or mantles draws further attention to these elements, providing a room with subtle drama and character.

Finials and Corbels

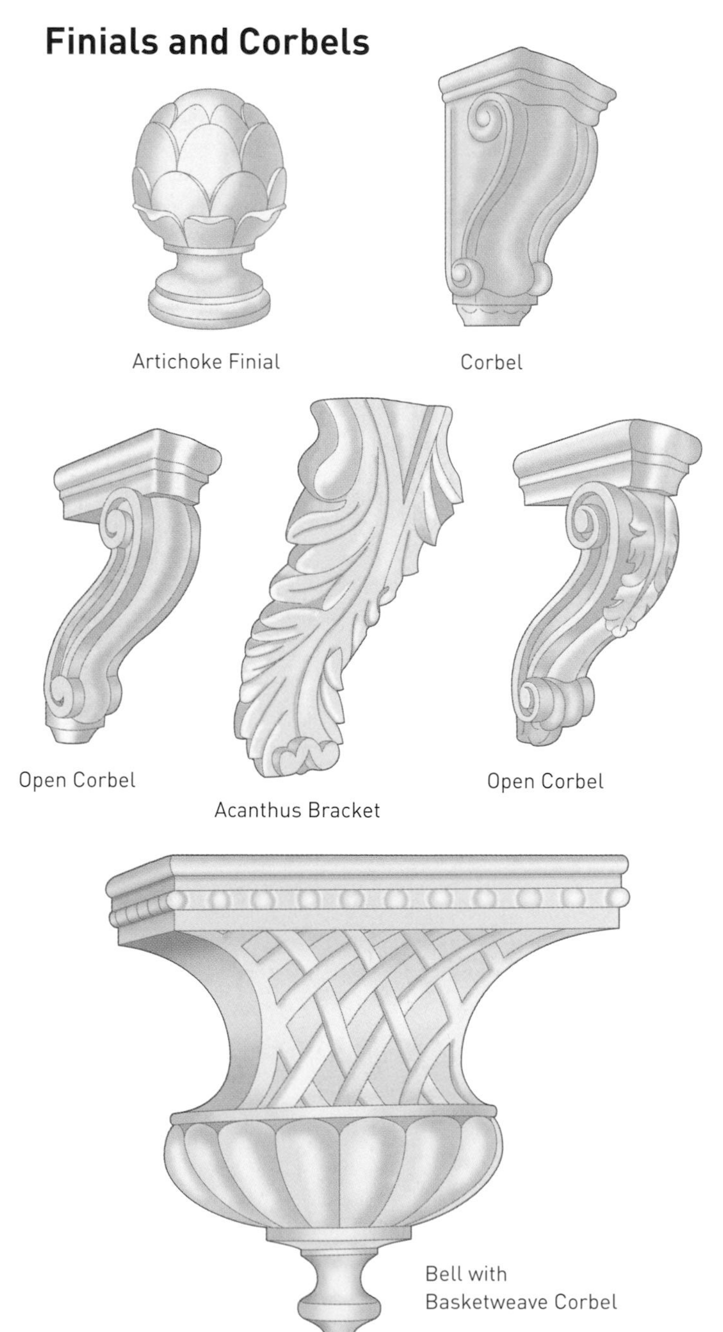

Above A gold-leafed corbel reinforces the formal tone set by the heavy deep cornice.

Ornaments

New Chapter 4 TRIM Shot List
1) Opener, 1 shot, page 1-2, 1-1/2pages.
Chopsaw, bench other power tools.
2) Prep Lumber, 5 shots, page 4, 1/6 page each.
4) Hand miter, 3 shots, page 7, 1/6 page each. Shot Done 4/25/01
1. clamp board, 2. swing saw, 3. cut.
8) Before shot 1
9) Before shot 2
10) After shot (maybe 2)
NAILS
EB14B
2000mAh 14.4v

Chapter 3

Tools and Techniques

Having the right tools for the job makes a do-it-yourself trim project easier and improves the final results. Experienced woodworkers can create elaborate trim projects that include fluted pilasters and moldings. But you can add a lot to the look of your home with more modest projects using only basic tools and techniques.

The person guiding the tools makes the real difference in the final look of a trimwork project. For do-it-yourselfers, this means you should steer clear of cheap, entry-level models. For example, cheap cutting tools won't hold a sharp edge and throwaway brushes will litter a finish with bristles.

On the other hand you don't need to invest a fortune in top-end professional tools. They certainly won't hurt your results, but most amateur woodworkers don't need the extra capacity. A heavy-duty router with a top-rated motor may pay off for a cabinetmaker who uses the tool five days a week, but it's overkill in most beginner home shops.

Do-it-yourselfers today are faced with an array of tools in a wide range of quality and prices. There are so many that once you start collecting them the urge to acquire more is irresistible. But for most trimwork projects you need only basic equipment and rudimentary woodworking skills to give your rooms a whole new look.

As a rule, a beginner will do well (while saving money) using mid-priced tools that do one job well. To get started, ask friends to recommend tools that they like.

A combination of hand and power tools will get the job done for most trimwork projects.

Layout Tools: A—measuring tape, **B**—electric distance finder, **C**—framing square, **D**—stud finder, **E**—chalk-line box, **F**—contour gauge, **G**—speed square, **H**—sliding T-bevel, **I**—compass, **J**—folding carpenter's ruler, **K**—combination square

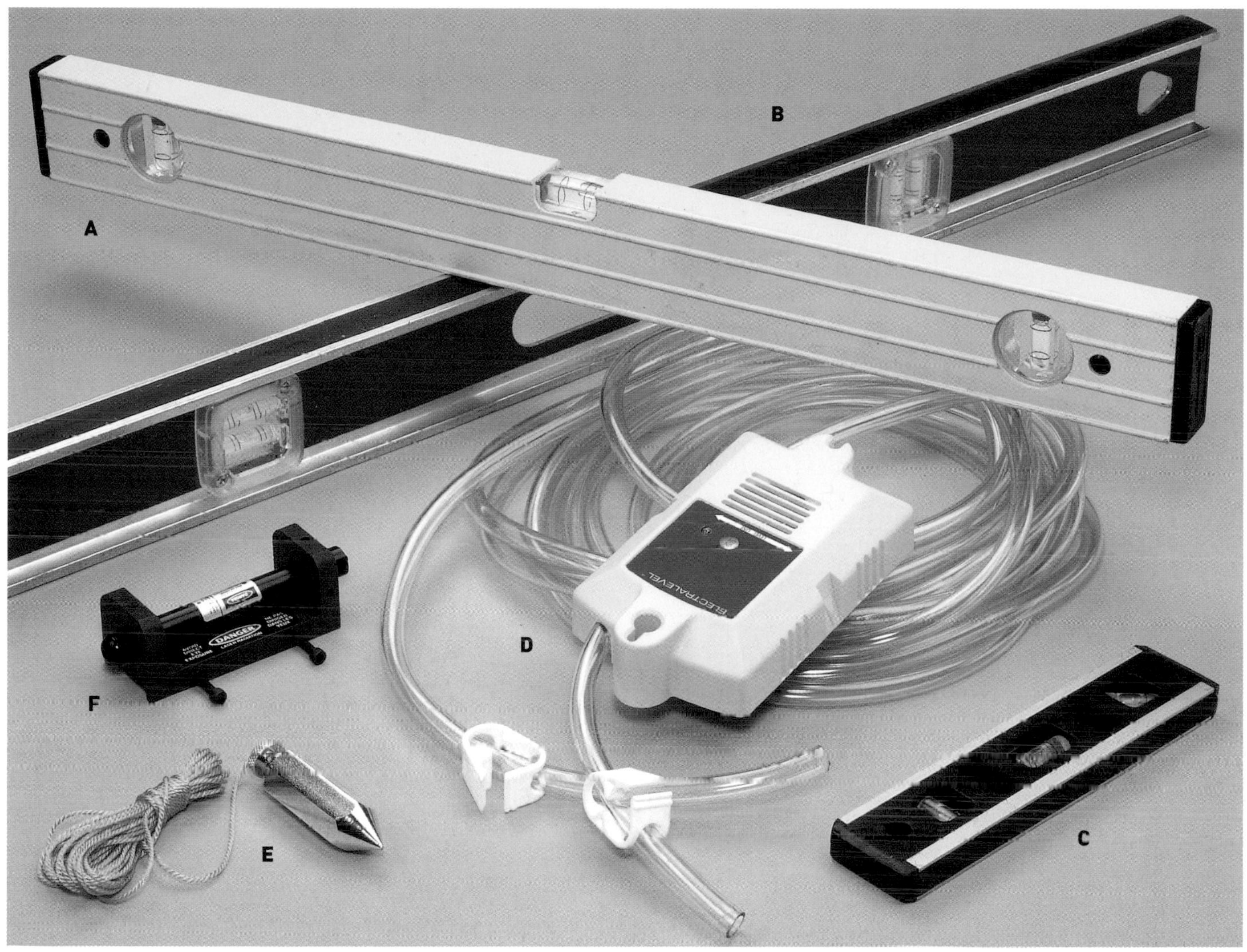

Leveling Tools: A—2 ft. spirit level, **B**—4-ft. spirit level, **C**—6-in. spirit level, **D**—water level with electronic level sensor, **E**—plumb bob and string, **F**—laser level, which can be attached to a standard level

Layout and Leveling Tools

Most trimwork is straightforward, but it's easy to make a mistake that can complicate a project and waste wood. The adage "measure twice and cut once" makes a lot of sense. To reduce the chance of duplicating an error, measure length by height the first time, then the other way around on your double check.

In a perfectly plumb and level room, you can make a precise layout. But in many houses you have to compromise. If you dead-level a chair rail, it may look out of kilter with the baseboard. If you dead-level a cornice, it may create gaps against the slightly sloped ceiling. Always step back and see how the trimwork elements look in the overall framework of the surrounding floors, walls, and ceilings.

Cutting Tools

There are different saws for different jobs. Miter saws miter and bevel stock. They come in two basic types: the simple version cuts miters or bevels in separate steps, while a compound miter saw handles both operations in one pass.

A saber saw has a vertical cutting blade that is generally used in freehand work, such as cutting curves. One type of saber saw features a barrel grip that you rotate in the direction of the cut. The other has a fixed top handle, requiring you to turn the entire saw to guide the cut.

Circular saws come in a variety of sizes, but the 7½-inch (blade diameter) model is ideal for most homeowners. Find a saw with good balance that is easy to adjust for blade angle and cutting depth. A table saw is the tool of choice for ripping boards accurately.

Coping saws are essential for cutting coped joints where two pieces of molding meet at an inside corner. The shape of the tool makes it easy to follow the profile of the molding.

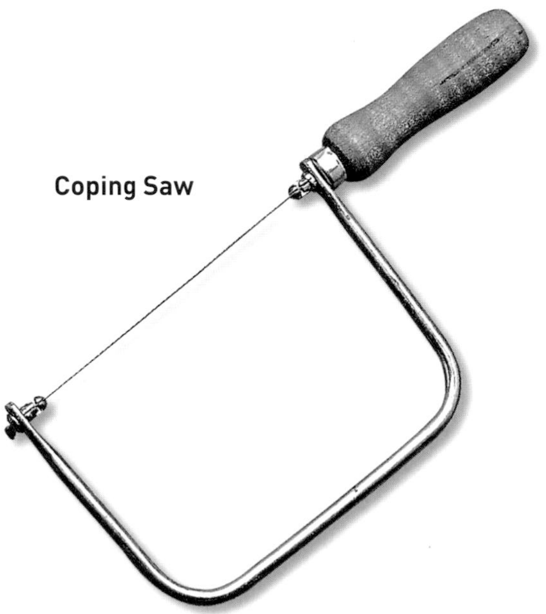

Coping Saw

Trim Blade

Crosscut Blade

Ripping Blade

1 A miter saw has a scale that is calibrated so you can make a straight crosscut at the 0-degree right up to 45-degree miters.

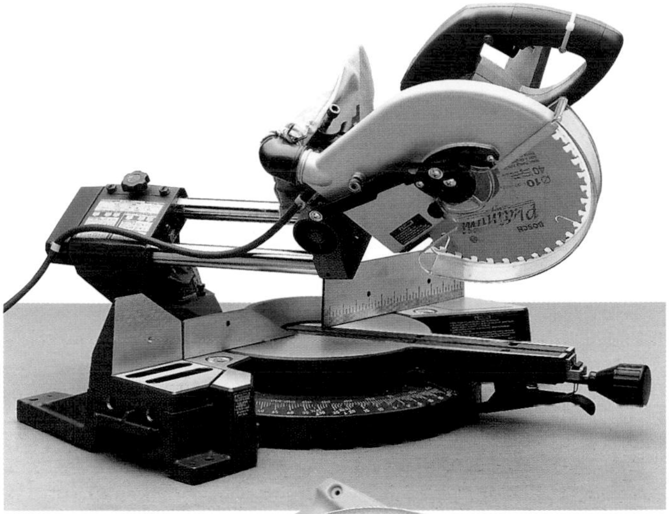

2 A slide compound miter saw increases cutting capacity with rails that enable the motor and blade to glide across the work.

3 Circular saws with comfortable main handles and an auxiliary handle up front make for more accurate cuts.

4 Versatile saber saws offer easy-changing blades, variable speed, and control of the blade-cutting angle.

5 A benchtop table saw is easy to move around the work area and stable enough once you clamp it in place.

Smart Tip **Picking Saw Blades**

Choosing the right blade will produce better results more quickly. Blades with more teeth and carbide tips generally produce the cleanest cuts. **Fine-toothed blades** are used to cut miters. **Ripping blades,** with widely spaced teeth, are used to cut long pieces of stock lengthwise. **Plywood blades** have smaller teeth spaced closer together. **Crosscut blades** are designed to cut cleanly across the grain.

Attachment Tools

Nail guns allow do-it-yourselfers to drive nails faster and more accurately than a hammer. A plate joiner, or biscuit joiner, makes joining two pieces of trimwork a breeze. An electric drill and a set of attachments can not only make quick and easy pilot holes, but will also allow you to drive in screws effortlessly.

2

1

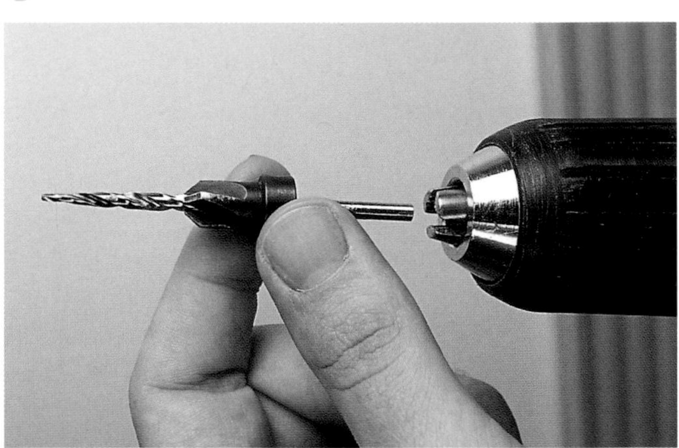

3

Safety Equipment

When using power tools, always check the manufacturer's operating instructions and follow the rules for safe operation. Guard against injury from woodchips and sawdust by wearing safety glasses or goggles, and in some situations, a dust mask or respirator. Gloves are handy for sanding and finishing work, and use knee pads when installing baseboards and wainscoting.

Safety Equipment: **A**—rubber gloves, **B**—work gloves, **C**—knee pads, **D**—safety glasses, **E**—safety goggles, **F**—particle mask, **G**—respirator, **H**—ear protectors

Other Useful Tools

Power planers can clean up board edges and remove thin shavings to create a perfect fit. Sanders can remove blemishes on the board surface and a lot of stock from the board's end. Rasps and flat files can help shape the final fit of two pieces of trimwork. Scrapers can help remove paint when refinishing existing moldings.

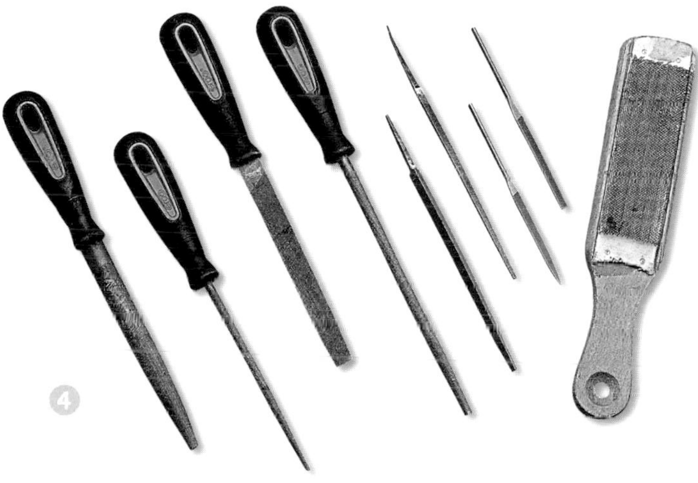

1 Nail clips, which you purchase by the box, quickly load into brad nailers (left) and finish nailers (right).

2 A hammer and nail set allows you to sink finishing nails below the surface of the wood.

3 A combination bit and drill makes clean, straight pilot holes. This bit is used for countersinking screws.

4 Large and small files help shape trimwork that joins together, and a handy file card (right) removes scrap wood from the teeth.

5 Powerful belt sanders are designed to remove a lot of stock from trimwork with a minimum of effort.

6 Sheet sanders are excellent for finishing with the grain and are easy to operate with one hand.

7 Random-orbit sanders not only remove stock from trimwork but also handle a lot of finishing jobs.

8 A basic router setup includes a rip fence with extension guides, straight-cutting bits, and molding profile bits.

Cutting Crown Molding with a Basic Miter Saw

Inside Corner, Left Side Cope

Place the molding bottom up on the saw's table. (Note that the cove detail is at the top.) Position the molding so that the excess will fall to the left.

Inside Corner, Right Side Cope

With the molding bottom up, reposition the miter gauge to the left 45-deg. mark. The excess falls to the right.

Outside Corner, Left Side Miter

With the gauge set on the left and the molding bottom up, cut so that the excess falls on the left.

Outside Corner, Right Side Miter

Move the gauge to the right. Turn the bottom of the molding up, and cut so that the excess falls on the right.

Cutting Trimwork

Do-it-yourselfers installing new molding will have to make miter cuts. A miter is the most basic joint in trimwork. It's a 45-degree cut where two boards join at right angles, such as at the corners of a window or door frame. It's common to most trimwork in the house.

There are several ways to make miters. The tool of choice for pros (and for amateurs tackling large projects) is a power miter saw. With a sharp, fine-toothed circular blade, you can make quick cuts at 45 degrees for miters because the saw is built with detents that allow you to lock in the correct angle. A power miter saw also adjusts to cut irregular angles. The technique for cutting a compound miter, which is a miter and a bevel cut, depends on the type of tool you are using.

Cutting Crown Molding with a Compound Miter Saw

Inside Corner, Left Side Cope

Tilt the saw to the correct angle, and set the miter gauge to the right. Place the molding so that the top faces the fence and the excess falls to the right.

Inside Corner, Right Side Cope

With the saw tilted, set the miter gauge to the left. Place the molding so that the bottom faces the fence and the excess falls to the right.

Outside Corner, Left Side Miter

With the saw tilted, set the miter gauge to the left. Place the molding so that the bottom faces the fence and the excess falls to the left.

Outside Corner, Right Side Miter

With the saw tilted, set the miter gauge to the right. Place the molding so that the top faces the fence and the excess falls to the left.

(See above for cutting crown molding with a basic miter saw and a compound miter saw.)

If you don't have a power miter saw, you can do very well making cuts on trimwork the old fashioned way: by hand. You can use a handsaw held in a guide or a special miter box that has a blade built into it, generally known by a common trade name, Lion Trimmer.

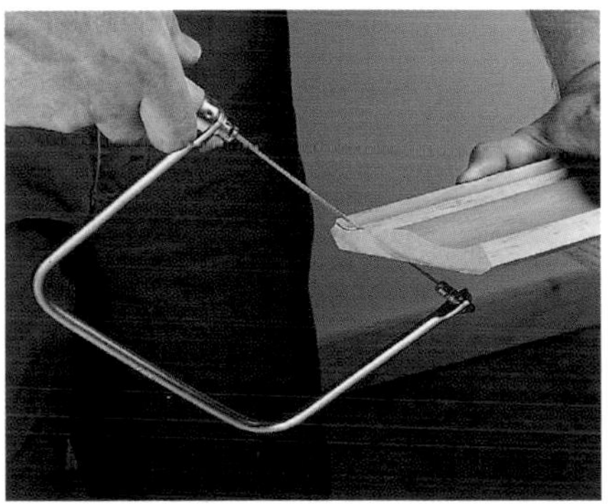

Left A coping saw, with its U-shape and thin blade, is essential equipment for cutting intricate molding shapes in coped joints.

Installation Tips

Most trimwork is attached with a hammer and finishing nails. But there are certain situations when a drill will come in handy.

To avoid narrow pieces of molding from splitting, especially at the ends, use a drill to make pilot holes. These holes also help start nails at the correct angle, preventing bent nails from marring molding.

Cleaning Up Edges

Even if you don't have a home shop full of stationary power tools such as jointers and planers, you can still prepare trimwork. It just takes a little longer using hand and portable power tools. Use a belt sander, right, to smooth surfaces and to provide finishing touches on the edges of boards. Use a power planer, below left, to reduce the width of boards in a hurry. Make a final pass with the rotating blade set to trim just a hair off the edge. Of course, you also can use muscle power and a hand plane, below right. Long planes are best for smoothing and straightening edges.

A belt sander has two drums that spin and guide a continuous belt of sandpaper over the work.

A power planer has a small rotating blade that you can adjust to remove a little or a lot of wood.

A hand plane with an adjustable blade and a long bed can true up and clean the edge of a board.

1 Metal or plastic anchors and screws can be a good solution when attaching trimwork to a wall with no stud.

2 Use a small sanding block to remove blemishes and rough spots from trimwork in tight spots.

3 Trim made of polyurethane requires construction adhesive and nails for installation.

4 Using a hand file to smooth out the rough ends of trimwork allows you to achieve a tight, perfect fit.

Part 2

Trimwork from the Bottom Up

Chapter 4

Base Treatments

Baseboard trimwork comes in many styles and profiles. As with all trimwork, the baseboard style you choose for a room should complement the rest of the molding. Baseboard molding is available in standard one-piece styles. But you can create more ornate built-up looks by combining standard pieces to produce unique details and designs.

The baseboard, base cap molding, and shoe molding make a handsome foundation for this bathroom cabinet and also complement the other trimwork styles in the room.

At its most basic, baseboard molding hides the gap between the wall and floor and for that reason is present in almost every room of the house. It was developed in the eighteenth century as owners of grand houses began to prefer plaster walls over wood paneling, and today it remains true to its purpose of protecting wall surfaces from shoes, furniture, and other domestic hazards. As an architectural detail, baseboard provides a foundation to a wall, as a base does to a column, giving the eye a starting point as it absorbs a room's decoration.

Through the years baseboard has diminished in stature if not ubiquity. Georgian and Federal homes had substantial base molding, sometimes made of marble, but always with its detailing in keeping with door and window casing. Victorian and Craftsman decorators also preferred deep baseboards, although with simpler profiles, the latter often favoring a wide flat board with a slightly rounded top edge. Modern homes typically have narrow ranch- or Colonial-style moldings, sometimes with the same type of trim also used for the window and door casing. Older homes typically have baseboard molding with more character. Rather than replace it, you might want to strip the trimwork and refinish it to bring out its period luster. If part of it is damaged, you can supply a section of undamaged molding to a millwork company that may be able to duplicate the profile.

Baseboard Molding

You have many options when it comes to choosing baseboard for a room. For example, you can buy stock Colonial-style bases as tall as 5½ inches, which may work well in most rooms. Although these boards are slightly less than ½ inch thick and often look too thin on their own, they can serve well as part of a built-up base treatment.

You can build up a base with combinations of different moldings. In most cases, you will be combining a base with a base cap and shoe molding. Both the cap and shoe molding add dimension to the base assembly and help to hide the gaps between the molding and the wall and floor. But you can also rout the details you like into plain-faced stock. When you plan custom bases, consider the height of obstructions such as baseboard heaters and electrical outlets.

Baseboard molding can be painted the same color as the wall above it, creating a look of harmony and seamlessness. Or to provide drama and tension, it can be stained or naturally finished to let the wood grain show through. Either way, baseboard is more than just a functional foundation for a wall; it is a vital component of the trimwork of the entire room.

1

2

1 The high, simple baseboard molding pairs beautifully with the door casing and wall frame.

2 The baseboard trimwork ties the window seat to the rest of the trimwork in the room and adds a fancy foundation.

3 The high, white baseboard molding contrasts smartly with the natural wood wainscoting, attracting the eye to it.

Smart Tip **Molding and Utilities**

Electrical receptacles, phone jacks, and video jacks may interrupt baseboard molding. You have two options. You can either butt two pieces of baseboard to the sides of the electrical outlet or phone jack, or you can allow for the outlet by measuring carefully and cutting out a section of molding for the component. Consider the height of the component before selecting a baseboard size.

A cutout was made in the baseboard molding to accommodate this combination electrical and video-jack receptacle.

1

2

3

4

1 The baseboard trim provides a clean linear feel and gives the eye a starting point in this room full of different trimwork profiles.

2 The natural finish on the baseboard complements the simple furnishings in the room.

3 The circular room requires trimwork that can be bent into shape.

4 A simple low baseboard allows the stenciled plank flooring to take center stage.

Base Molding Profiles

Most period houses contain baseboard molding that consists of flat one-by stock topped with a decorative base cap and finished with shoe molding installed where the baseboard meets the floor. A modern alternative is to choose a one-piece molding profile that contains a milled design, such as the profiles shown here. They range in height from 3½ inches to over 9 inches and are available at home centers and from specialty millwork companies. The designs range from simple to highly elaborate.

Above The simply painted trimwork in this room underscores the elegance of the traditional decor.

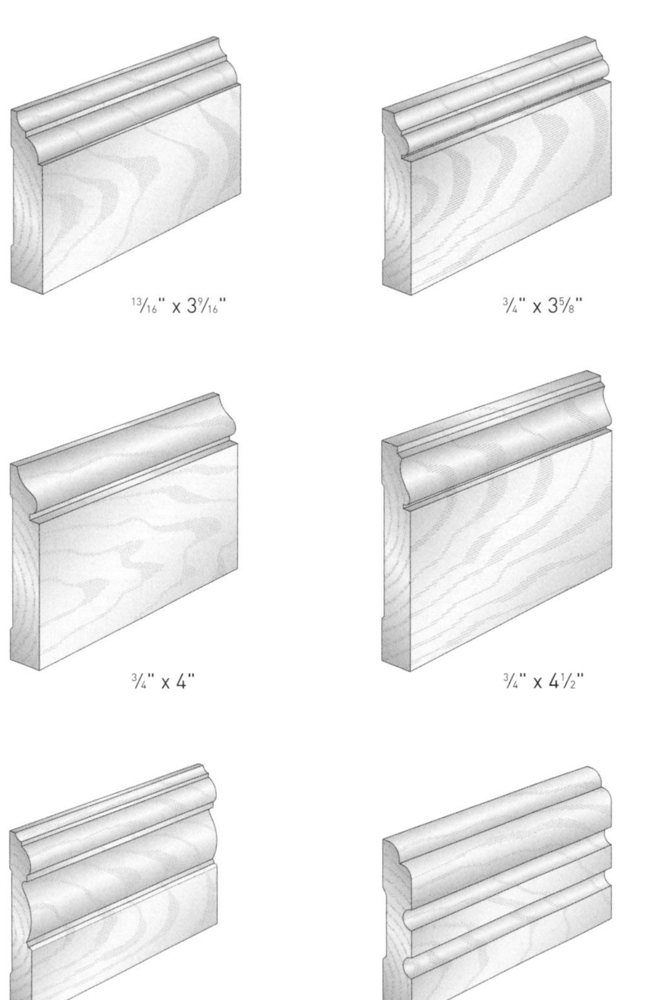

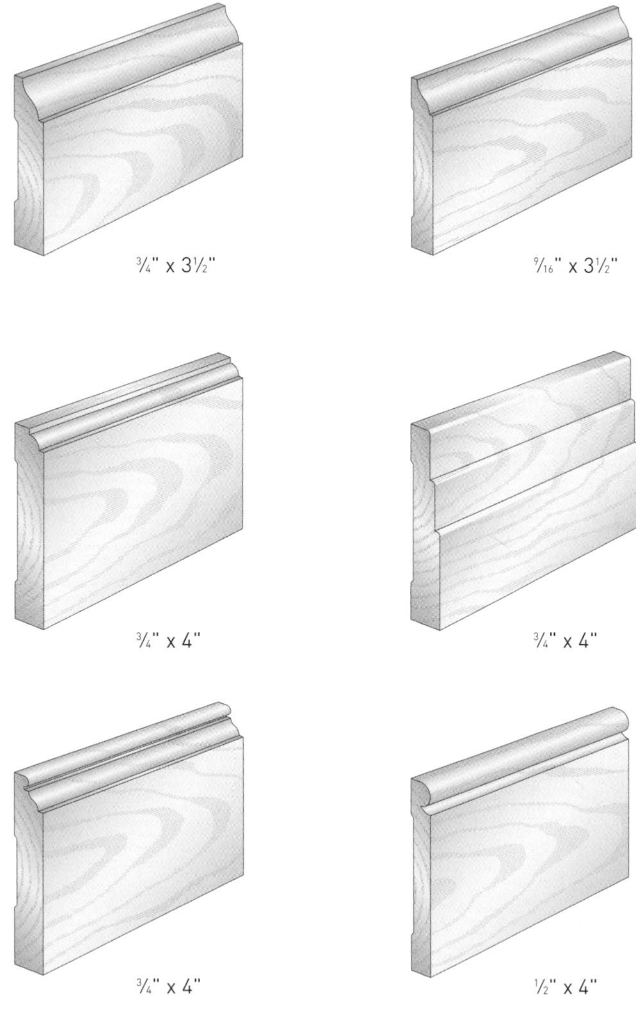

Using Corner Blocks

Using decorative corner blocks with baseboard molding can save you a lot of time and effort. Because the sections of molding butt up against the corner block, there is no need to make miter joints at outside corners and the more-difficult coped joints at inside corners. They also punctuate long and short runs of molding with eye-appealing decoration.

Decorative corner blocks can heighten the drama of already ornate natural finish baseboard molding.

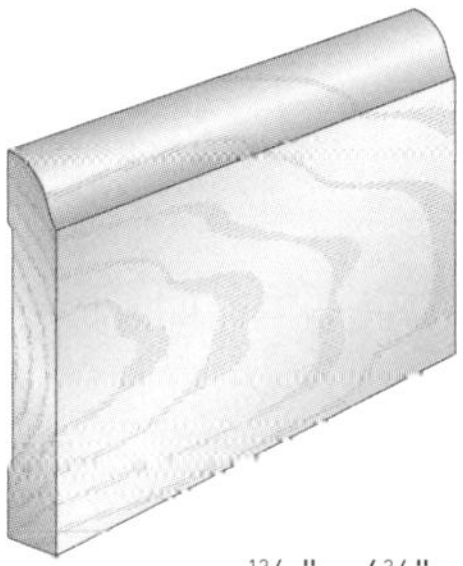

13/16" x 4 3/4"

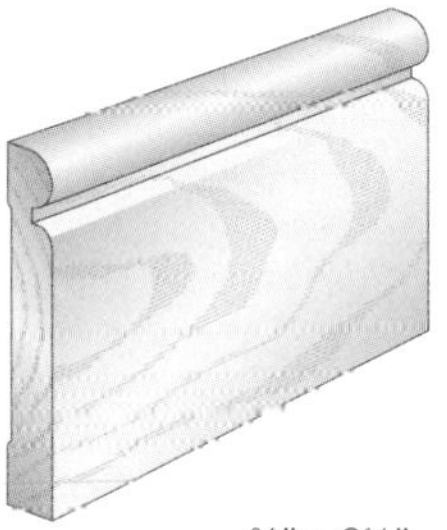

3/4" x 3 1/2"

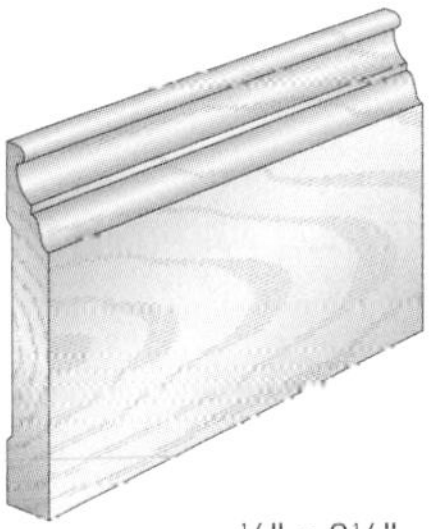

1/2" x 3 1/2"

9/16" x 3 1/2"

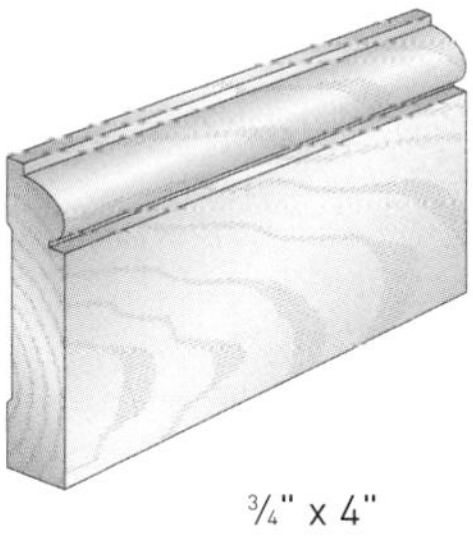

3/4" x 4"

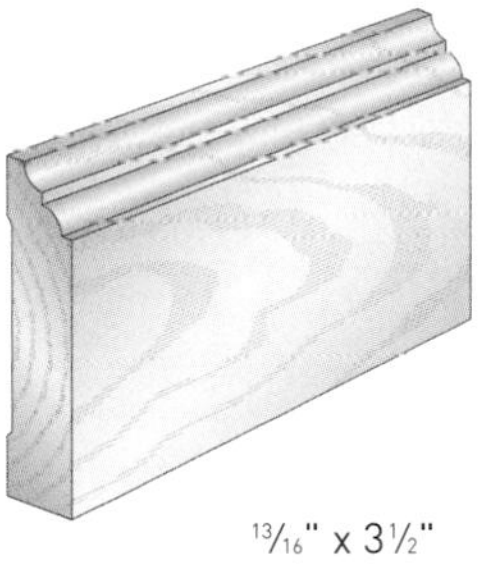

13/16" x 3 1/2"

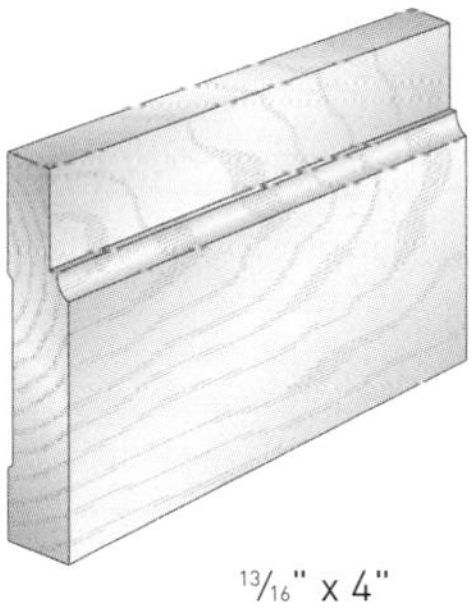

13/16" x 4"

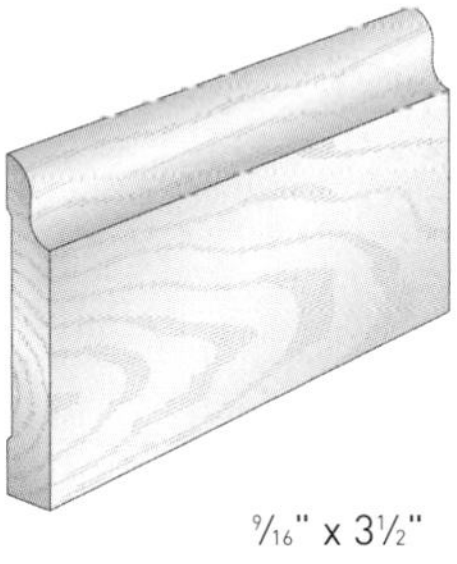

9/16" x 3 1/2"

1/2" x 4"

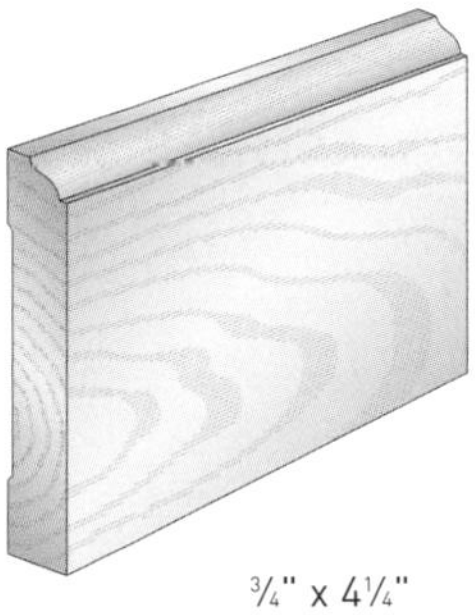

3/4" x 4 1/4"

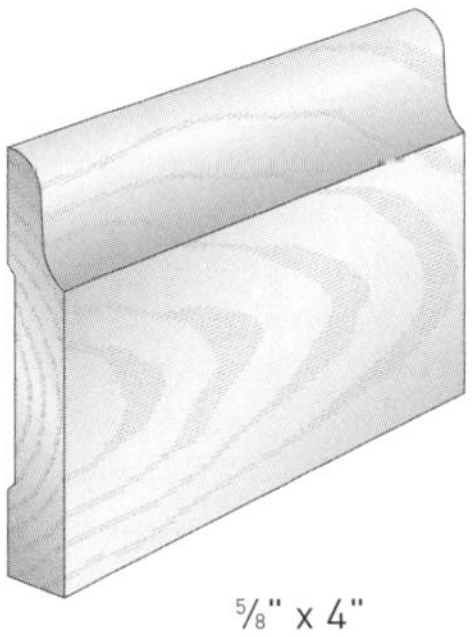

5/8" x 4"

9/16" x 4 3/16"

Baseboard Nailing

Most baseboards require two finishing nails at each stud. You can also drive nails into the bottom plate. For built-up baseboards, install the main board first; then add the cap and other accent moldings. When nailing the bottom of the baseboard, make sure you do it close enough to the floor so that the shoe molding will cover the nailholes. Toenail through the top edge of the baseboard into wall studs so that the cap molding will conceal the nail holes. Nail the base shoe to the floor so that it can move independently of the baseboard and prevent gapping.

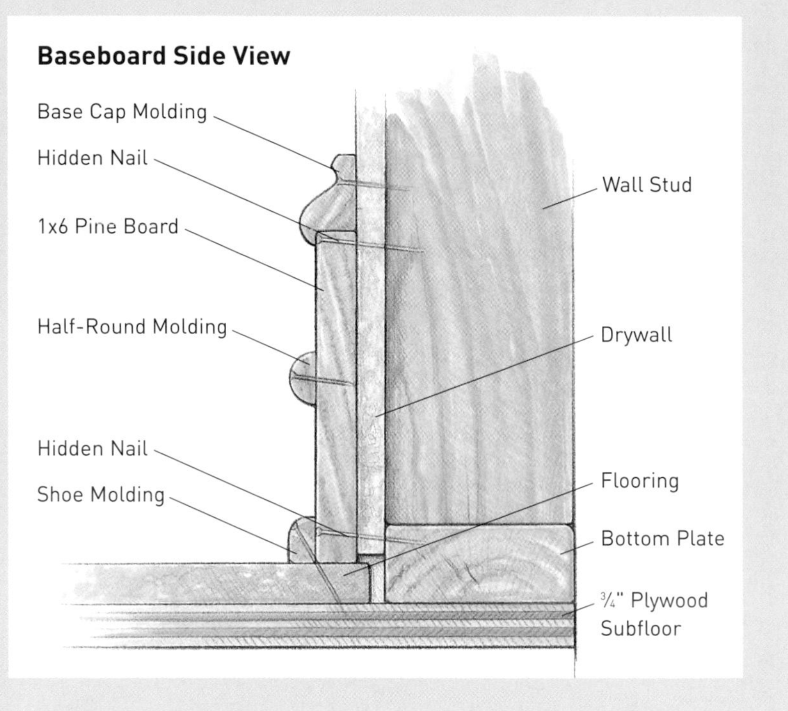

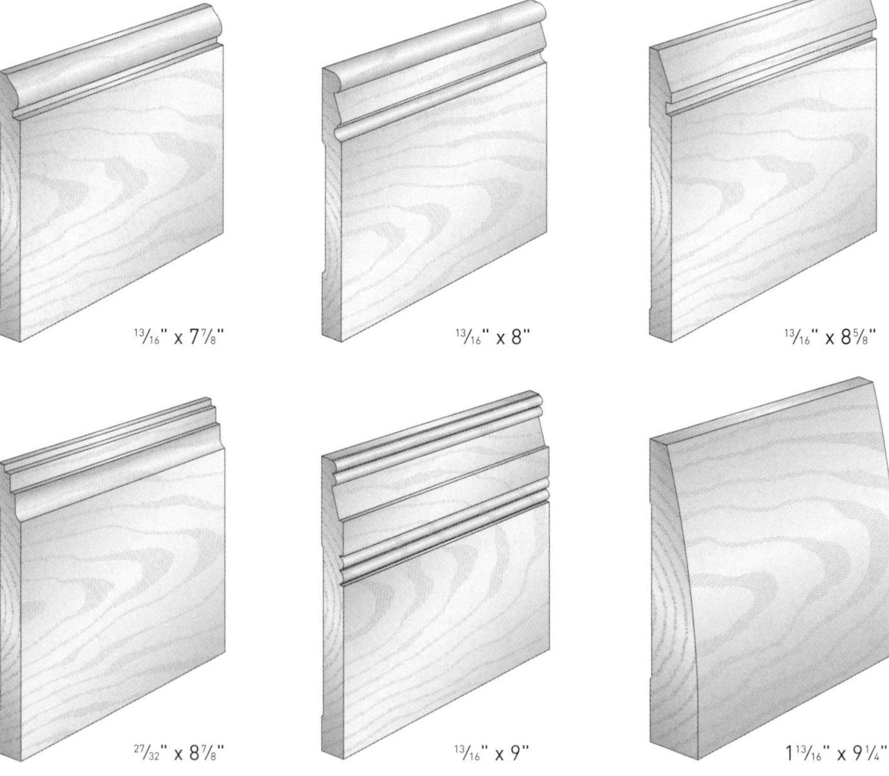

Above The base trim on this Arts and Crafts bottom rail is a simple baseboard with cap and shoe molding.

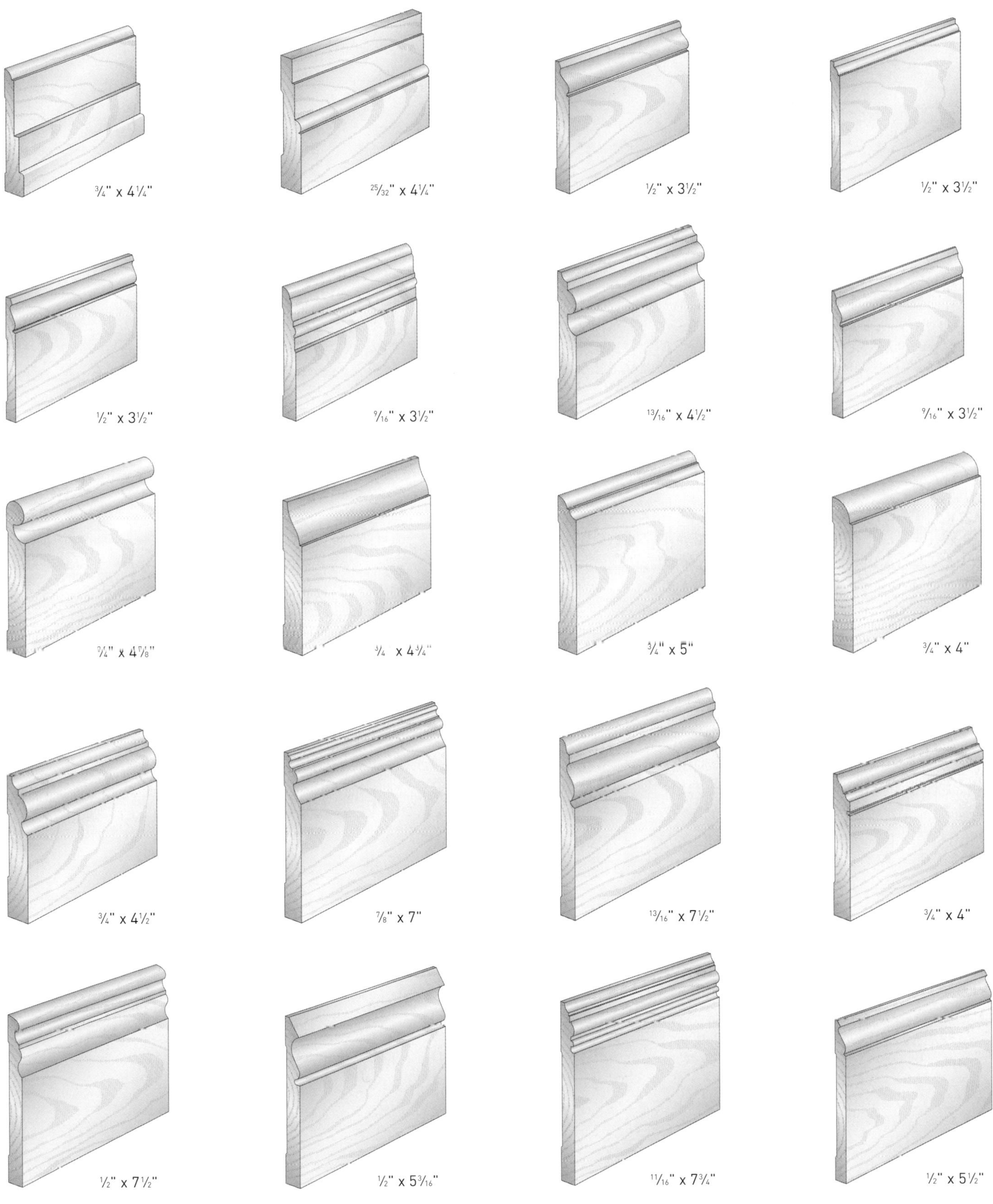
3/4" x 4 1/4"
25/32" x 4 1/4"
1/2" x 3 1/2"
1/2" x 3 1/2"
1/2" x 3 1/2"
9/16" x 3 1/2"
13/16" x 4 1/2"
9/16" x 3 1/2"
3/4" x 4 7/8"
3/4 x 4 3/4"
3/4" x 5"
3/4" x 4"
3/4" x 4 1/2"
7/8" x 7"
13/16" x 7 1/2"
3/4" x 4"
1/2" x 7 1/2"
1/2" x 5 3/16"
11/16" x 7 3/4"
1/2" x 5 1/2"

Base Cap Molding

Base cap moldings enhance the look of just about any baseboard, making a nice finishing detail to the molding. There are any number of base cap options to choose from, as you can see below and to the right. Make sure that any base cap you do decide on complements the base—as well as the window and door casing—and doesn't compete or seem out of character with it.

On a typical three-piece base molding, the cap serves as a transition between the flat stock of the base and the wall.

Above The base cap molding profile echoes the profile of the wall frame above it.

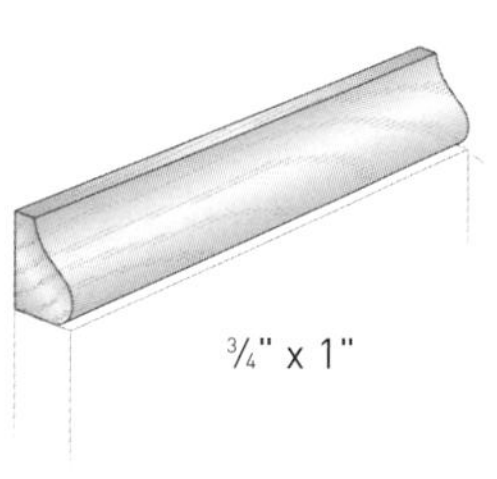

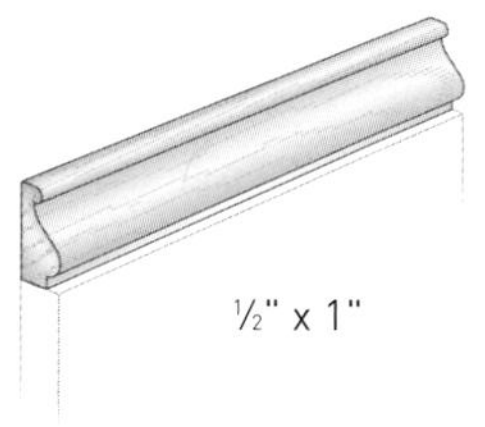

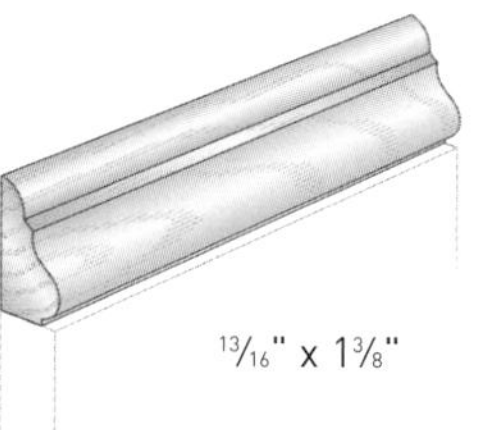

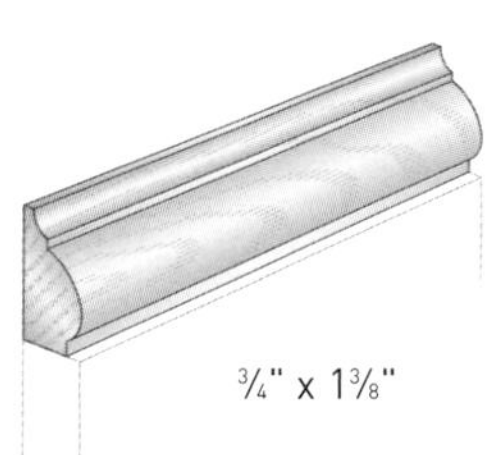

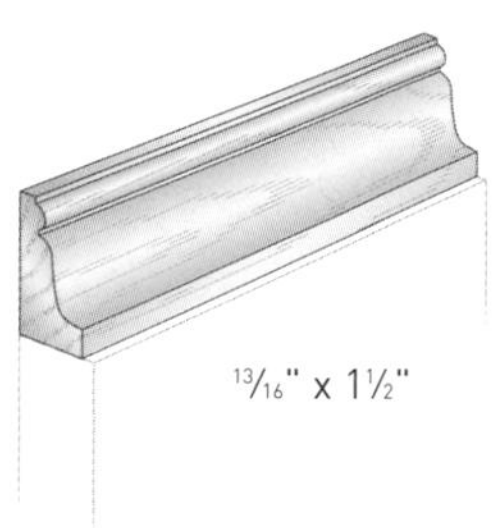

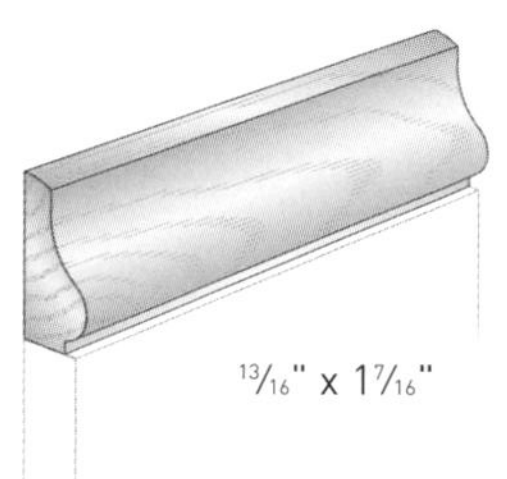

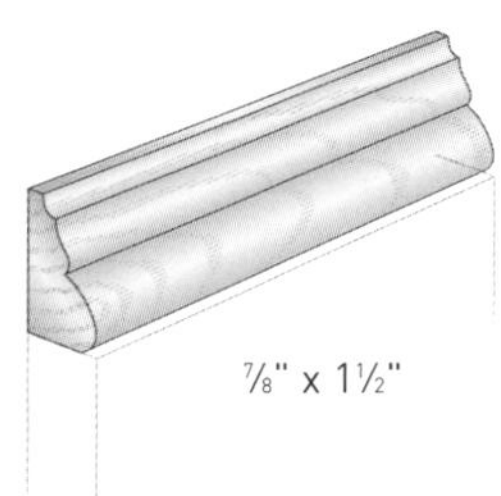

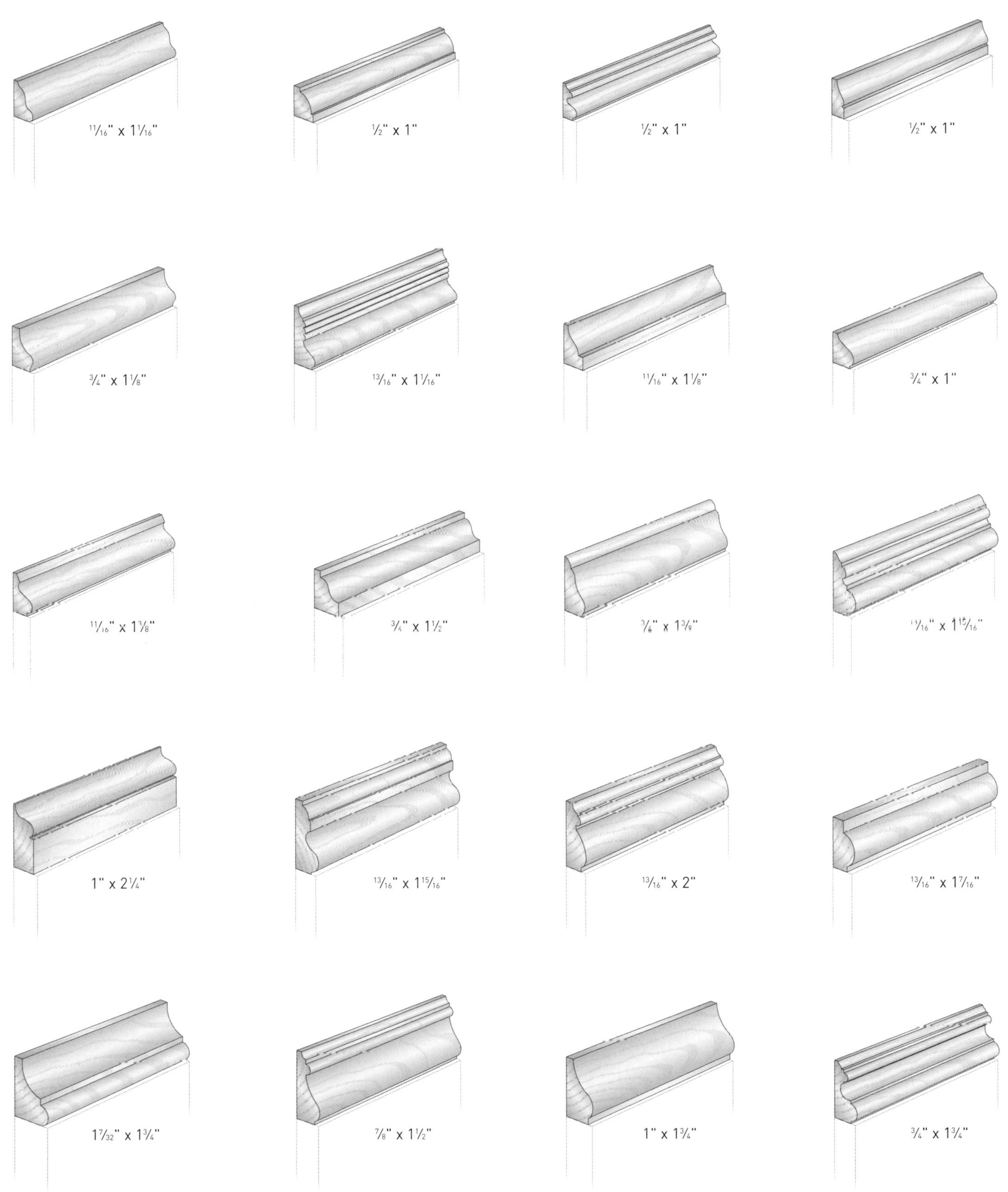
11/16" x 1 1/16"
1/2" x 1"
1/2" x 1"
1/2" x 1"
3/4" x 1 1/8"
13/16" x 1 1/16"
11/16" x 1 1/8"
3/4" x 1"
11/16" x 1 3/8"
3/4" x 1 1/2"
3/4" x 1 3/8"
13/16" x 1 15/16"
1" x 2 1/4"
13/16" x 1 15/16"
13/16" x 2"
13/16" x 1 7/16"
1 7/32" x 1 3/4"
7/8" x 1 1/2"
1" x 1 3/4"
3/4" x 1 3/4"

Smart Tip **Determining Whether Corners Are Square**

One of the most accurate ways to square up corners relies on a simple bit of mathematics you may remember from your high school geometry class. The idea is to use the proportions of a 3-4-5 triangle. Here's how it works: when the three sides of a triangle are in the proportion of 3 : 4 : 5, one of the corners has to be exactly 90 degrees, no matter what unit of measurement you use, inches or feet, or how long the measurements are.

You don't have to remember the Pythagorean theorem. Here is a very simple way to figure out whether your room's corners are square before installing trimwork. On one side, mark a point 3 feet from the corner. On the other side, mark a point 4 feet away from the corner. If the distance between the two marks is exactly 5 feet, the corner is square.

As a double check, measure the length of the diagonals in the room. If the project is square, the distance between two opposite corners will equal the distance between the other two corners.

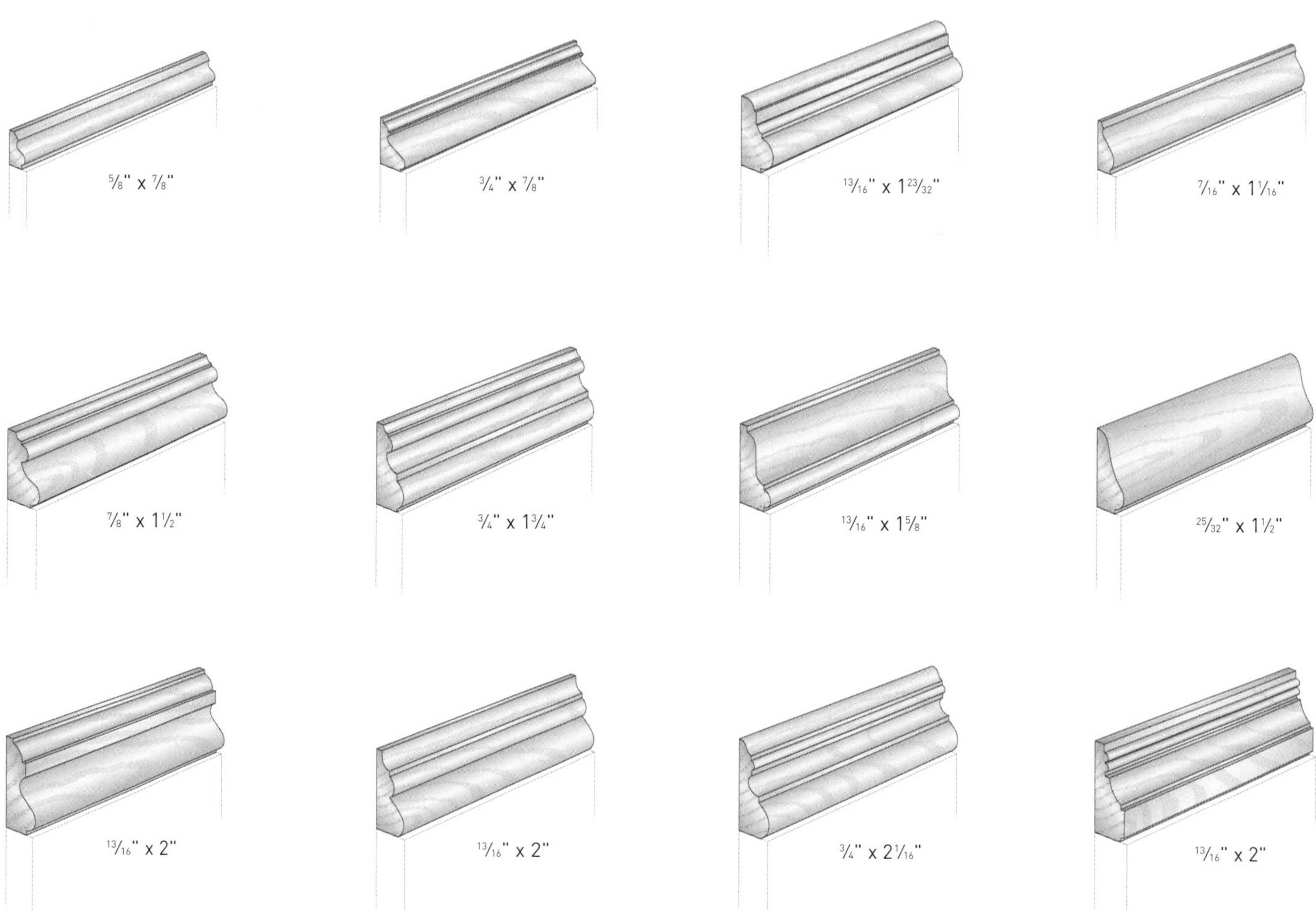

Above Finish base trim with shoe molding and base cap molding that matches the surrounding trim style. Think of all of the trim in a room as part of the same design.

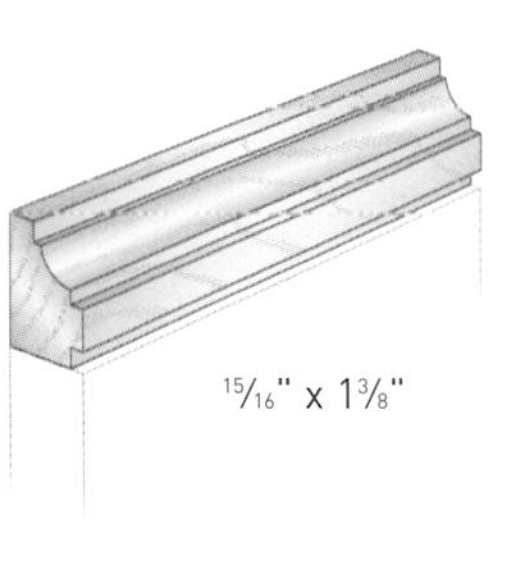

15/16" x 1 3/8"

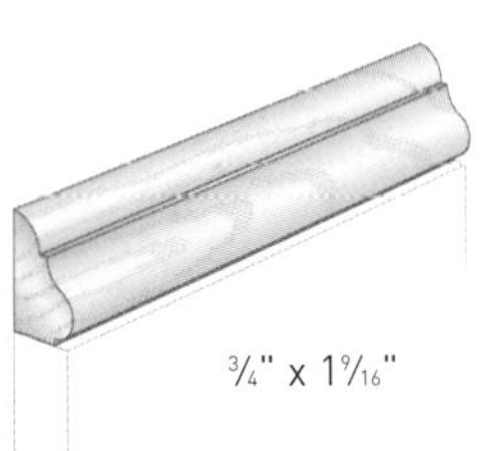

3/4" x 1 9/16"

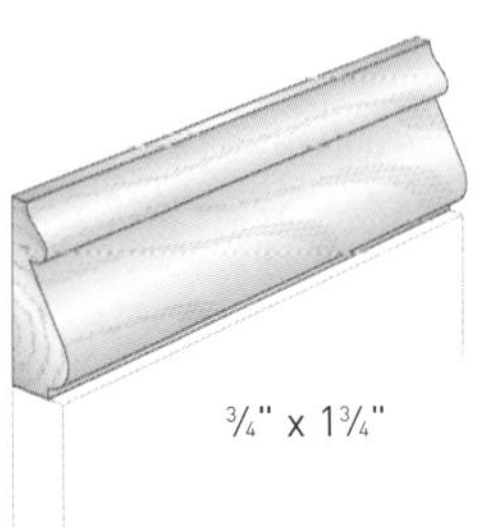

3/4" x 1 3/4"

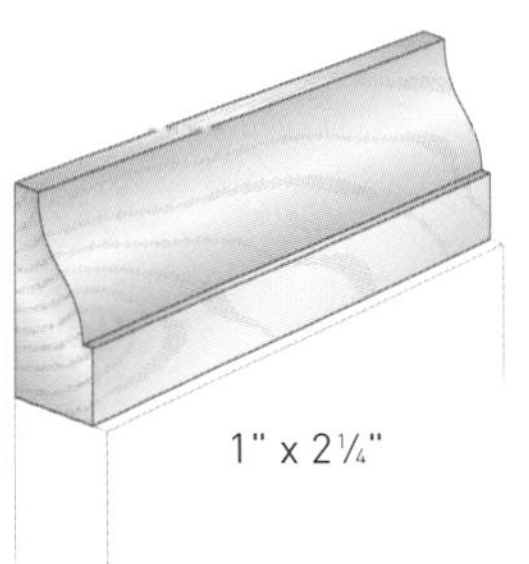

1" x 2 1/4"

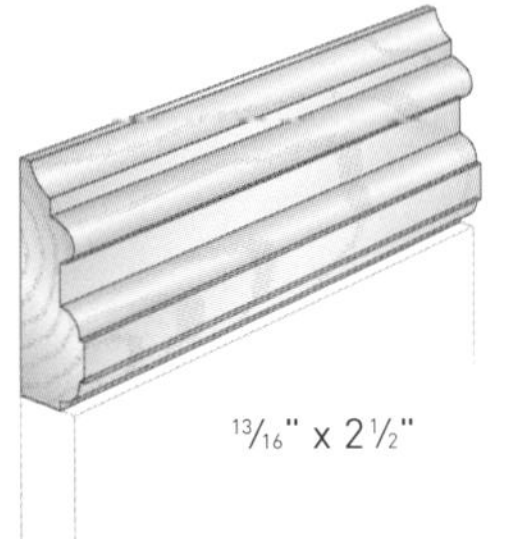

13/16" x 2 1/2"

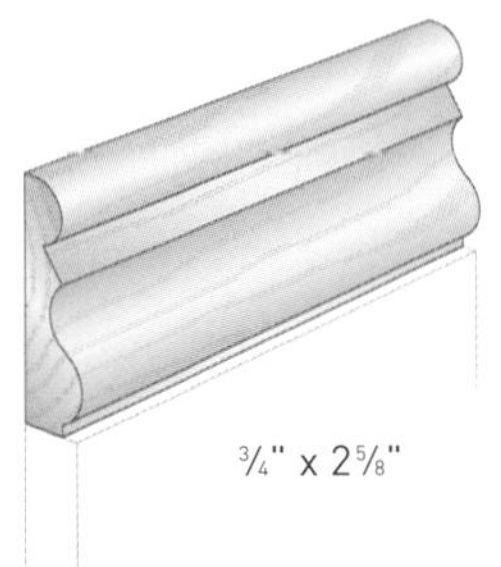

3/4" x 2 5/8"

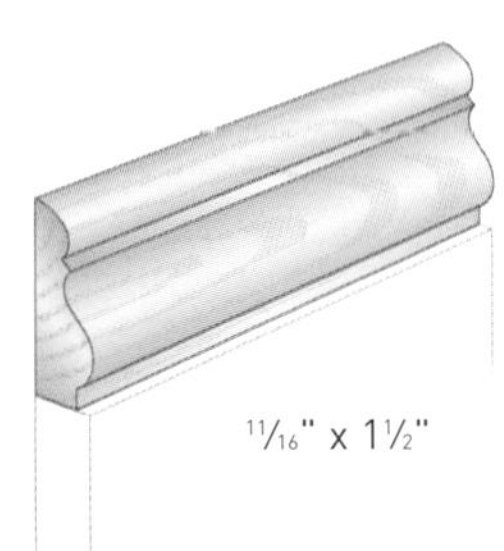

11/16" x 1 1/2"

Special Installations

In many homes, the baseboard is interrupted by heating and cooling registers. It takes some time and close work to do the job right, but the results are usually worth the effort. To prevent splintering when cutting these short sections of molding, place a thin strip of wood not much taller than the base cap between the cap and the saw fence.

One approach is to butt the sides of the register and run the base cap over the exposed top. Another approach is to add a reveal for greater definition. Or set the base cap molding and the top inch of the baseboard over the register so that the register appears to be inset in the molding.

Above Run base cap up and over the top of heating registers for a finished appearance.

Register Options

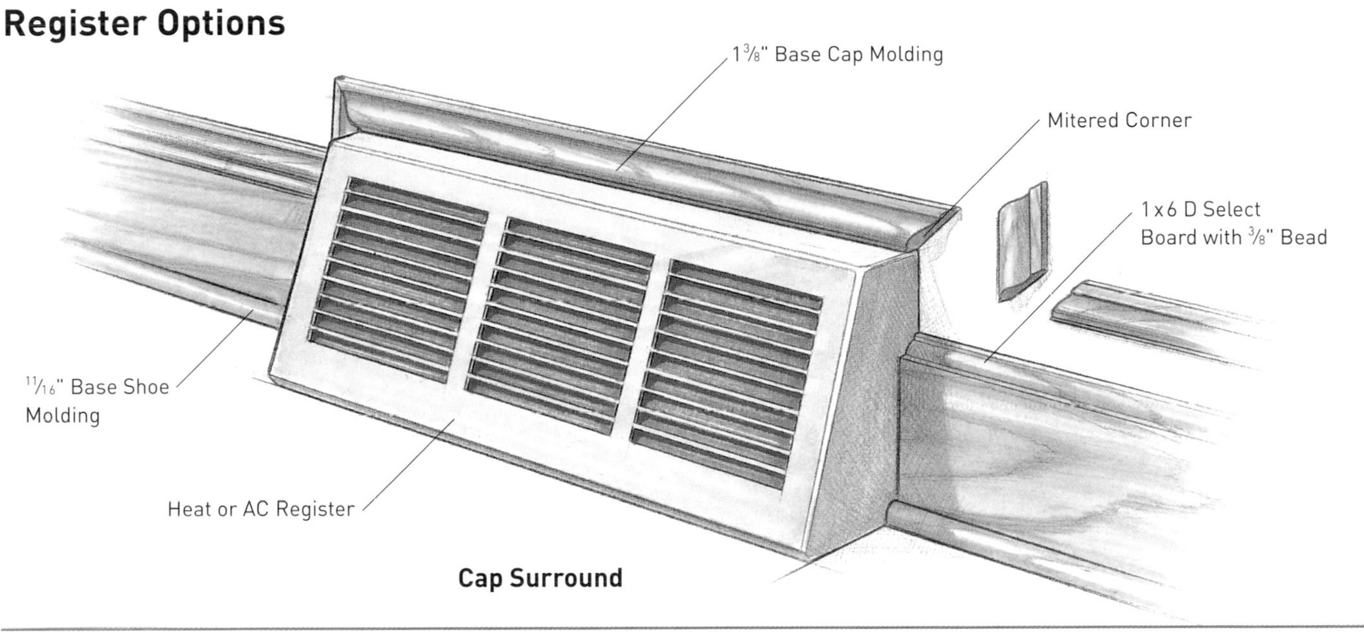

Cap Surround

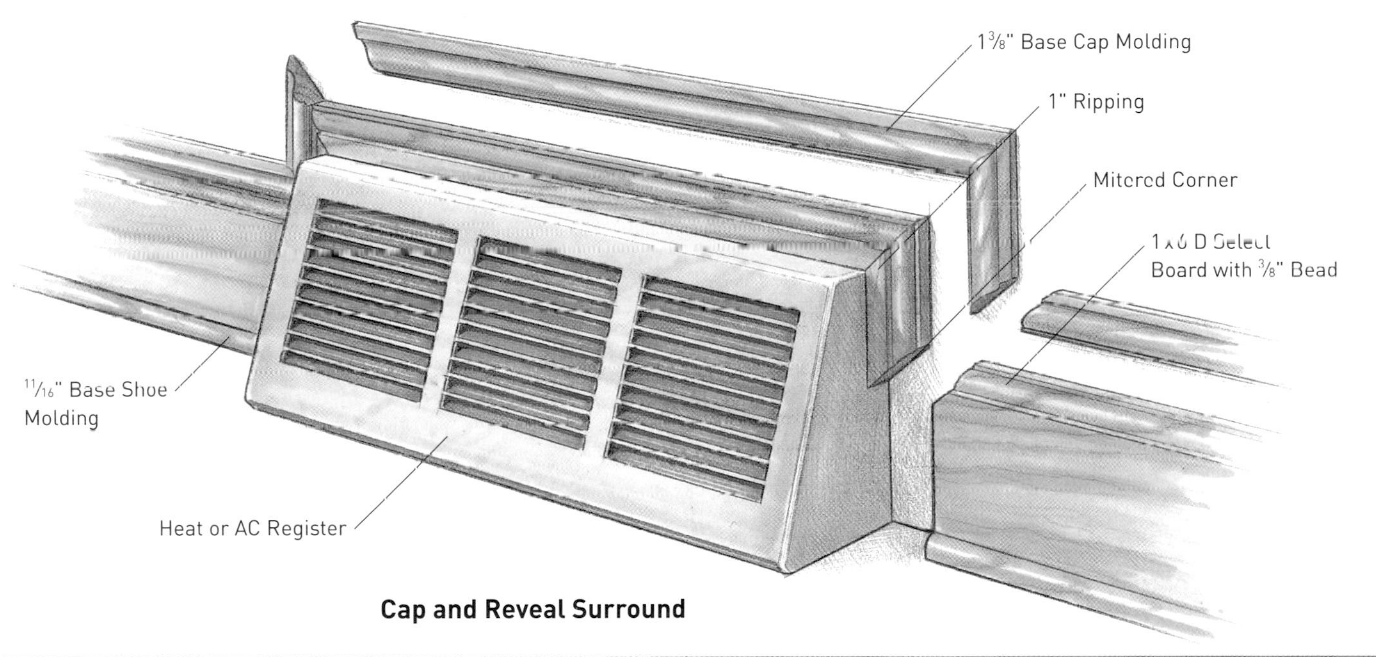

Cap and Reveal Surround

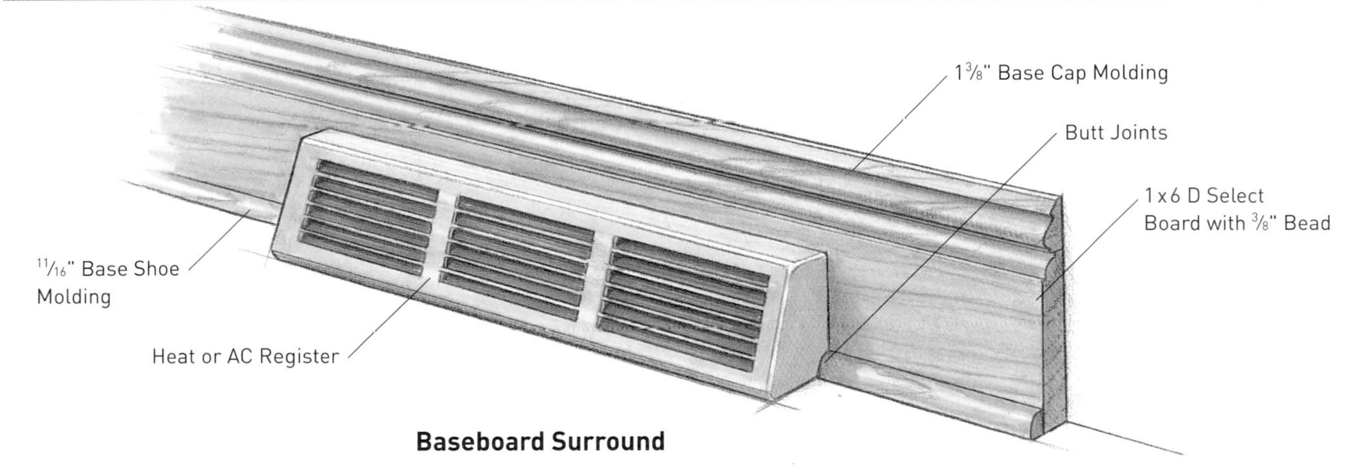

Baseboard Surround

Establishing Floor Levels

In rooms with level floors and plumb walls, installing trim is a straightforward job. If the floor has a few ups and downs, it's a little more complicated.

Generally, if the floor is out of level no more than ½ inch, you can install the baseboard level and cover any gaps with base shoe molding. If the floor is out of level more than ½ inch, you'll need to make adjustments so that the baseboard accommodates the slope of the floor. If you plan to install wall frames or wainscoting, the top

Base Gap Detail

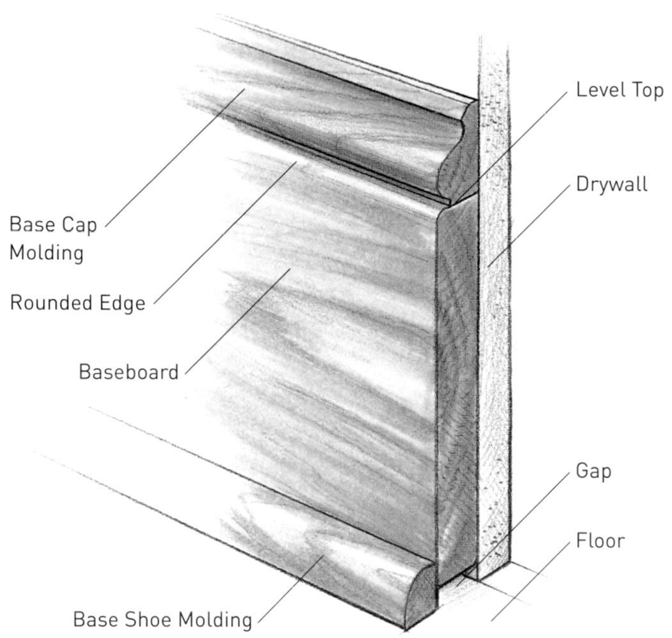

Small Gaps

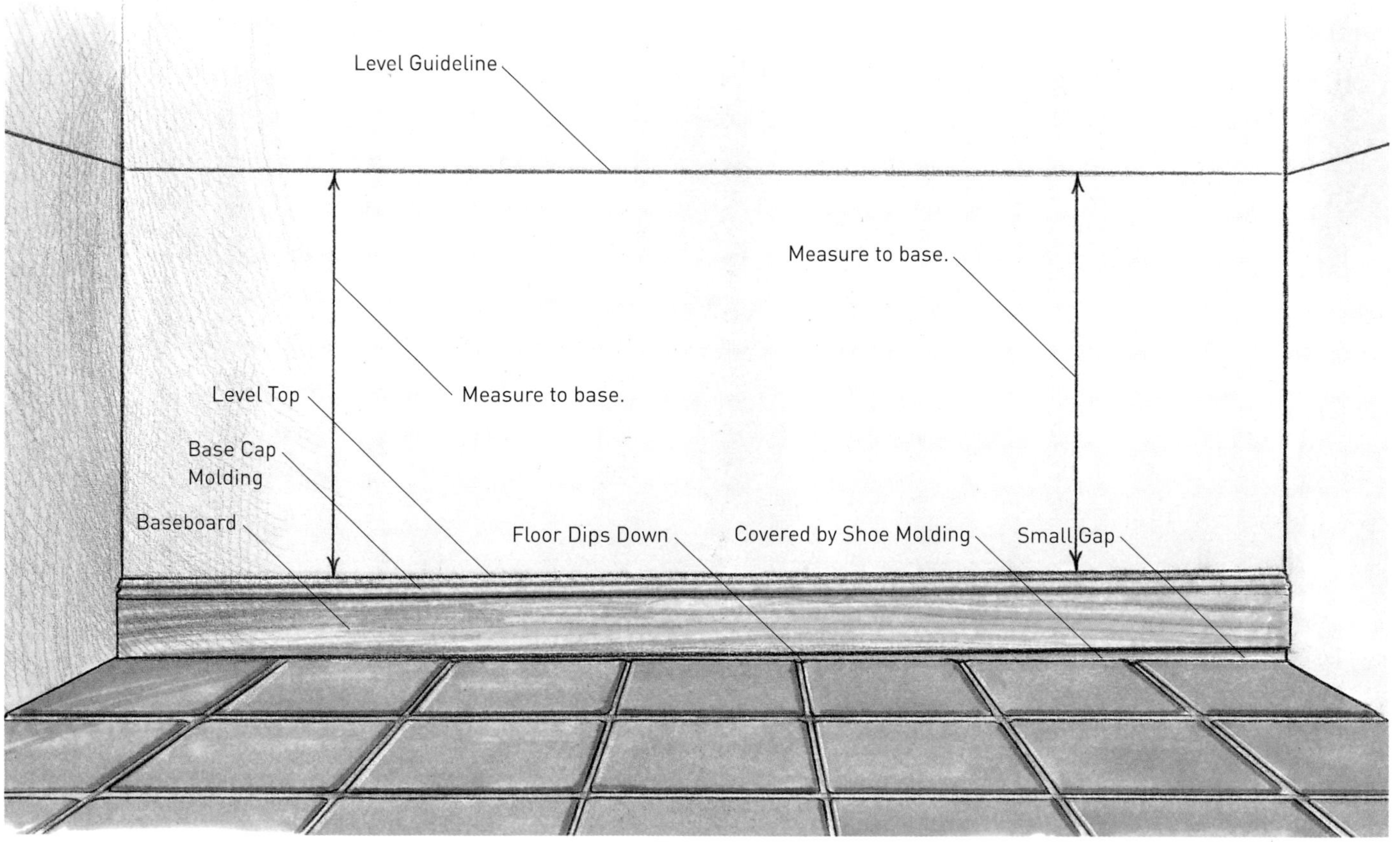

of the base trim needs to be level all around the room.

To establish a floor level, work off a level reference line that you draw on the wall around the room, determining the distance from the line to the floor on each side of the room and at both sides of all doorways and passageways. The shortest distance between the reference line and the floor indicates the floor's high point. The longest distance indicates the floor's low point. The illustrations opposite bottom and below show how to determine the size and location of any gaps.

If the difference between the low and high points is more than ½ inch, it's best to trim the bottom of the baseboard where it traverses the higher floor areas. Scribe a cut line on the trim and make the cut carefully. Remember that you have some margin to play with because the shoe molding or carpeting will hide gaps. As a general rule, you can raise the base over the lower areas of the floor by about ½ inch, which reduces the amount of trimming you will have to do. The important thing to remember is that the top of the base must be level.

Large Gaps

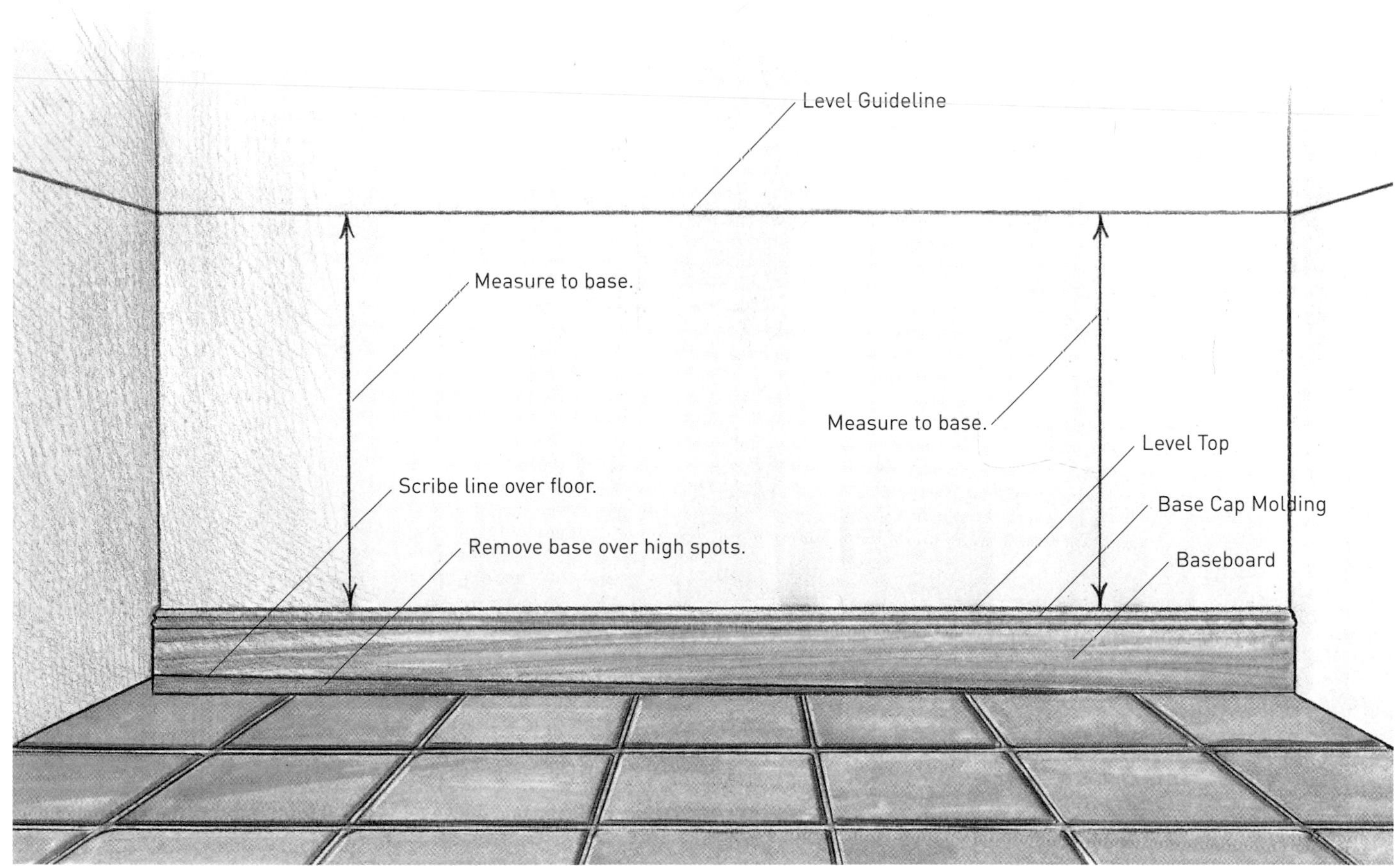

Chapter 5

Trimwork for Windows and Doors

Casing surrounds door and window openings, hiding the gap between the wall finish and the jambs of the door or window frames. In most cases, the same casing is used for the doors and windows, although main entry doors often carry different trim than internal doors. There are many profiles and styles of trim for windows and doors.

The natural finish Gothic arch echoes the window arches in the room and adds classical charm to contemporary furnishings.

Casing plays an important and unique decorative role because it frames passages, affecting the view of what lies beyond the passage, just as a picture frame contributes to the visual impact of the painting it contains.

Most casing styles can be grouped into one of two broad categories: tapered and square. Tapered casing is heaviest along its outside edge and tapers around the edge that contacts the door or window jamb. This type of casing is almost always installed with mitered corners (like a picture frame). Stock Colonial and clamshell casings are tapered casings.

Square casing has the same thickness on both sides and, if not smooth, has symmetrical detailing across its face. Square casing can be mitered at the corners or can be combined with decorative corner blocks and plinth blocks, adding visual weight and substance to the treatment. These casings often look more decorative than stock Colonial-style casings, and they are easier for most do-it-yourselfers to install because you don't have to miter square casings.

In addition, door and window casings can be built up with molding to form more formal or elaborate treatments. Visually connect passageways and banks of windows with a surround of trim that ties into baseboard and chair rail moldings.

1

1 The window header above the gracefully curved French doors adds drama and airiness to this passageway.

2 The window casings pick up the staircase motif, reinforcing the playful feel of the stenciled walls.

3 Architectural elements like this ornate cap can enhance arched trimwork in an entryway.

Window and Door Casing

Door casing consists of a horizontal head casing joined to two vertical leg casings. The simple window surround most common in modern homes consists of tapered casing along all four sides of the window. A more traditional style is the stool-and-apron treatment, in which a flat, horizontal stool, or windowsill, projects out from the window and an apron finishes the underside of the stool.

In addition to casing, doors and windows in older homes often carry attractive header treatments. Classical pediments were common in homes from the Georgian through the Colonial Revival periods; now they're available through architectural product dealers. Even more popular is the big frieze header: a broad horizontal frieze board topped with crown and other moldings. Variations of the frieze header are easy to make using stock lumber and standard molding.

3

2

1

2

3

Smart Tip **Hiding Joints with Caulk**

It's difficult to get perfect miter cuts with large casings, but it you plan to paint the molding, you can fill small gaps with paintable caulk and still achieve professional-looking results. Read the label closely. Always apply the caulk sparingly; wipe off the excess with a damp sponge; let dry according to the instructions; and apply a coat of primer to the molding. Once dry, finish with paint.

5

4

1 The oval trimwork and curvilinear grillwork on the window provide a beautiful focal point in this bathroom.

2 Elaborate header treatments capping these passageways add continuity and draw the eye toward the skylight.

3 The attractive header treatment adds architectural interest to this bank of plain windows.

4 The plain window casing ties in the counter and shelving below it.

5 A decorative header, built up from many different styles of trimwork, adds a classical formality to the passageway.

1

2

3

1 The decorative caps and fluted trimwork on the windows and wall cabinet add eye appeal.

2 Corner blocks, built-up door casings, and plinth blocks add architectural interest to this passageway.

3 Add drama to a passageway by painting doorway and ceiling details with a contrasting paint or stain color.

Creating and Trimming a Pass-Through

Designing and building a pass-through is not a difficult project. The construction involved is fairly simple, provided the wall is a nonbearing partition. There are many ways to finish a new pass-through or add trim to an existing one. One popular treatment is to wrap the inside of the opening with jambs of finish lumber; then install casing on both sides, like a window surround.

To add a shelf, notch the ends of the shelf to create horns that will receive the bottom ends of the side casing and add an apron board below the shelf in the style of a stool-and-apron window surround. Adding shutters or doors to enclose the pass-through keeps the space private and adds a decorative feature to the opening.

Pass-Through Construction

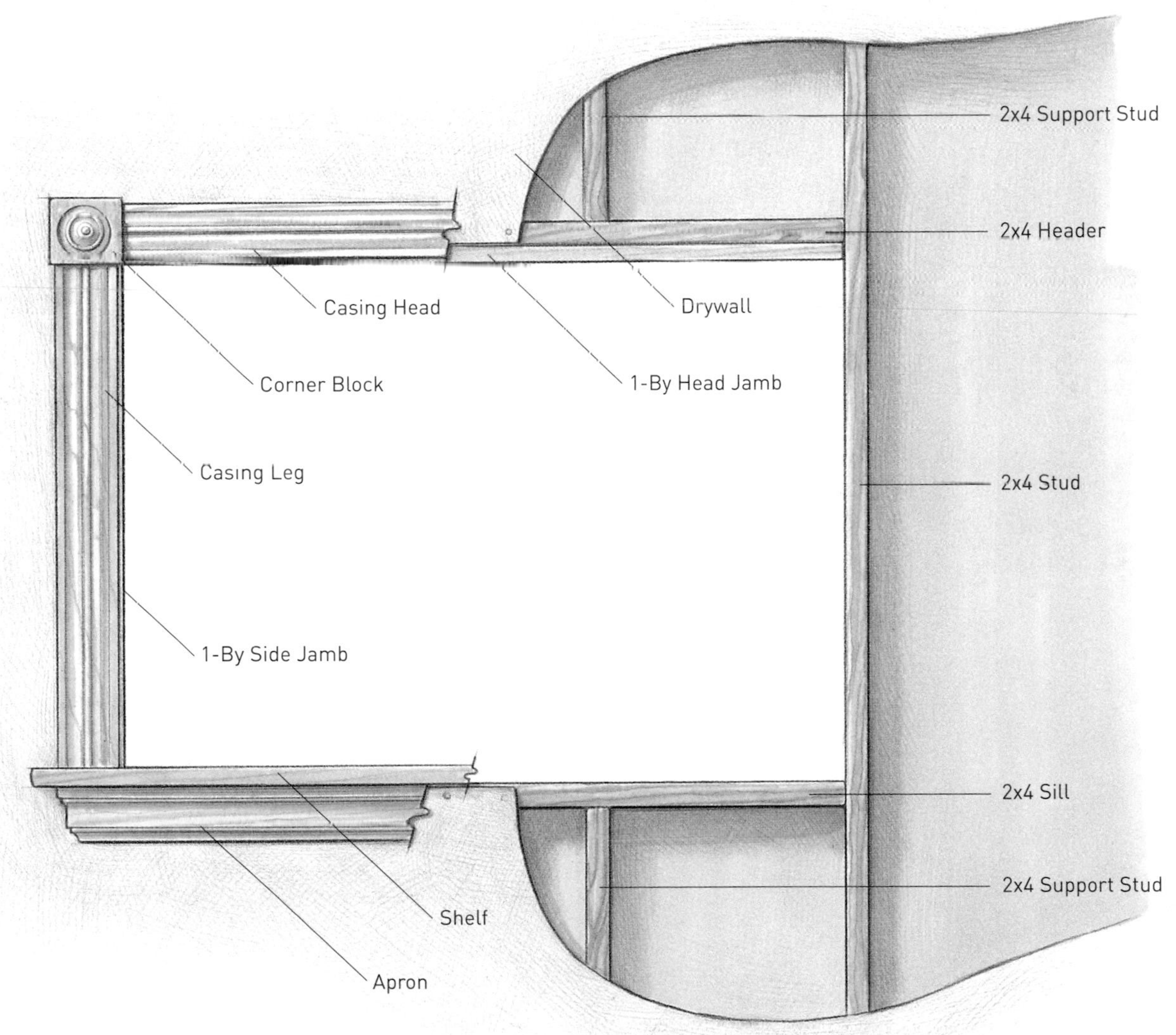

Ideas for Arched Openings

An arched passageway opens up a room and adds classical charm to any home. You can add an arched passageway to your home with a do-it-yourself archway trim kit. Such kits are available from architectural product dealers and generally come in a few different neoclassical styles. To install a kit, remove any trim from the existing opening; add blocking and triangular drywall pieces at the top corners; then fit and attach the arch and columns.

Another way to create an arched passageway is to use prefabricated arch corners that are installed directly over wood or steel framing. The corners butt flush against standard drywall and do not require finishing along the curved edges.

Victorian detailing

Smooth-surface archway

Gothic design

Arch with decorative keystone

Classic trimwork

Casing Profiles

There is a wide variety of casing profiles for windows and doors. As with other trimwork, the style of your home will play a role in trim selection around doors and windows. Details should be in proportion to the rest of the room.

Most home centers carry many standard types of trim. If you are looking for custom molding, millwork shops, mail-order companies, and the Internet offer any number of period moldings. Another option is to visit a salvage shop for architectural elements like pediments to embellish passageways and banks of windows. Columns can dress up passageways, adding a classical touch to a modern home.

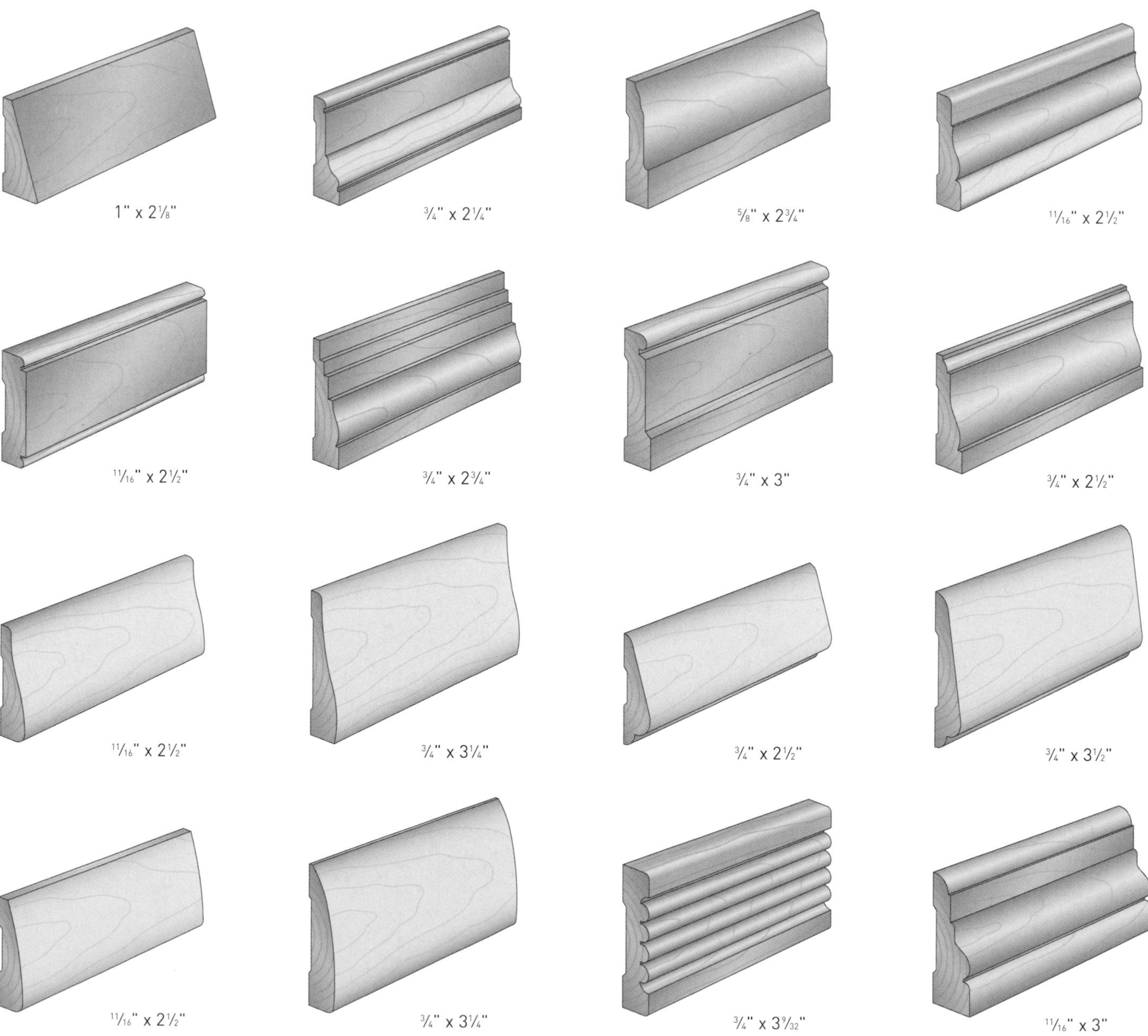

Building a Window Cornice

A traditional cornice like the one shown here starts with a simple wooden box. Cover the box with any combination of molding, fabric, or decoration.

Cut the side, top, and front pieces for the box from ¾-inch plywood or MDF, or one-by paint-grade lumber. Plan so that the top piece overlaps the edges of the side and front pieces. If the corner joints will not be covered with molding, fit the side and front pieces together with mitered joints so that no end grain is exposed. Assemble the box with wood glue and screws. Test-fit the box over the window, and mark the wall for a 2x2 nailer or metal L-bracket for mounting the cornice. Fasten the nailer or brackets to the window header using screws.

Finish the cornice by adding molding. Crown molding provides an attractive angled profile to the top, while base cap, panel cap, or small chair-rail molding works well along the bottom. You can also install a flat bead molding (glass bead) so that it covers the bottom edges of the box.

Mount the cornice by screwing through the top piece into the nailer or through the L-brackets into the top piece.

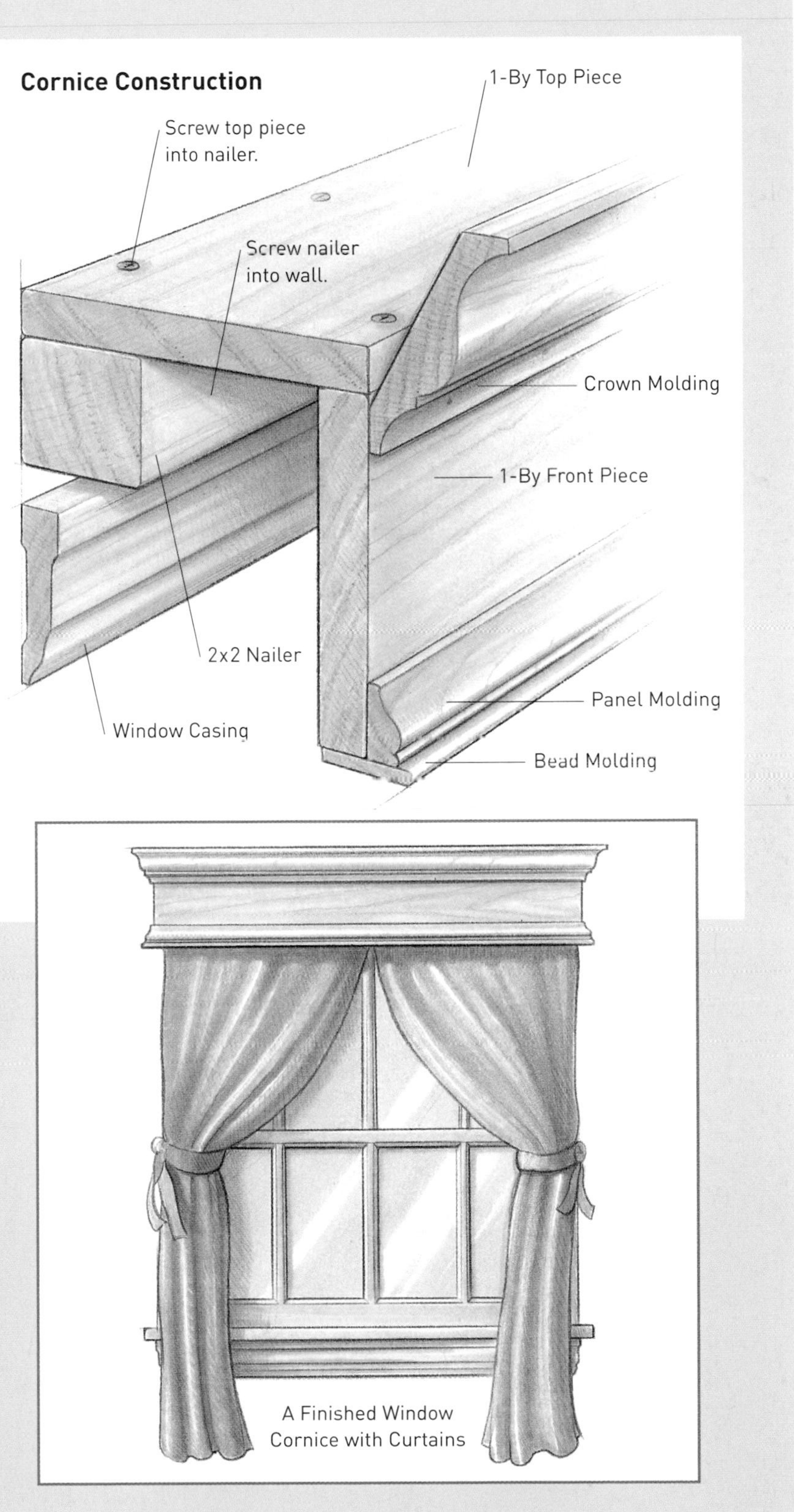

A Finished Window Cornice with Curtains

Installing Window and Door Casings

The first step to installing casing is establishing the reveal: the narrow strip of jamb that is left exposed when the casing is installed. Most reveals are about ⅛ inch. When you decide what looks best, make light pencil marks representing the reveal on each jamb at the corners of the opening. Use these marks for measurement.

To install mitered casing, cut the casing pieces and temporarily tack them in place; then make sure the joints fit tightly before permanently attaching the casing. Nail the casing to the jamb edges with small (4d or so) finishing nails; then nail through the outer edges of the casing into the wall framing, using 6d finishing nails.

If you're using corner and plinth blocks, install them first; then cut the casing to fit in between.

Butted Casing with Mitered Backband

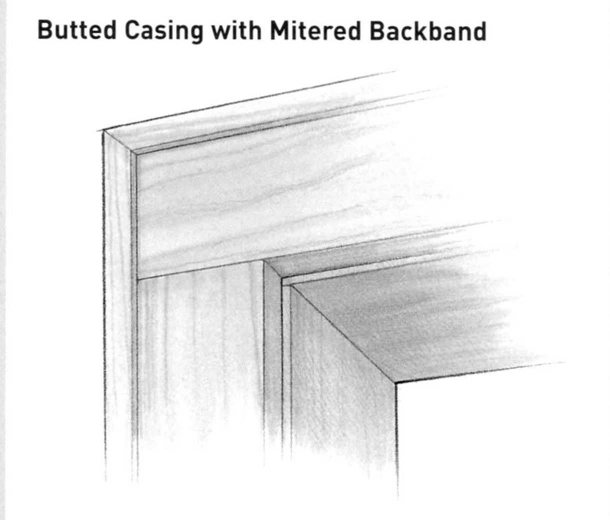

Butted Casing with Reveal

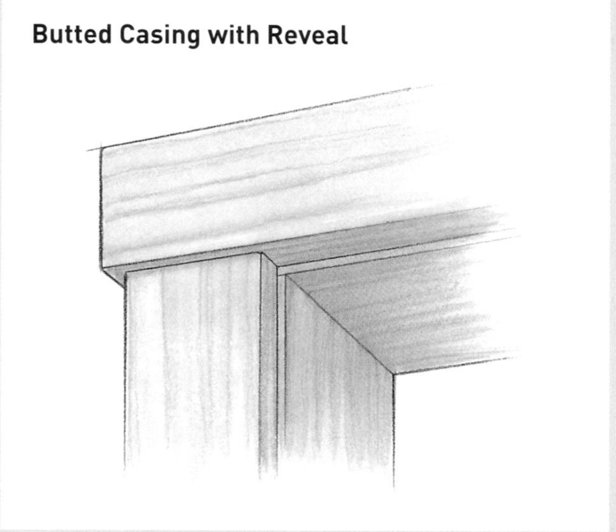

Mitered Casing

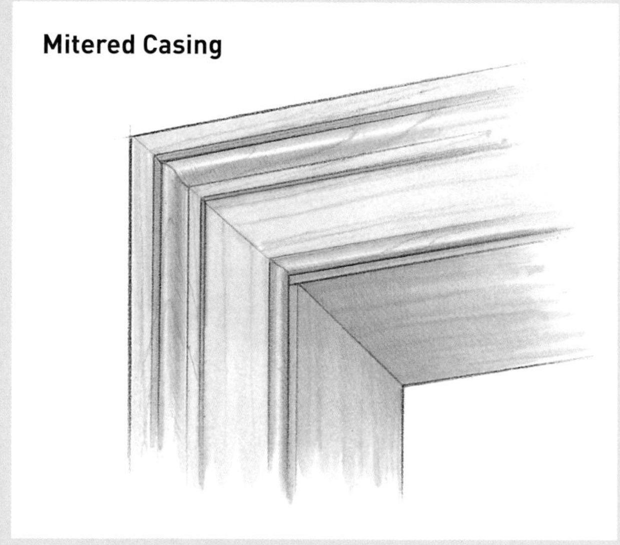

Casing with Corner Blocks

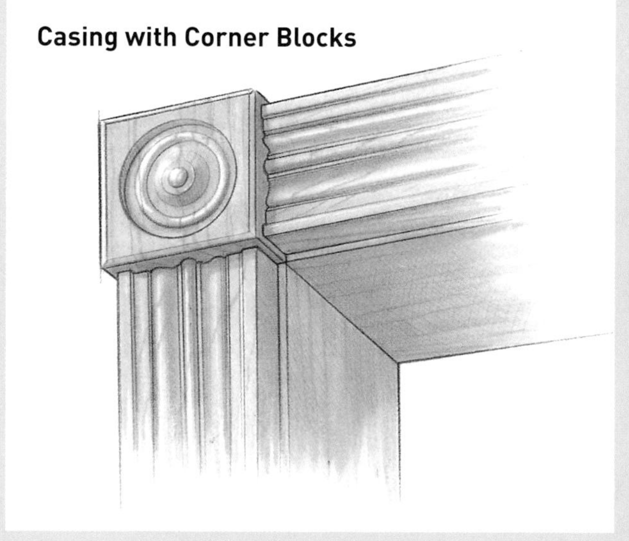

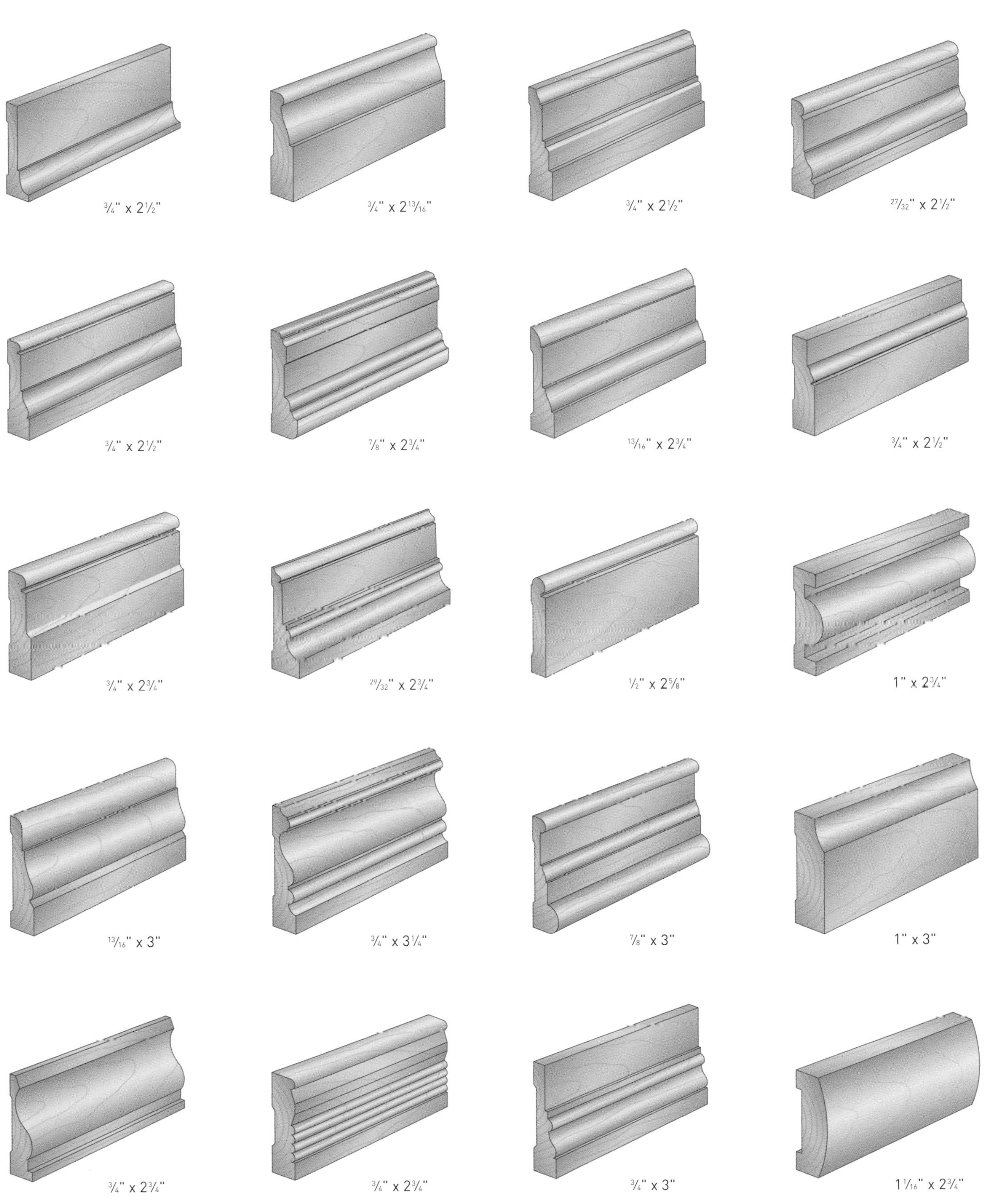

3/4" x 2 1/2"
3/4" x 2 13/16"
3/4" x 2 1/2"
27/32" x 2 1/2"
3/4" x 2 1/2"
7/8" x 2 3/4"
13/16" x 2 3/4"
3/4" x 2 1/2"
3/4" x 2 3/4"
29/32" x 2 3/4"
1/2" x 2 5/8"
1" x 2 3/4"
13/16" x 3"
3/4" x 3 1/4"
7/8" x 3"
1" x 3"
3/4" x 2 3/4"
3/4" x 2 3/4"
3/4" x 3"
1 1/16" x 2 3/4"

Arts and Crafts-Style Casing

A hybrid approach to trimming openings resembles the Arts and Crafts style in some respects but blends with a simplified version of the neoclassical approach. The leg casings are not fluted, because Arts and Crafts detailing calls for a flat profile and sometimes almost rugged-looking use of lumber.

You can use the illustration below as a model, but alterations should be made to suit the style of your house. For example, if you want to stay closer to pure Arts and Crafts style, you may avoid elaborate cornice molding with end returns at the top of the assembly and use something basic, such as strips of backband molding.

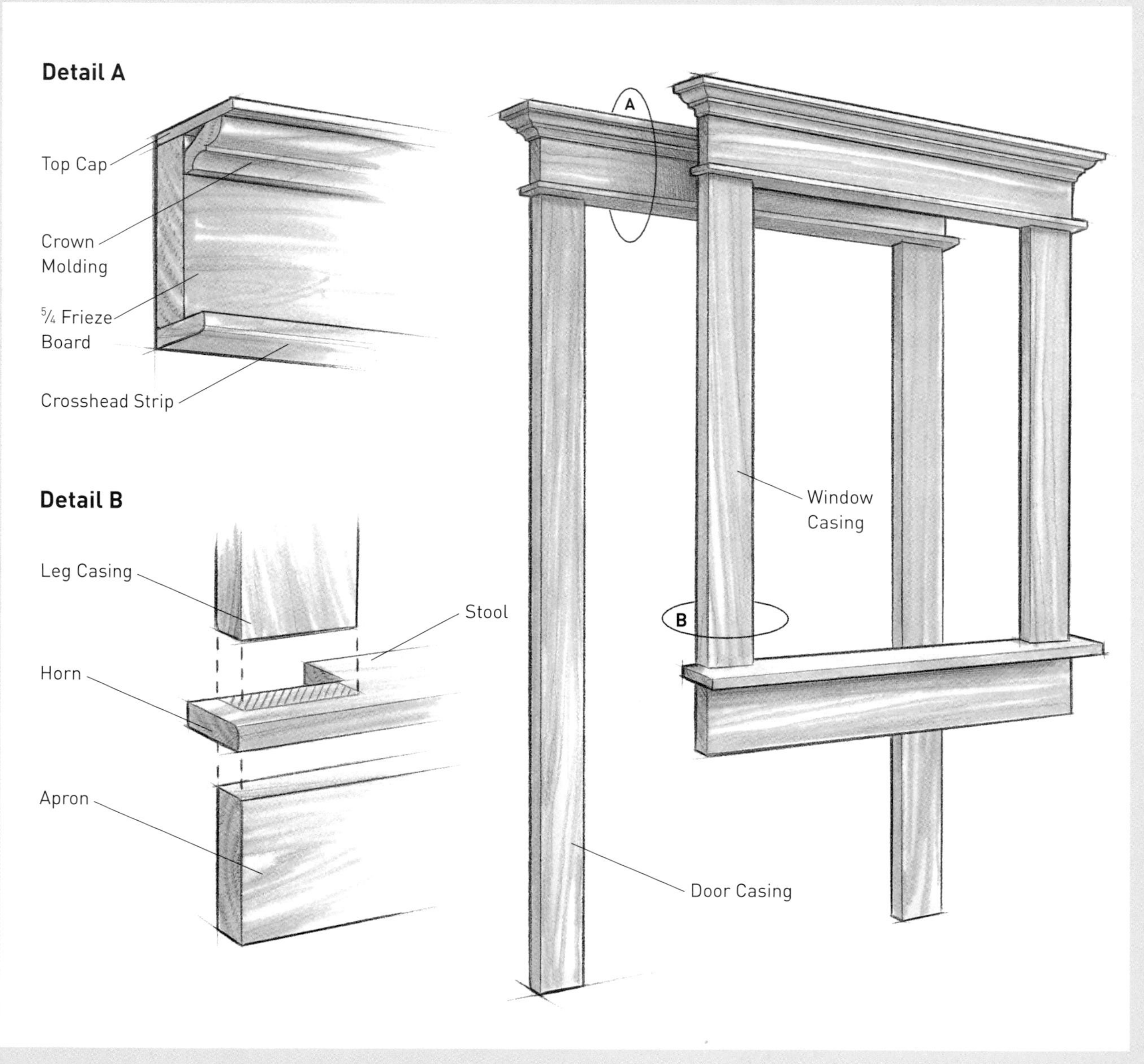

13/16" x 2 5/8"
13/16" x 3 1/16"
3/4" x 3"
13/16" x 3"
3/4" x 3 1/4"
3/4" x 3 1/2"
11/16" x 3 1/4"
13/16" x 3 1/4"
3/4" x 3 9/16"
7/8" x 3 9/16"
1" x 3 1/2"
3/4" x 3 5/8"
13/16" x 3"
25/32" x 3"
3/4" x 3"
11/16" x 3"
7/8" x 3 1/2"
13/16" x 3 31/32"
3/4" x 3 1/2"
5/8" x 3 3/4"

Corner Blocks and Casing

Corner blocks are a charming addition to any door or window casing. The rosette blocks shown below combine well with a wide range of leg and header casings. One approach is to use a combination square to draw reveal lines on the jambs. The inside edges of the casings will follow these lines. You should set each corner block with its lower inside corner flush with the corner formed by the side jamb and head jamb. This arrangement is easy to lay out and install, but you should check that the casing follows the reveal on the jamb and is centered on the corner block.

You might want to tack the blocks into position first and center the narrower casings on the wider blocks to establish the reveal along the jamb. Be sure that you make square cuts on the ends of the leg casings to assure a tight joint against both the top corner blocks and lower trim detail. Nail the pieces with glue in the joints and dabs of panel adhesive on the back of the casings.

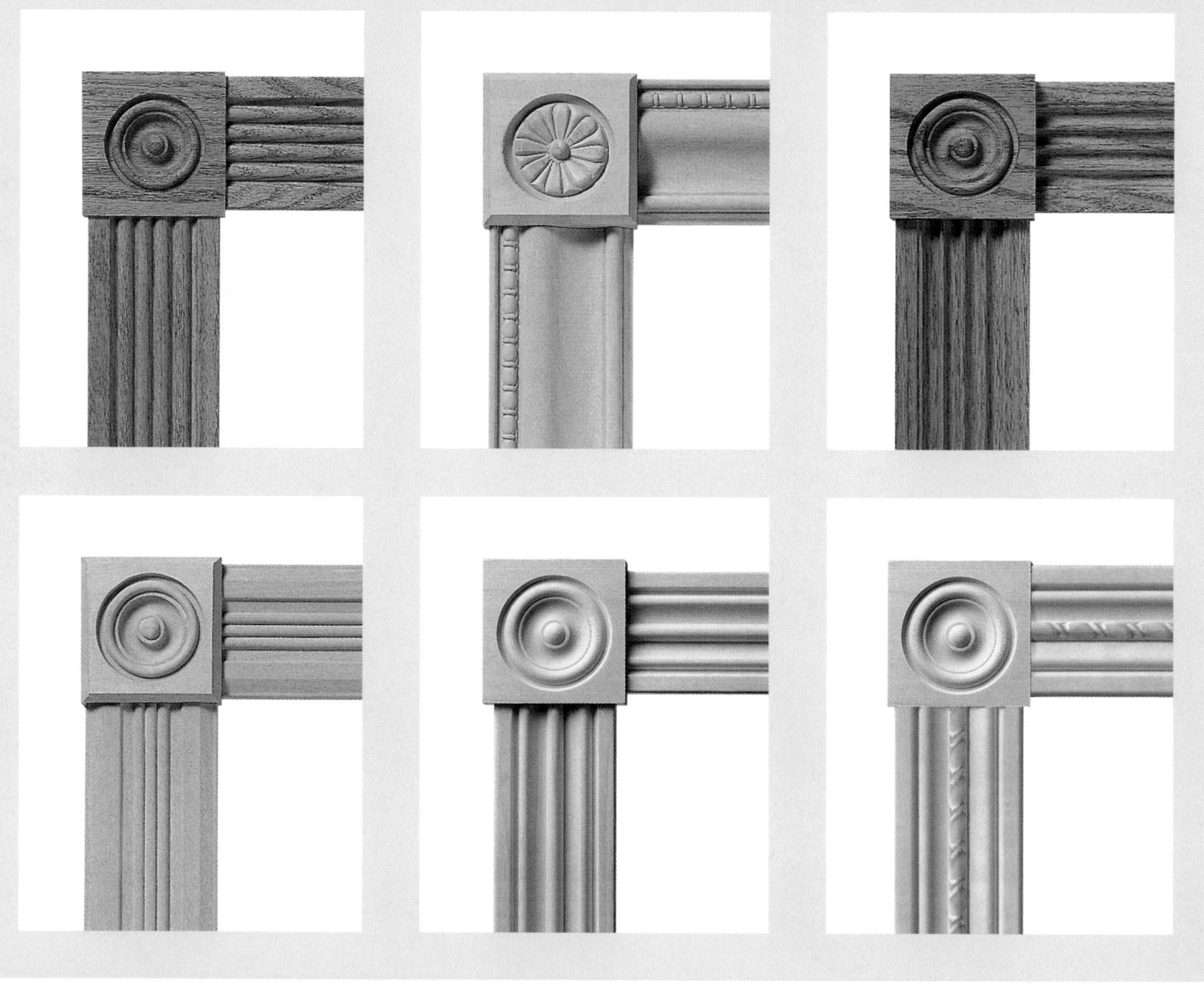

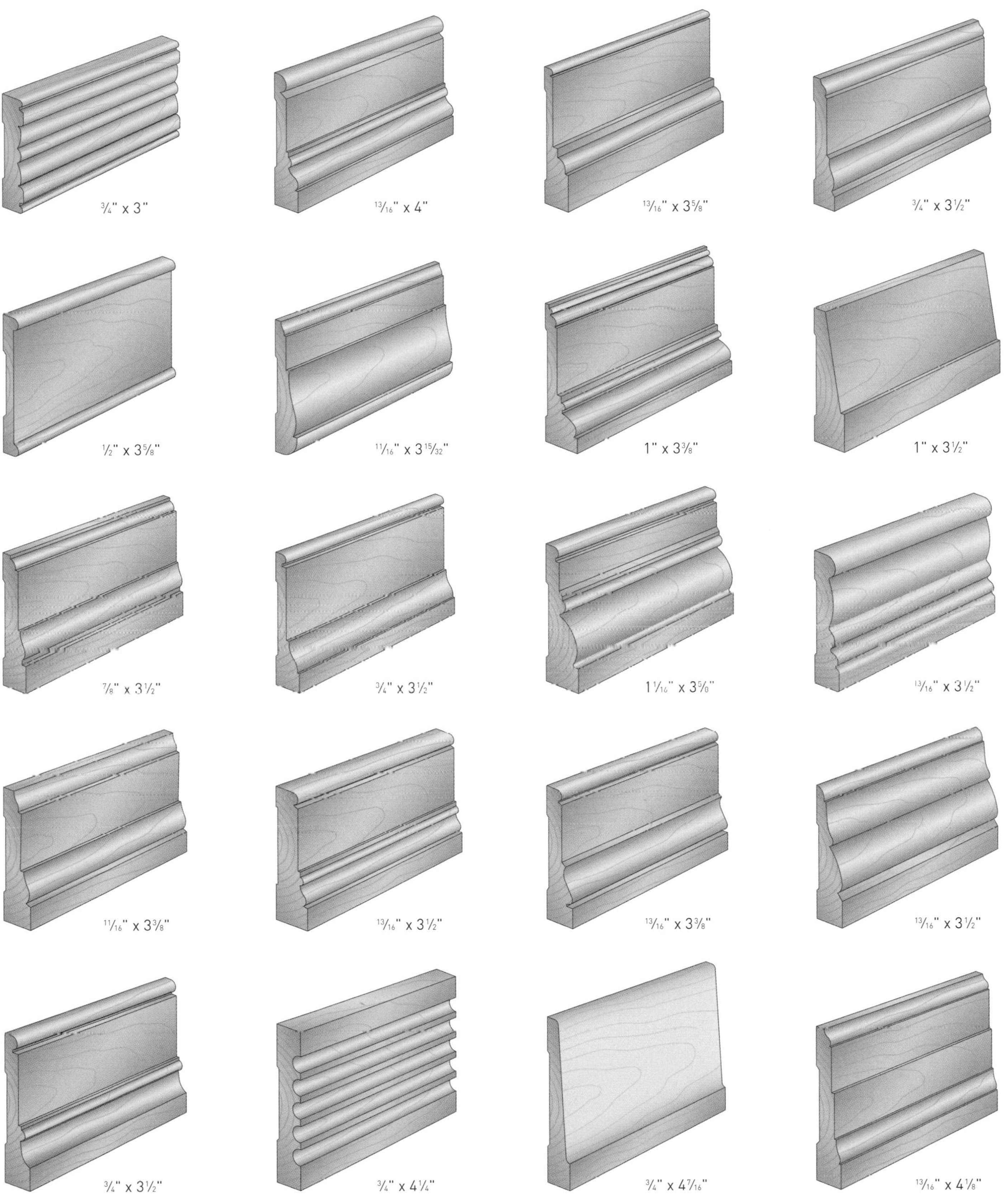
3/4" x 3"
13/16" x 4"
13/16" x 3 5/8"
3/4" x 3 1/2"
1/2" x 3 5/8"
11/16" x 3 15/32"
1" x 3 3/8"
1" x 3 1/2"
7/8" x 3 1/2"
3/4" x 3 1/2"
1 1/16" x 3 5/8"
13/16" x 3 1/2"
11/16" x 3 3/8"
13/16" x 3 1/2"
13/16" x 3 3/8"
13/16" x 3 1/2"
3/4" x 3 1/2"
3/4" x 4 1/4"
3/4" x 4 7/16"
13/16" x 4 1/8"

Victorian Casings

The common element of Victorian decor is the love of ornament. Victorian window and door casings add period charm to any room in the house.

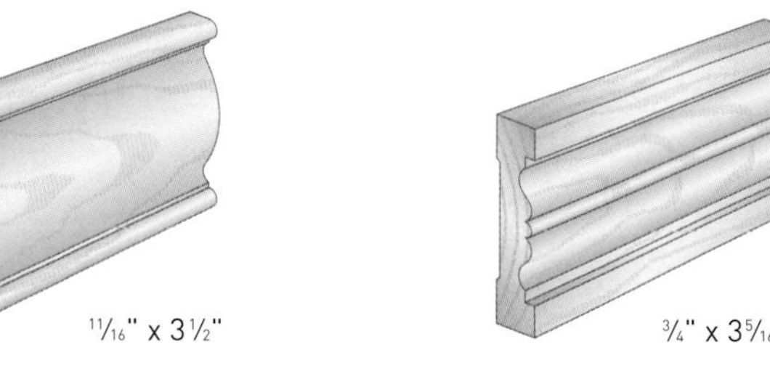

11/16" x 3 1/2"

3/4" x 3 5/16"

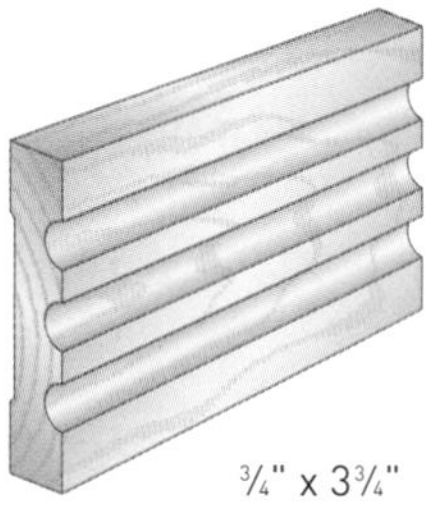

3/4" x 3 3/4"

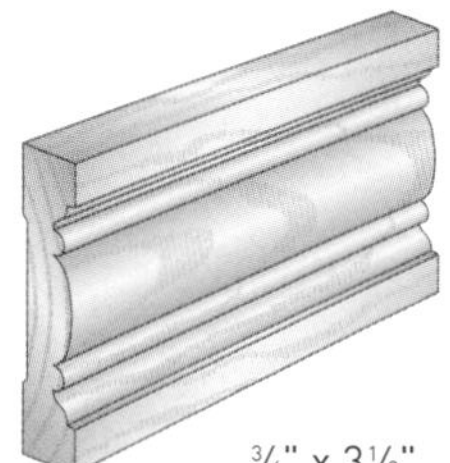

3/4" x 3 1/2"

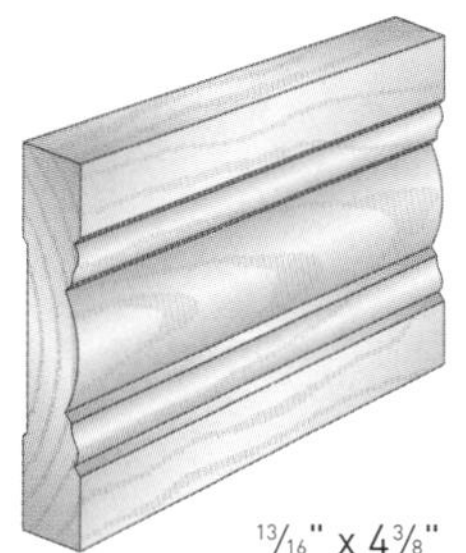

13/16" x 4 3/8"

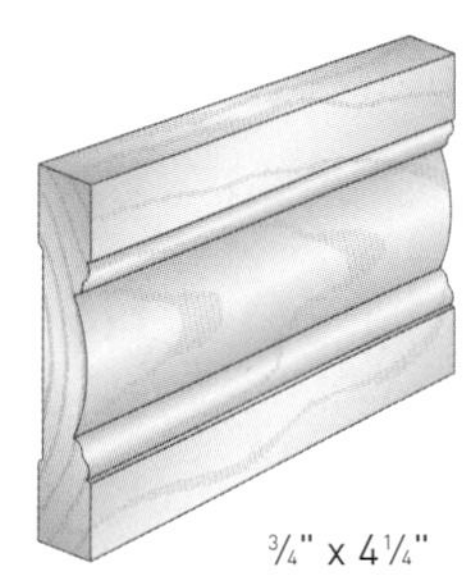

3/4" x 4 1/4"

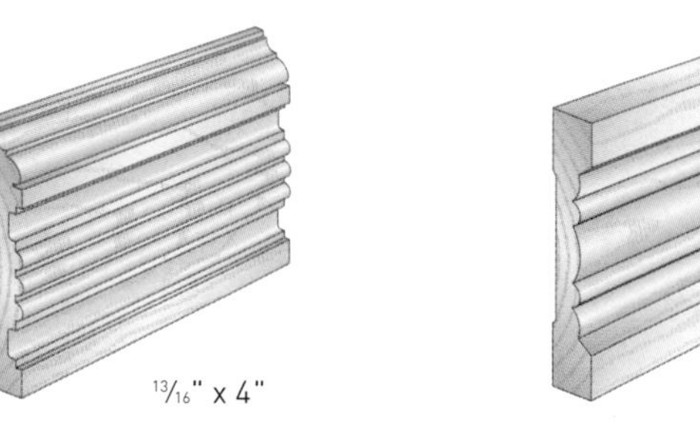

13/16" x 4"

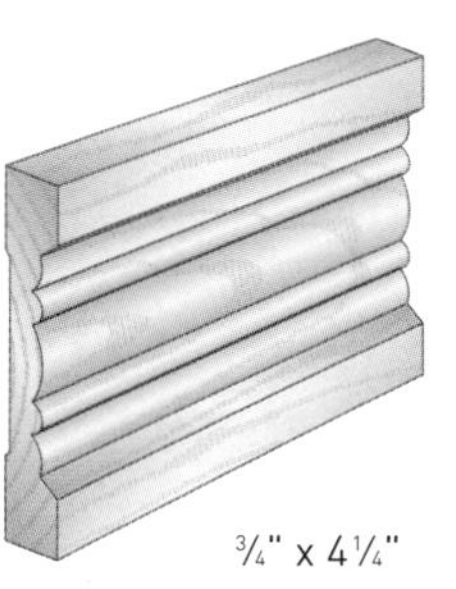

3/4" x 4 1/4"

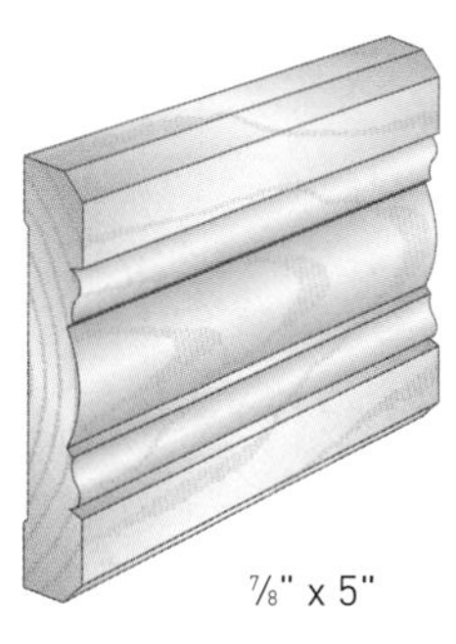

7/8" x 5"

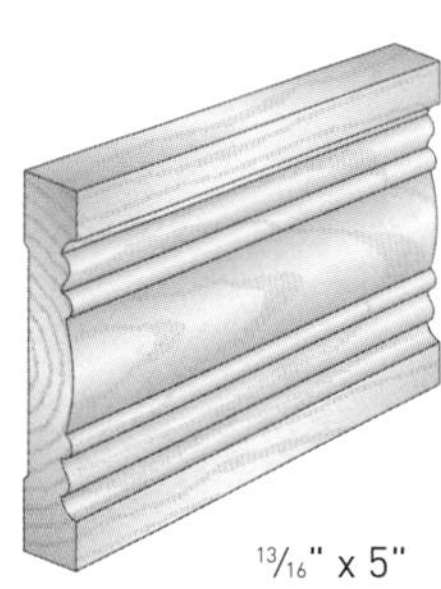

13/16" x 5"

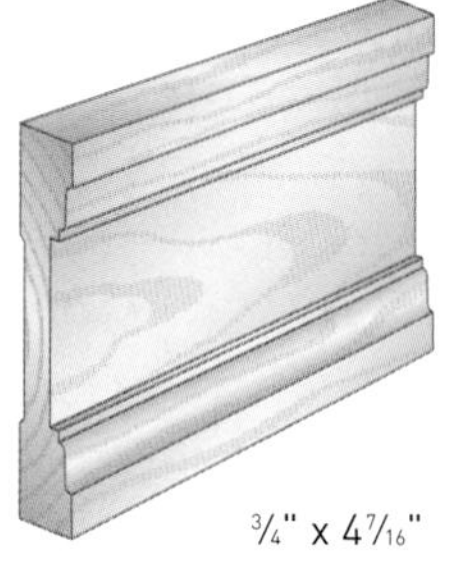

3/4" x 4 7/16"

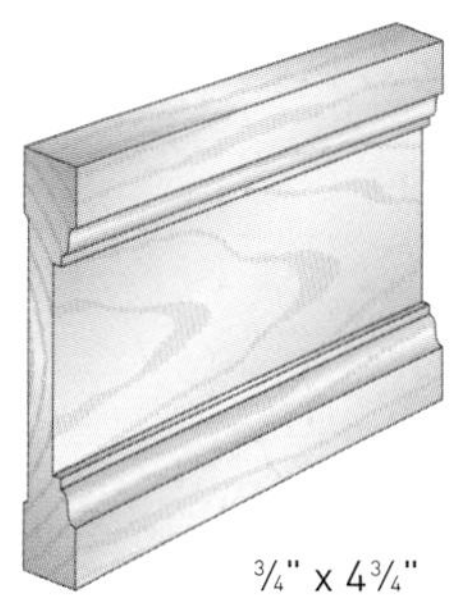

3/4" x 4 3/4"

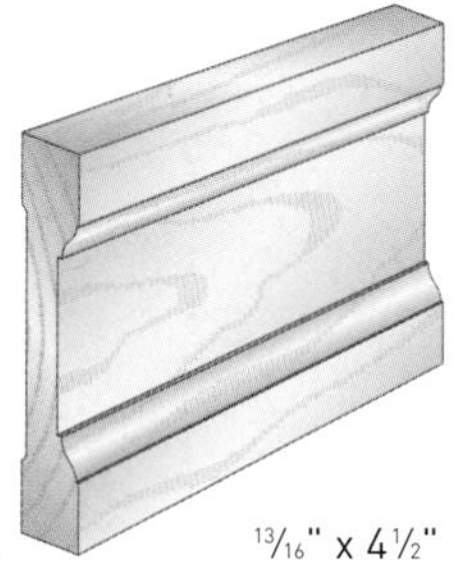

13/16" x 4 1/2"

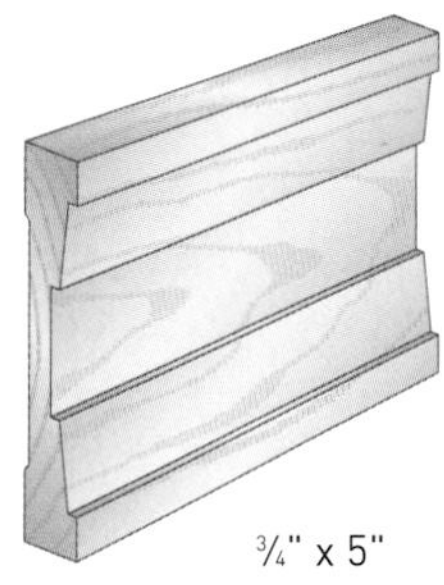

3/4" x 5"

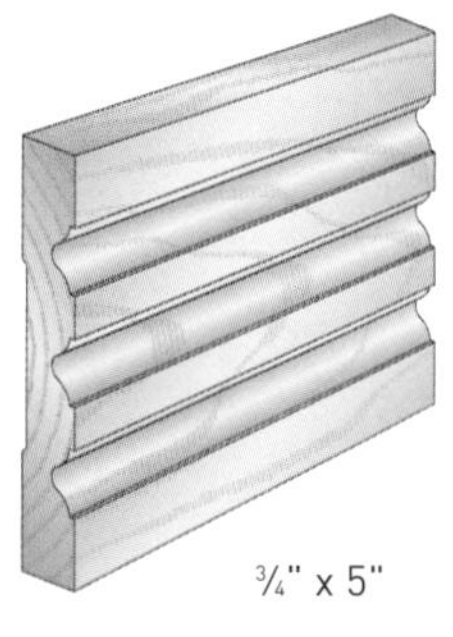

3/4" x 5"

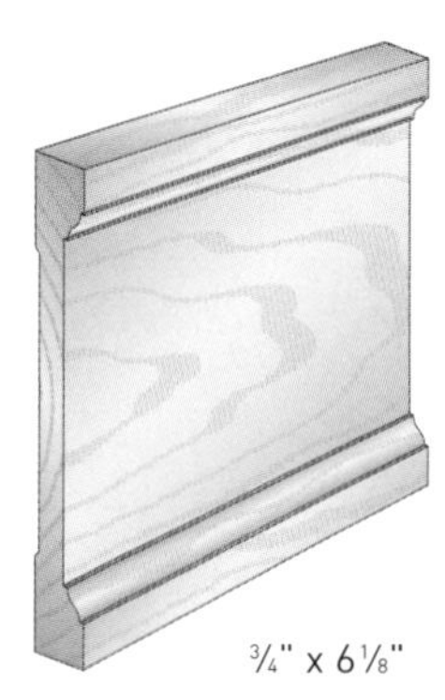

3/4" x 6 1/8"

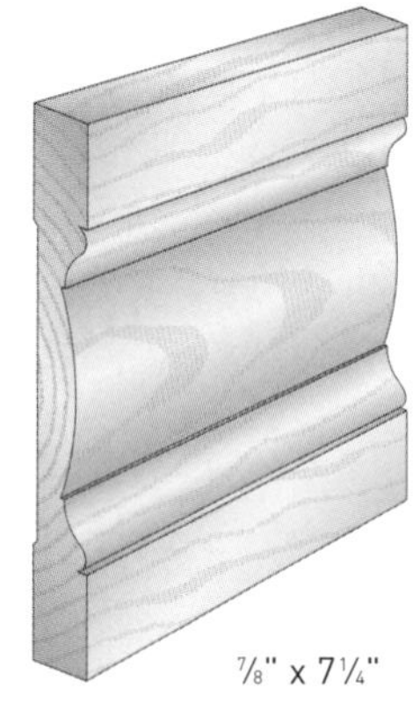

7/8" x 7 1/4"

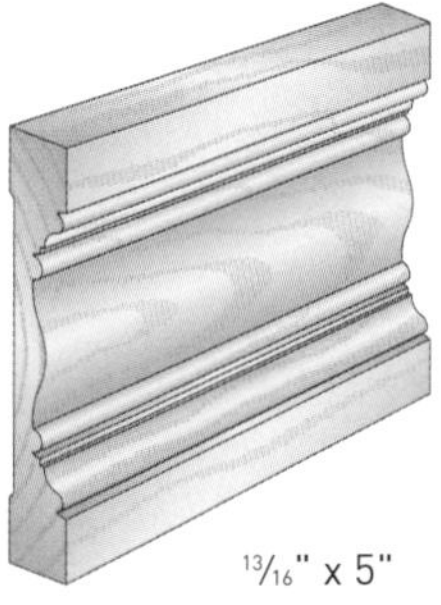

13/16" x 5"

Victorian Bellyband Casing with Rosette

Victorian bellyband casing is the hallmark interior detail in many older homes. It still looks good today and offers a major benefit that novice do-it-yourselfers will appreciate: no mitering. You can install this style of molding simply by butting the casing legs against the blocks. You still need to make a careful layout and allow for reveals. They can be a little tricky on corner-block jobs because the casing legs are always slightly narrower than the blocks.

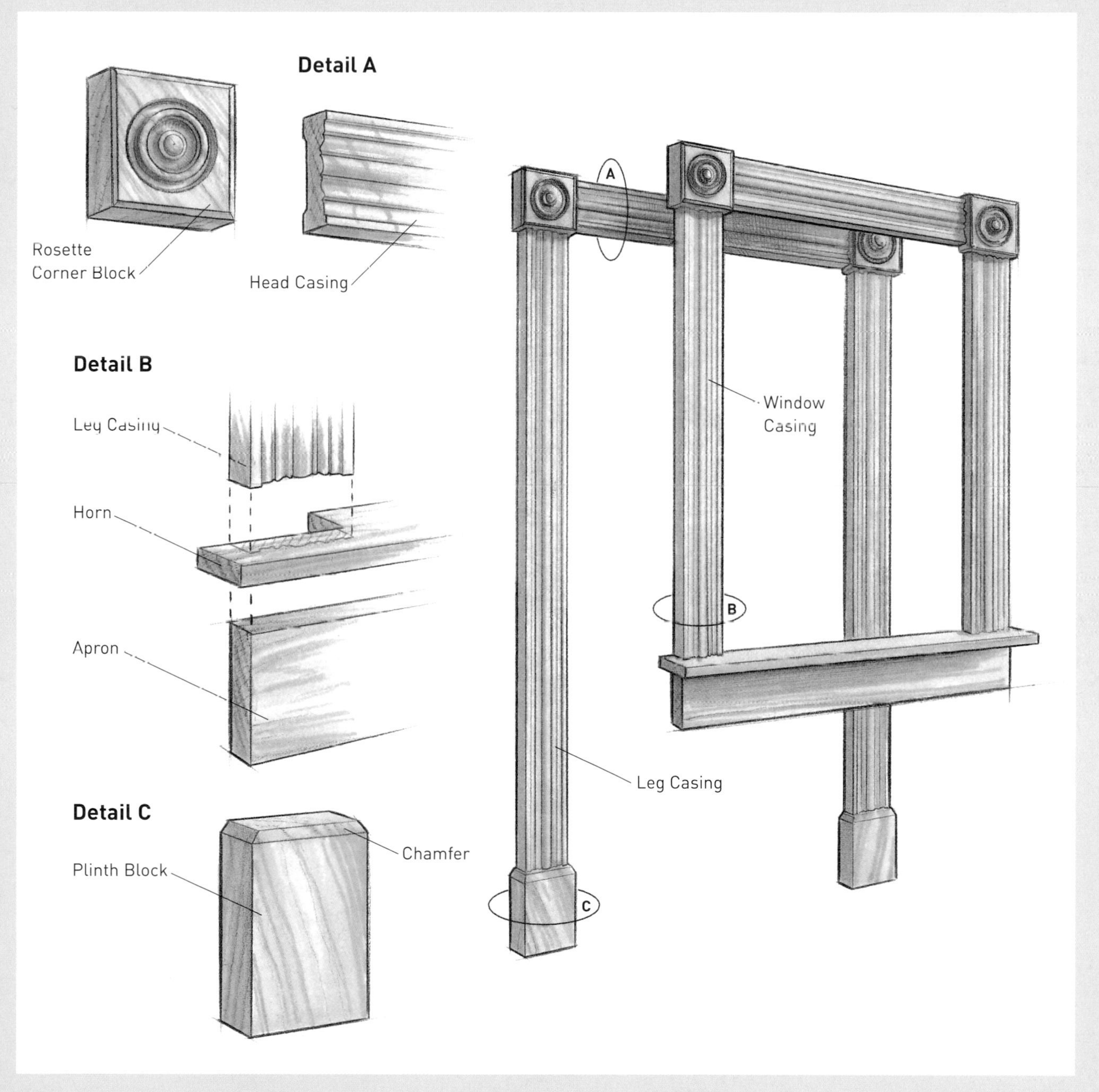

Plinth Molding

Plinth blocks add a decorative design where the door trim meets the base molding. They evoke the look and timeless feel of historical homes. The general rule for matching a plinth with baseboard and the door casing is that a plinth can be used with any molding as long as the molding isn't wider or thicker than the block. Plinths are sold in precut blocks (photo at right and illustration on page 129) or by the linear foot in a tapered profile (illustrations at right).

While many plinth blocks consist of only one piece, there is a vast array of caps that can be nailed or joined to the top of the block. Caps, similar to base cap moldings for baseboard, can dress up the block itself and the surrounding door casing. To install plinths, first glue them in position; then use finishing nails to secure them. When using plinth blocks, you don't have to miter baseboard or casings.

Right A plinth block completes the decorative door casing above it and suggests the base of a column.

Smart Tip **Painting around Casing**

You can mask the trim's edges with a quick-release tape that you can remove after the cut-in paint has set, or use a steady hand to guide the brush. When masking chair rails and base moldings, use tape that is wide enough to protect the trimwork from any misting or spraying from the roller. Now, using a trim brush, cut in a 2- to 3-inch strip of paint all around trim.

Tapered plinth profiles shown with door side to the right and base-molding side to the left.

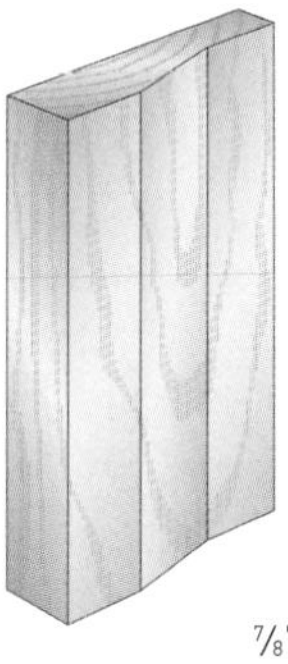

7/8" x 3 1/2"

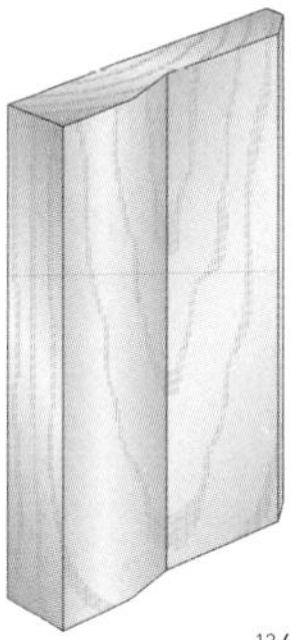

13/16" x 3 7/8"

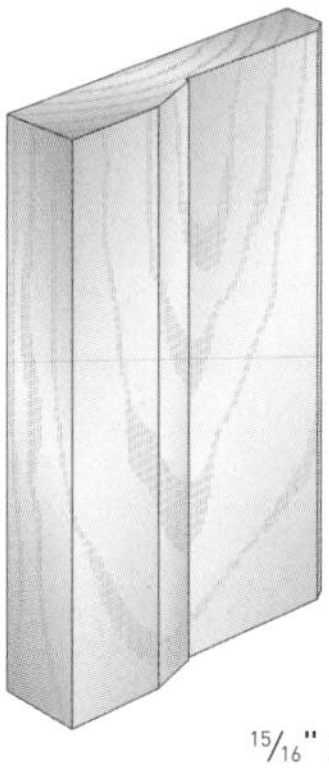

15/16" x 5"

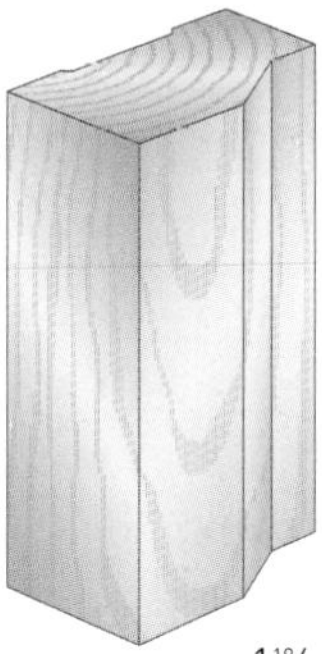

1 19/32" x 3 5/16"

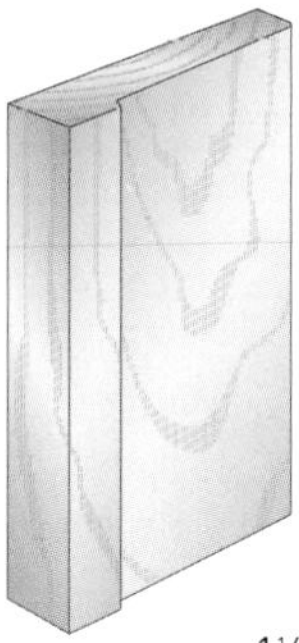

1 1/16" x 4 1/16"

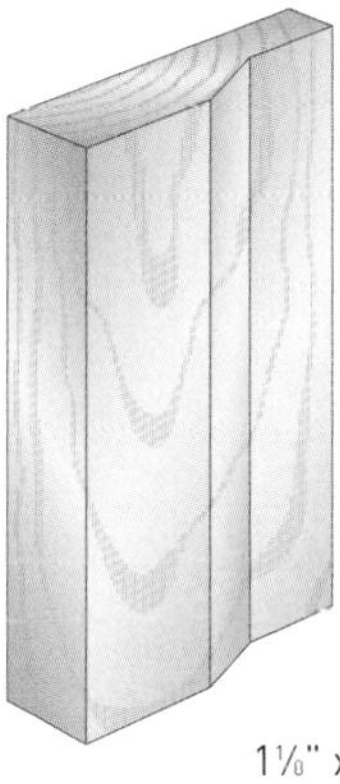

1 1/0" x 4 1/4"

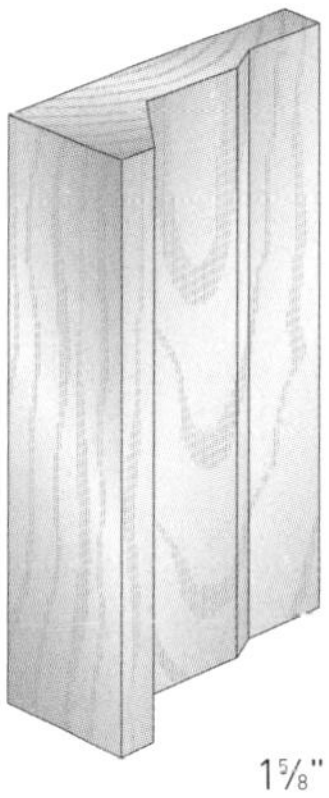

1 5/8" x 4 1/8"

1 5/8" x 4 3/4"

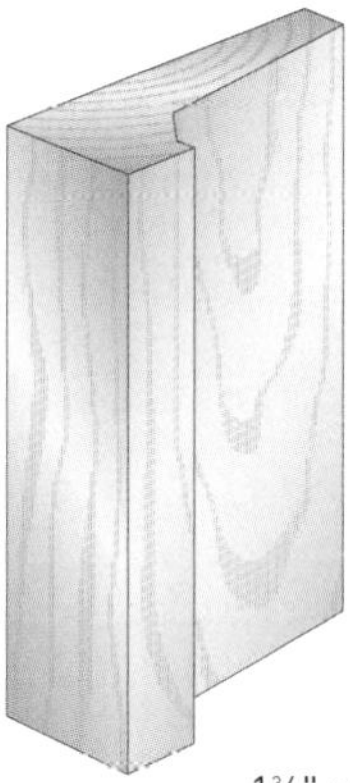

1 3/4" x 4 1/2"

7/8" x 4 1/2"

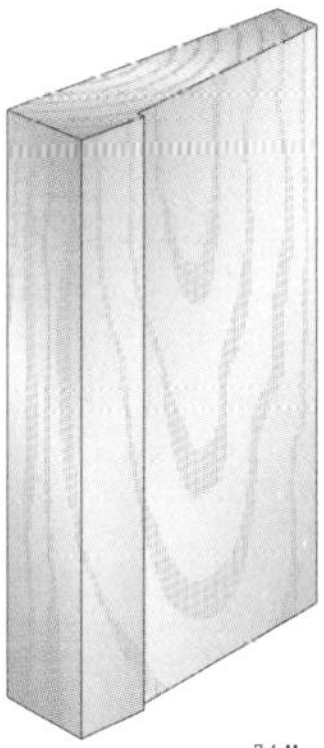

7/8" x 3 3/4"

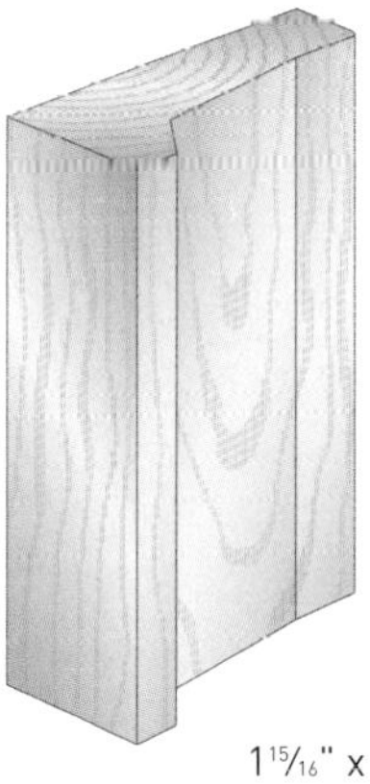

1 15/16" x 4 1/2"

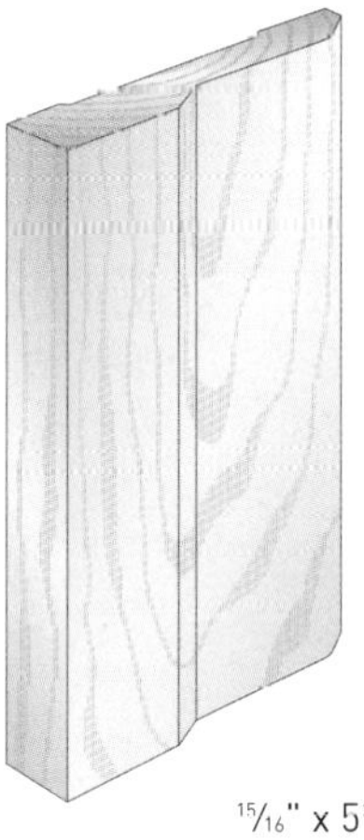

15/16" x 5 3/16"

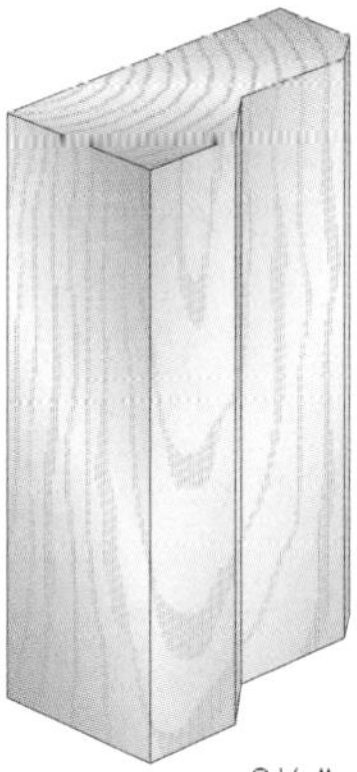

2 1/16" x 4 1/8"

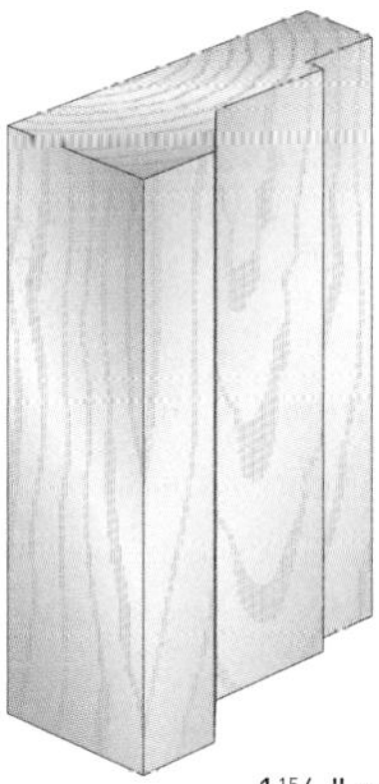

1 15/16" x 4 1/2"

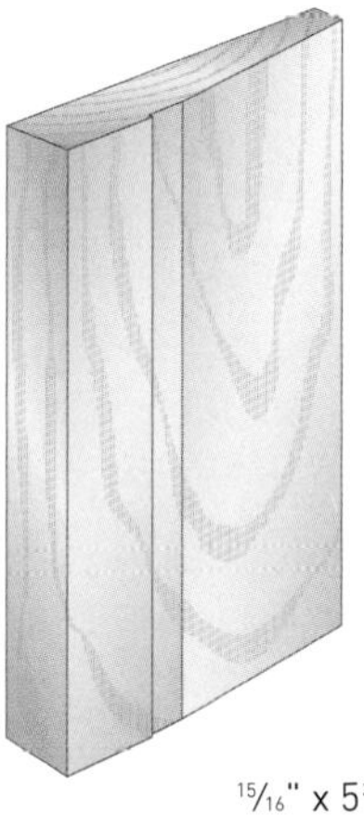

15/16" x 5 3/16"

1 13/16" x 6"

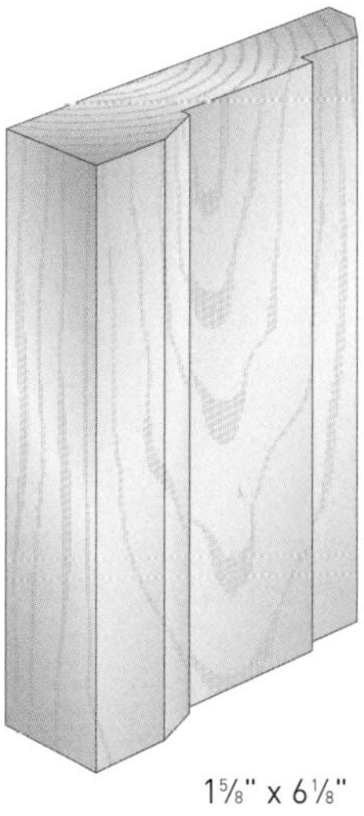

1 5/8" x 6 1/8"

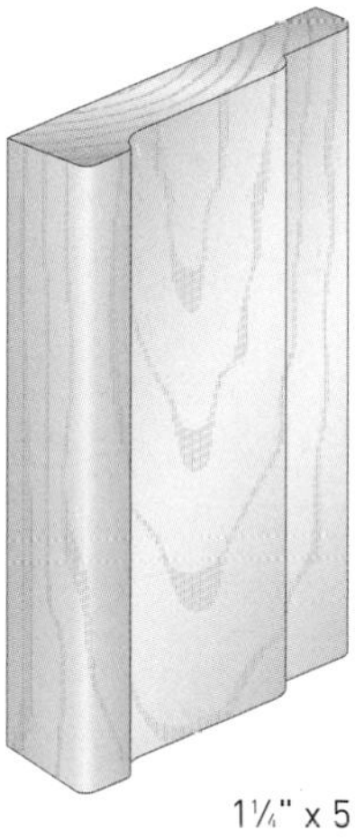

1 1/4" x 5 1/8"

Apron Molding

An apron is a flat board usually made of the same material as the stool (or sill) but often thinner. An apron finishes the underside of the stool and can be plain or ornate. Your choice will depend on the style and profile of the head and leg casings. When introducing a new trim design, it's probably best to tack sample apron under the stool so that you can step back and take a look.

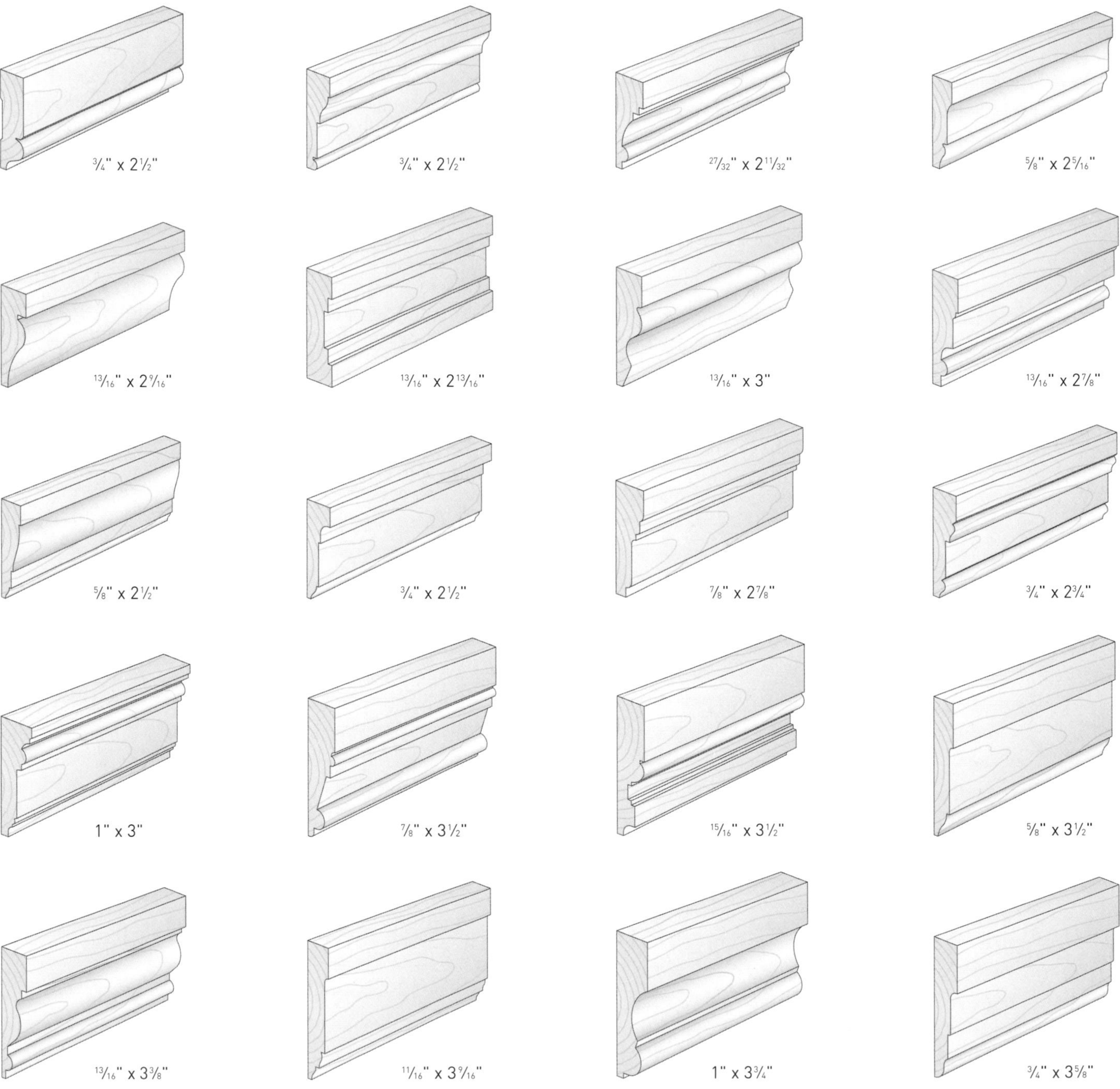

Cutting Clean Miters

A miter is the most basic joint used in trimwork. With a clean miter, the decorative surfaces and patterns of the molding flow cleanly from one board to the next. The tool of choice for mitering is a power miter saw. You can also make tight-fitting miters by hand using a miter box and a sharp saw.

One way to assure tight miters is by undercutting the miter with a block plane. This technique will also help you correct slightly inaccurate cuts. After making the initial cut using the saw, back bevel the lower edge of the board using a block plane as shown in the top photograph. Shaving this area means the top edge of the boards will fit together tightly. Many pros like to install the molding using both adhesive and nails.

Use a metal plane to smooth mitered edges so that they fit tightly when joining together at a corner around a window or door.

A clean miter cut is important: it enables casing to align and flow smoothly from one board to the next.

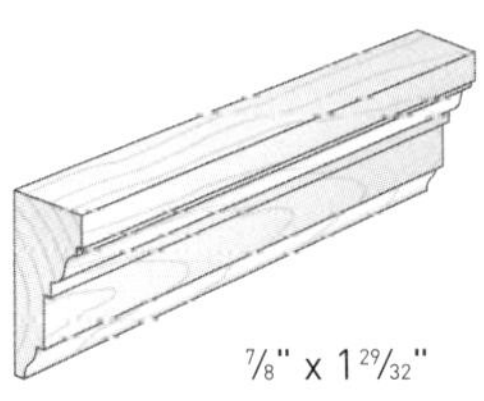

7/8" x 1 29/32"

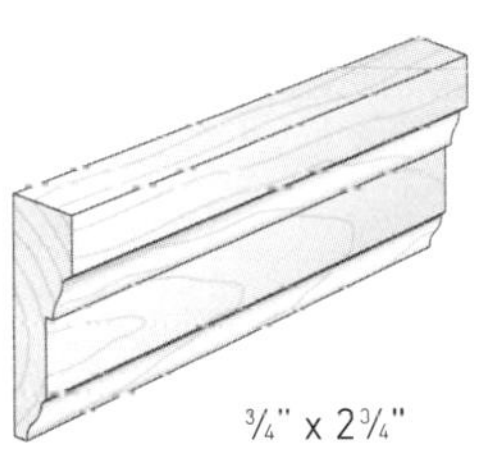

3/4" x 2 3/4"

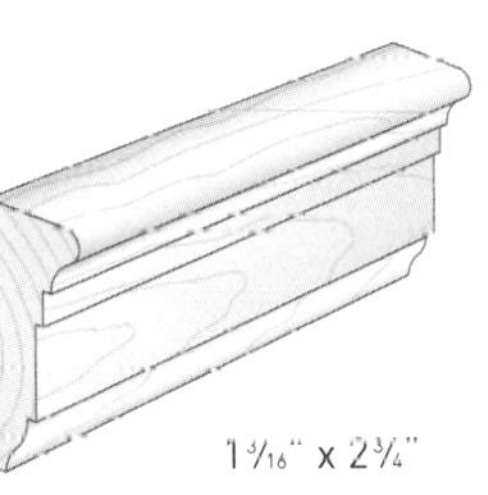

1 3/16" x 2 3/4"

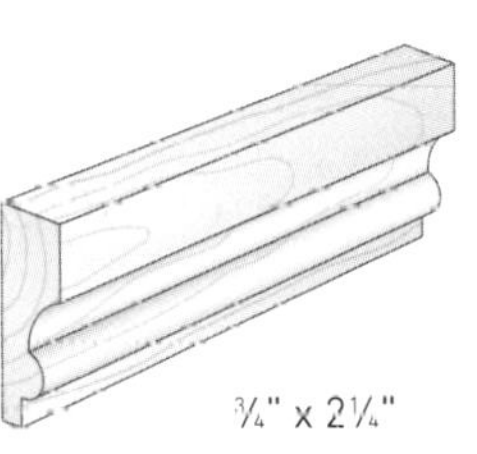

3/4" x 2 1/4"

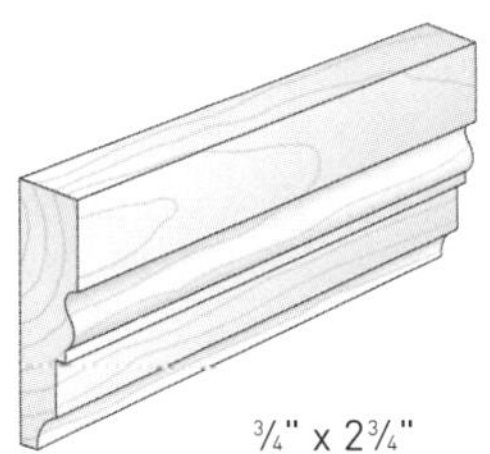

3/4" x 2 3/4"

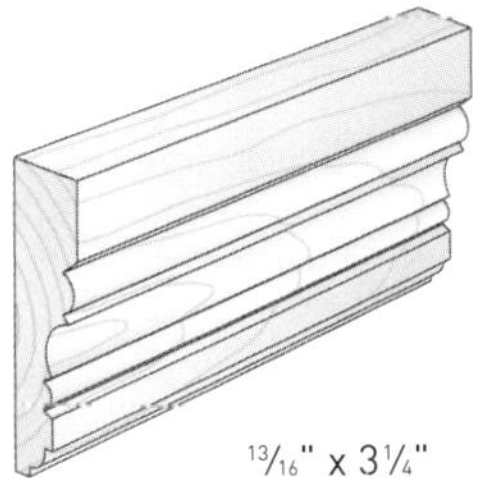

13/16" x 3 1/4"

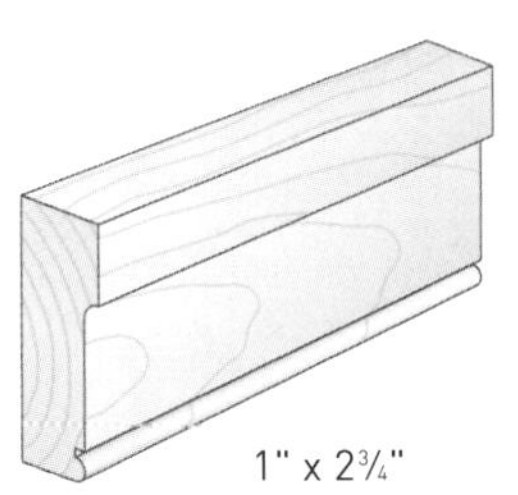

1" x 2 3/4"

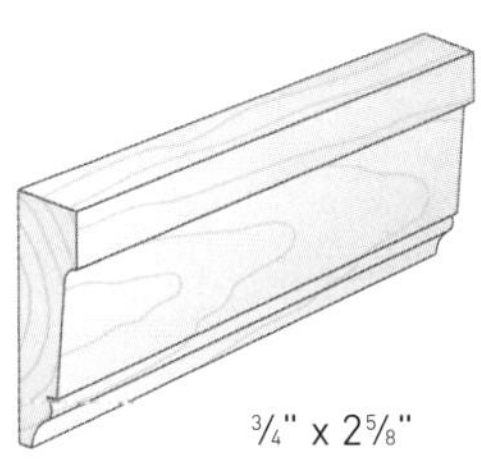

3/4" x 2 5/8"

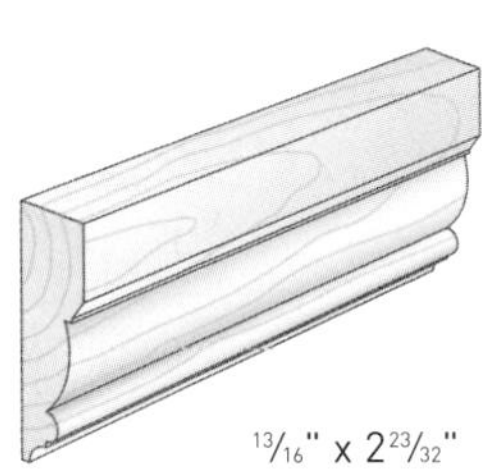

13/16" x 2 23/32"

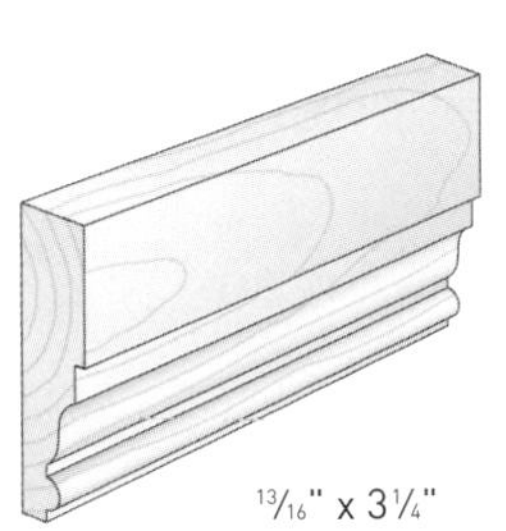

13/16" x 3 1/4"

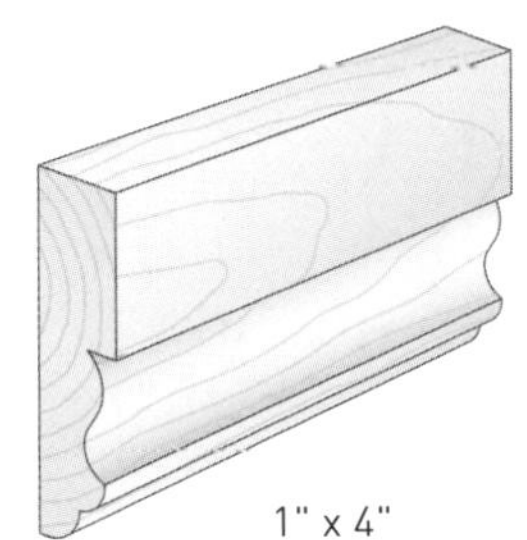

1" x 4"

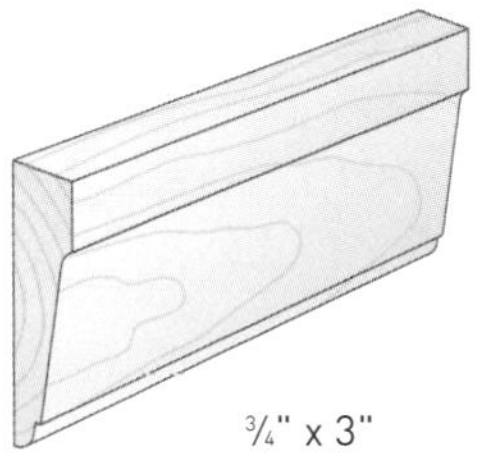

3/4" x 3"

Stools and Sills

The main difference between adding molding around a door and a window is that a window has a fourth side to trim. How you handle the lower section of molding depends mostly on what type of casing you're using.

When large casings were in fashion, most windows were trimmed out with two pieces: a window stool and an apron. A stool, or a sill, extends past the jamb into the room like a small shelf. The section at each end of the stool that extends onto the wall is called a horn. For good looks and sufficient strength, the horns should extend about 1 inch beyond the outside edge of leg casings.

Opposite Make sure window stools and horns sufficiently support casings.

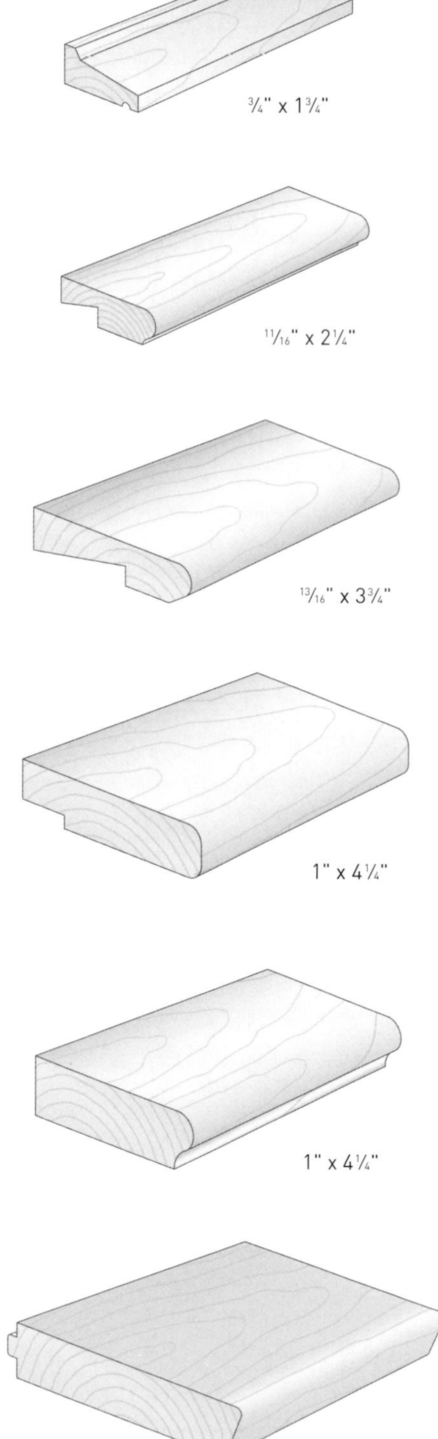

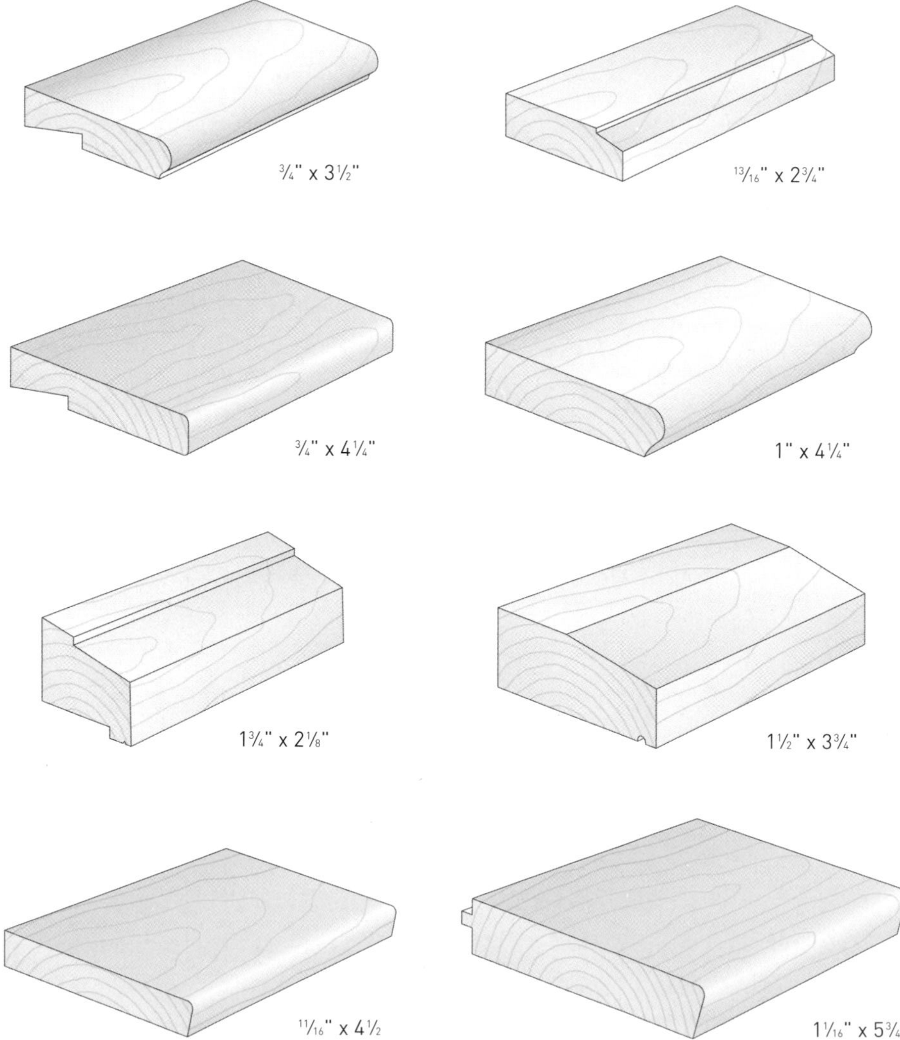

Chapter 6

Wall Treatments

Walls present you with many design opportunities when it comes to trimwork. Wainscoting, wall frames, wall panels, chair rails, picture molding, window seats, shelving, and mantels can be custom designed to accommodate a variety of situations and room configurations. As with all trimwork, wall treatments should complement other trimwork in the room.

Wall frames look like a series of large picture frames along the wall. They may simply provide a raised pattern of trimwork on a single-color wall, or they may be more complex, enclosing painted surfaces that give a more intense three-dimensional illusion of different depths and densities.

Some of the most popular molding treatments through the years have been based on wainscoting. The term covers a wide variety of materials and moldings that you can combine in frames and panels to create a decorative treatment for the lower portion of the wall.

Chair rails, which originated to prevent a chair from damaging the wall behind it, provide a room with a horizontal element that unifies the room. Picture rails, developed to hang framed pictures without damaging plaster walls, are similar in design.

Built-in shelving can lend character to a generic floor plan and adds more to your home than economical storage space—namely, striking architectural interest.

Wall treatments are a great way to breathe life into an ordinary room. But as with any other addition to your home, there are principles to be learned and rules to be followed. Learn these basic ideas, and you won't be disappointed with the results.

High and low wall frames, along with built-in shelves, create eye appeal as well as storage and display space.

Trimwork for Walls

A wall treatment is an easy way to transform an empty box into a room that looks more spacious, warm, elegant, and complete. Chair rails, wall panels, and wainscoting are horizontal components that tie everything together while adding character and beauty to a room. You can create accents on a wall by adding a strip of picture rail molding below a ceiling cornice. This creates a narrow section of wall called a frieze.

You can extend wall frame themes to include the walls of a stairwell. Unlike wall frames in, say, a room or hallway, where all the frames have simple right-angle corners, stairwell wall treatments require angles that vary from 90 degrees.

Adding a built-in bookshelf, a window seat, or an elaborate fireplace mantel to a home brings a sense of craftsmanship and lends character to a modern floor plan. When incorporating such elements into a room, keep basic design principles in mind: scale and proportion, balance, rhythm, emphasis, and harmony.

1 The neutral color of the walls provides a background that calls attention to the dark stain on the chair rail, shelf, and other trimwork in the room.

2 The natural finish of the wainscoting lends a formal character and rhythm to this spacious dining room.

3 The arched built-in bookshelf provides architectural drama and echoes the arched window on the adjoining wall.

1

2

3

1

1 The wall treatment's classical motif is reinforced with a freestanding column and figure from Greek mythology.

2 These striking built-in display shelves are completed nicely by the raised-panel doors below.

3 The vertical design of the wallpaper and the framed artwork complement the wainscoting underneath it.

4 Floor-to-ceiling wall panels make a grand architectural statement in this sitting room.

2

3

4

Chair Rails

Chair-rail trimwork comes in a wide range of styles and profiles. You can buy one-piece chair-rail profiles, such as those shown here, or build your own custom trim by combining different styles of trim. (See page 144 for examples.) The choice depends partly on how you will treat the space between the rail and the base molding along the floor.

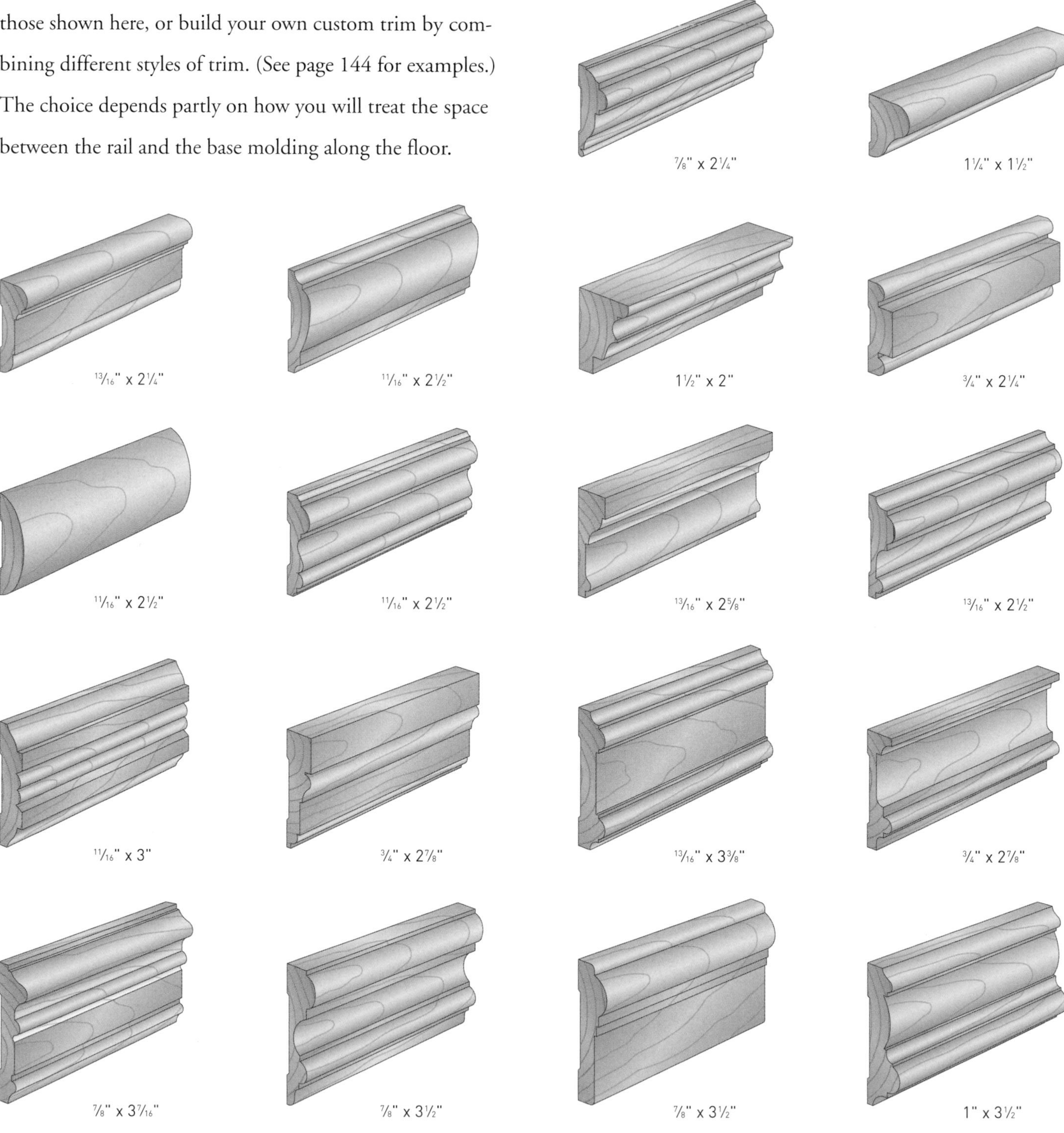

Embossed Chair-Rail Designs

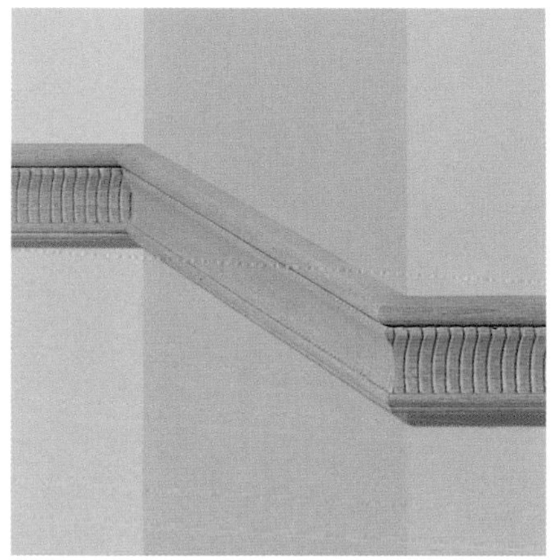

Shallow flutes

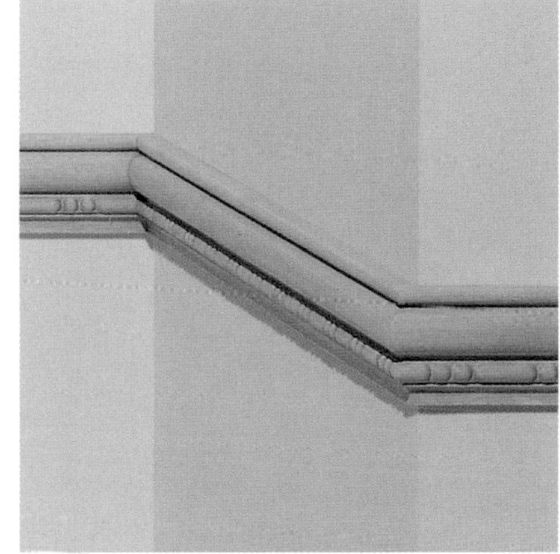

Bead and billet

Egg and dart

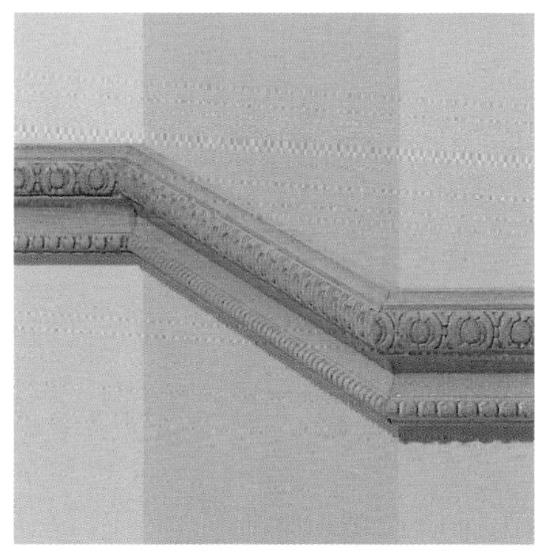

Rosettes and foliage

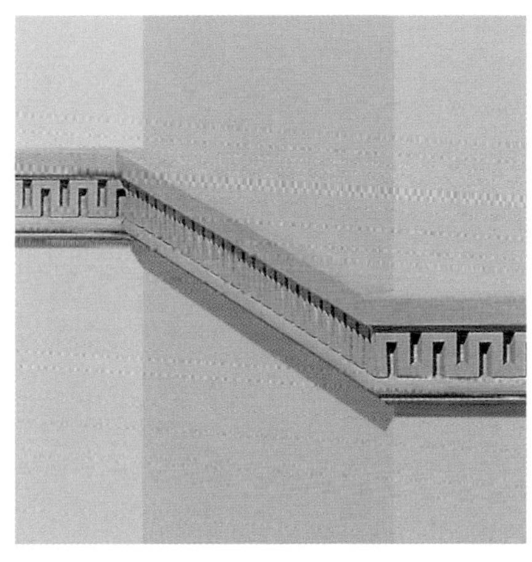

Key fret

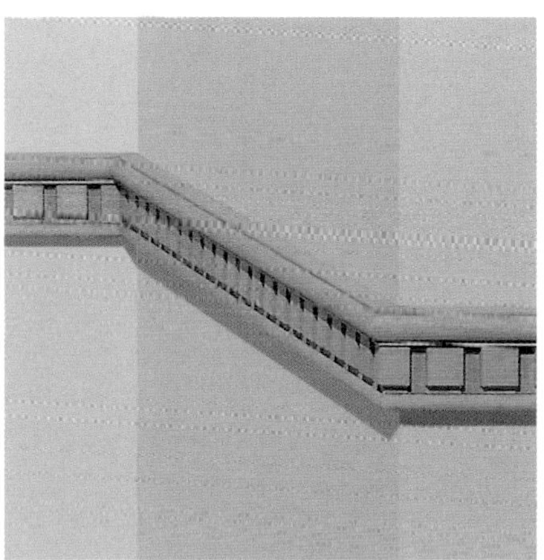

Dentil

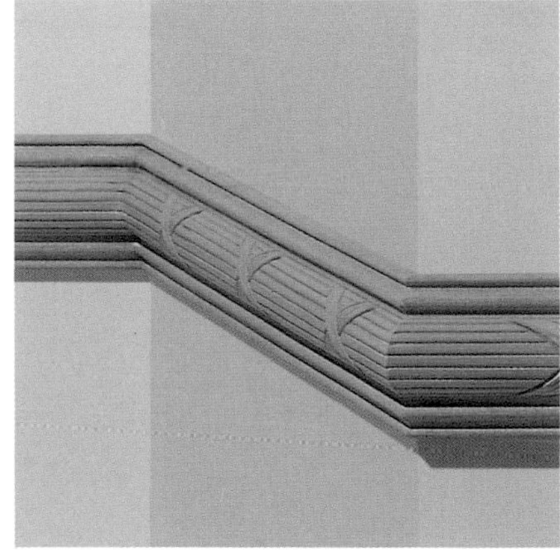

Bundled reeds

Dart and basket

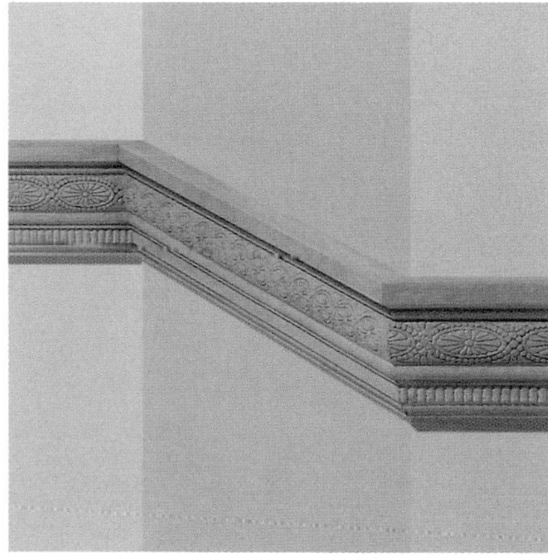

Floral with bead

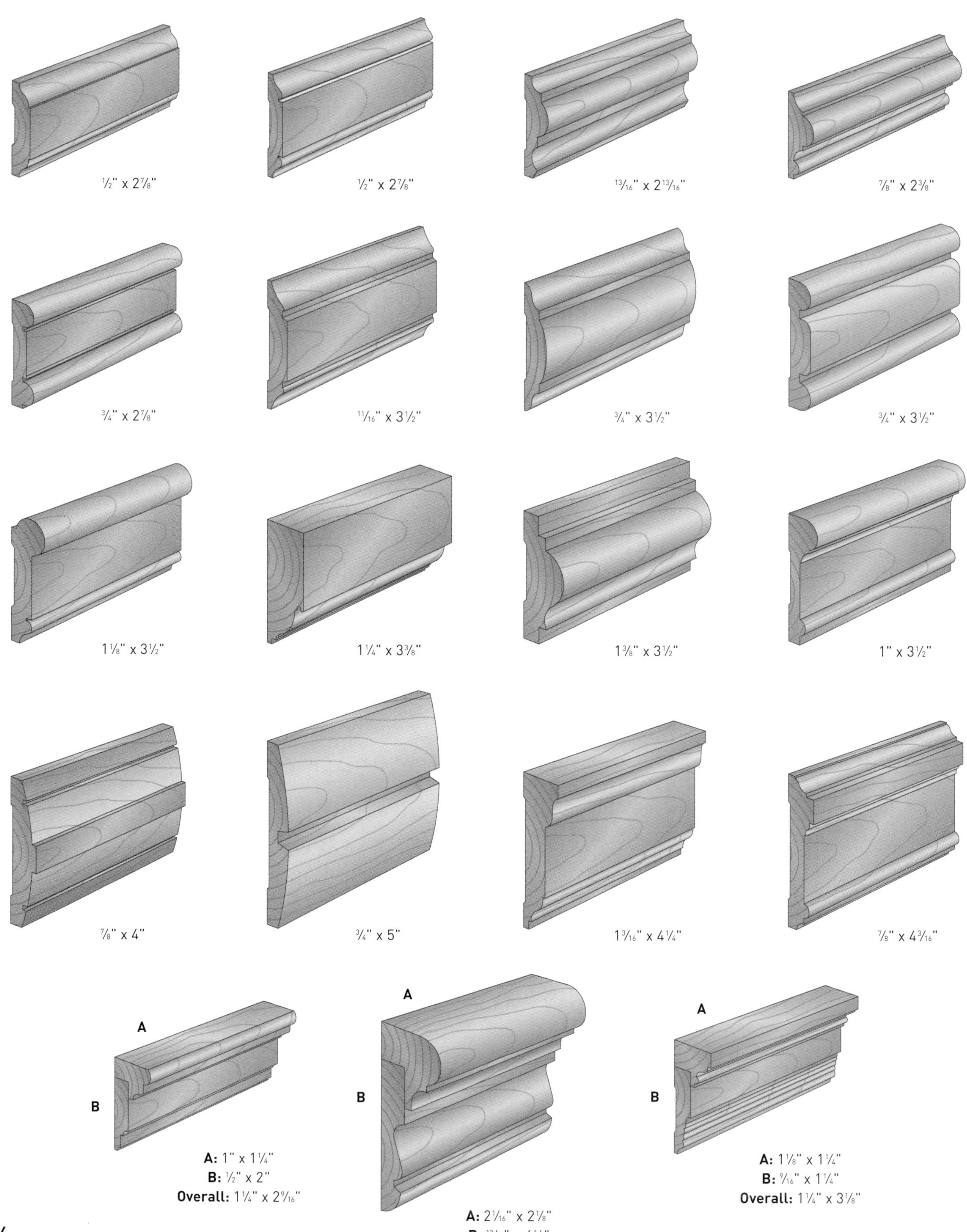
1/2" x 2 7/8"
1/2" x 2 7/8"
13/16" x 2 13/16"
7/8" x 2 3/8"
3/4" x 2 7/8"
11/16" x 3 1/2"
3/4" x 3 1/2"
3/4" x 3 1/2"
1 1/8" x 3 1/2"
1 1/4" x 3 3/8"
1 3/8" x 3 1/2"
1" x 3 1/2"
7/8" x 4"
3/4" x 5"
1 3/16" x 4 1/4"
7/8" x 4 3/16"
A
B
A: 1" x 1 1/4"
B: 1/2" x 2"
Overall: 1 1/4" x 2 9/16"
A
B
A: 2 1/16" x 2 1/8"
B: 13/16" x 4 1/8"
Overall: 2 1/16" x 6 1/4"
A
B
A: 1 1/8" x 1 1/4"
B: 9/16" x 1 1/4"
Overall: 1 1/4" x 3 1/8"

Return Options

Not every piece of molding joins another. There are three ways to treat the exposed end: one is to leave a square cut; another is to cut a 45-degree angle across part of the exposed edge (photo at left). The third way is to cut a mitered return. Although the most challenging, this solution offers the most sophisticated look (photo at right).

Left Beveling the exposed end of a piece of molding helps to create a finished look at the edge of the wall.

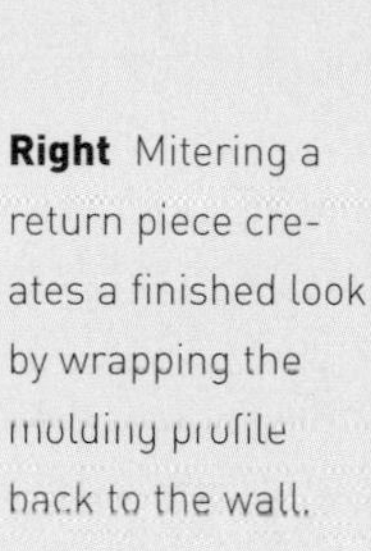

Right Mitering a return piece creates a finished look by wrapping the molding profile back to the wall.

Right The chair rail in this child's room separates wall coverings above and below the rail.

Wainscoting

When it comes to installing wainscoting, your options may seem limitless. You can use wainscoting in classic arrangements that originated in the nineteenth century, in which narrow tongue-and-groove boards are set vertically, or you can run panels up to chair-rail height or higher and cap them with a thin strip of trim or a wide shelf. Wainscoting treatments are extremely versatile. You can combine wainscoting with short walls, pillars, and pilasters at room openings. Wainscoting panel profiles are shown here.

Above Tongue-and-groove wainscoting is capped by a decorative chair rail that complements the door casing.

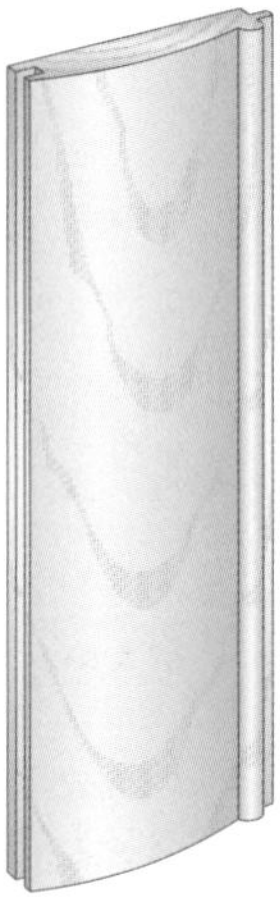

9/16" x 2 3/4"

11/16" x 3 1/2"

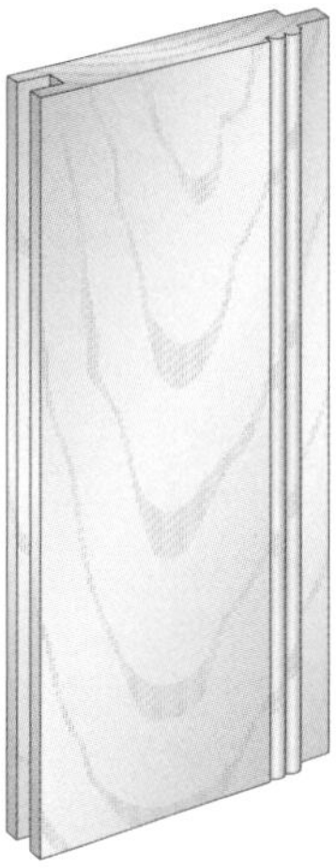

5/8" x 3 1/2"

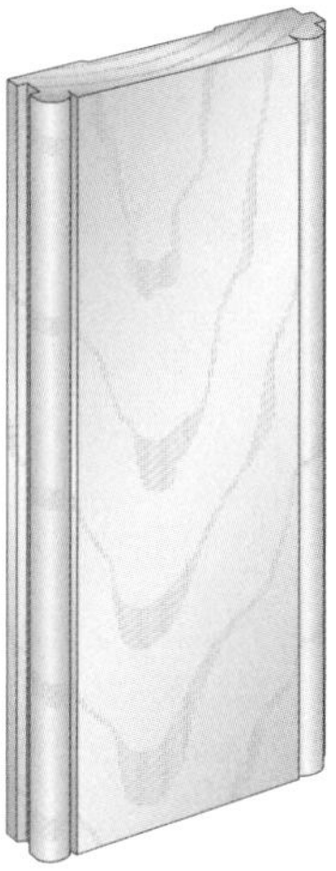

3/4" x 3 1/2"

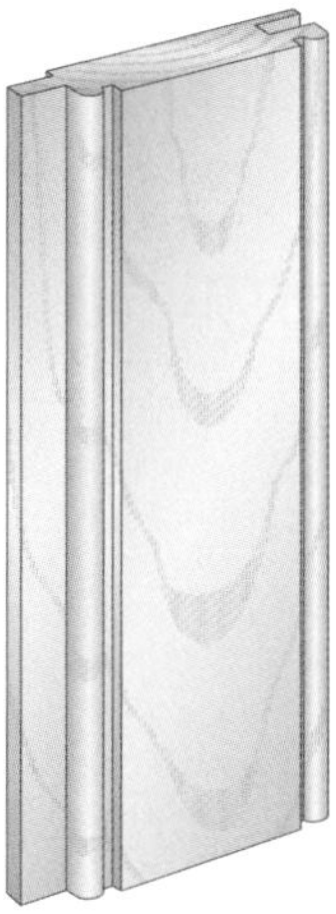

3/4" x 2 3/4"

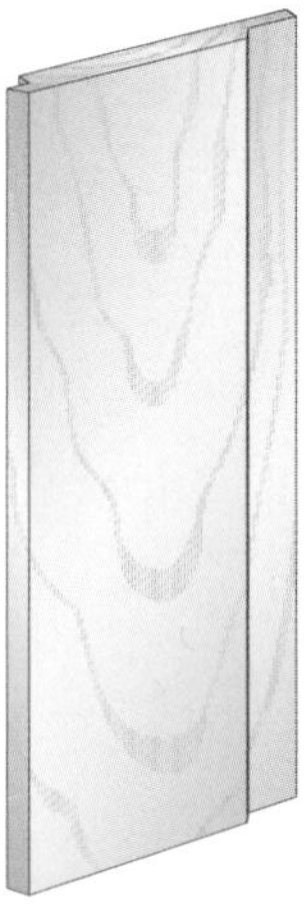

3/8" x 3 3/16"

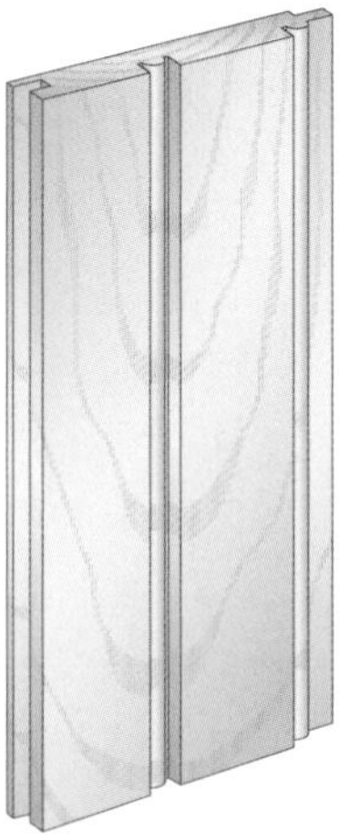

9/16" x 3 25/32"

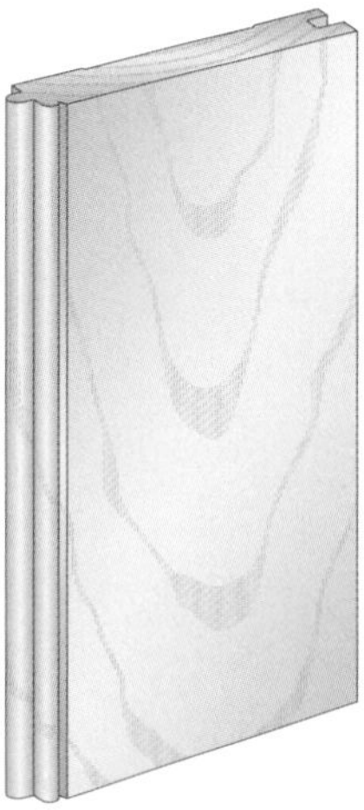

9/16" x 2 3/4"

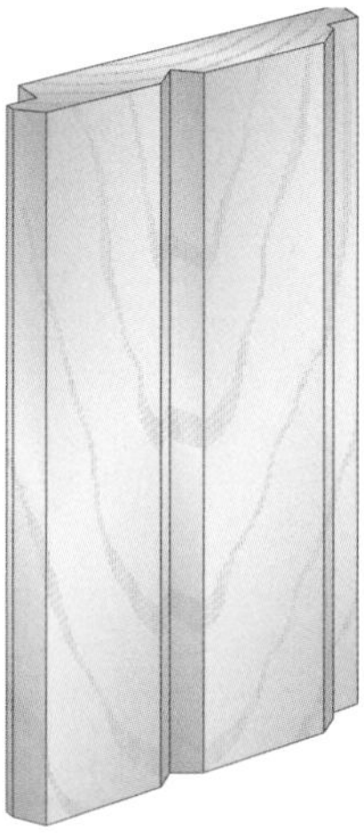

3/4" x 4 3/8"

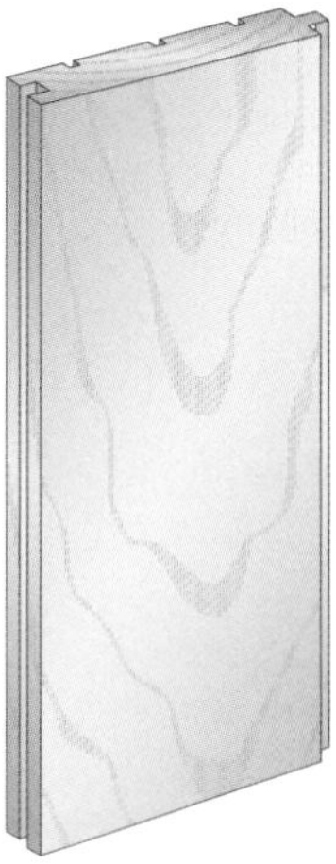

3/4" x up to 9"

Bead-Board Wainscoting

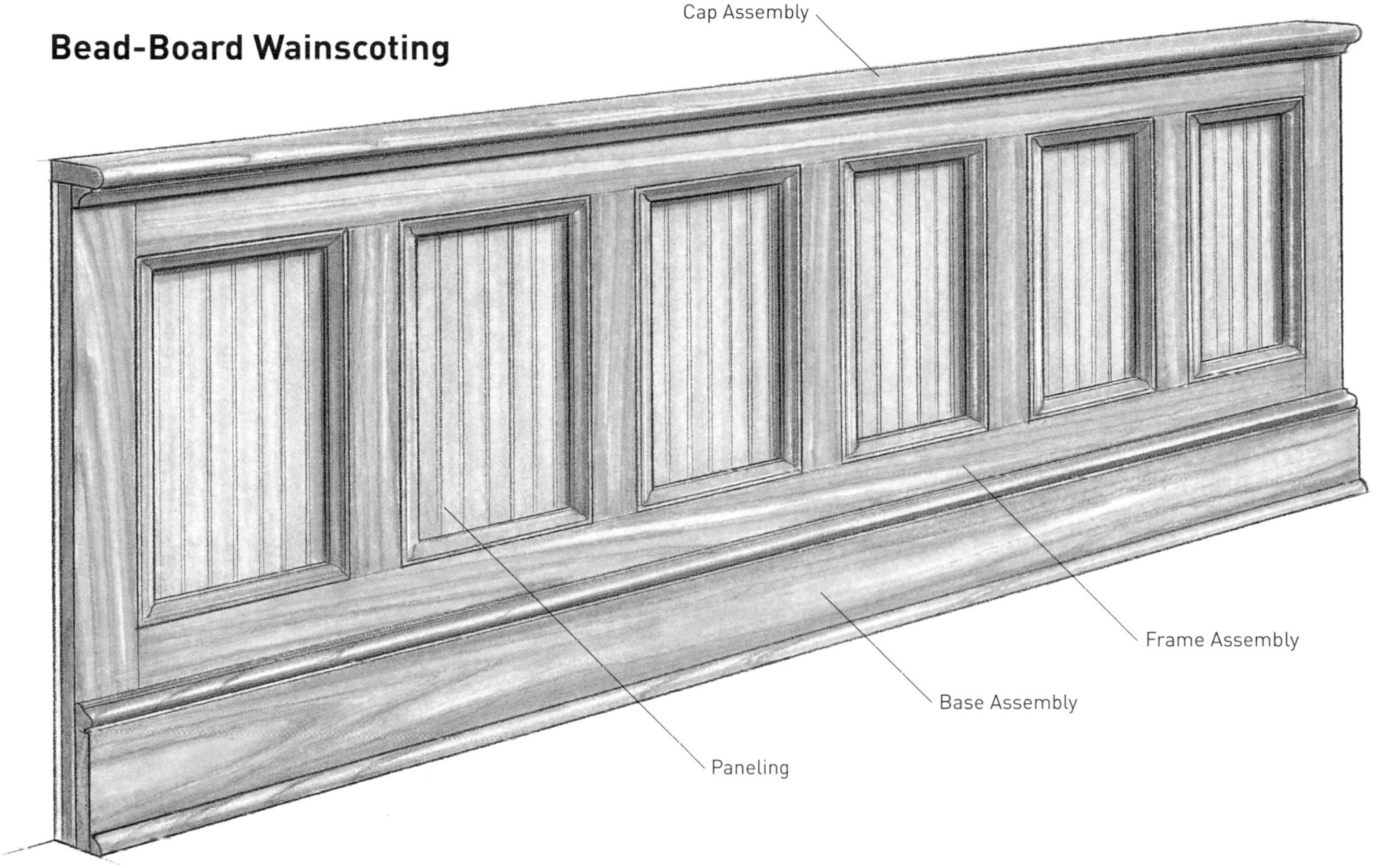

Cap Assembly
Frame Assembly
Base Assembly
Paneling

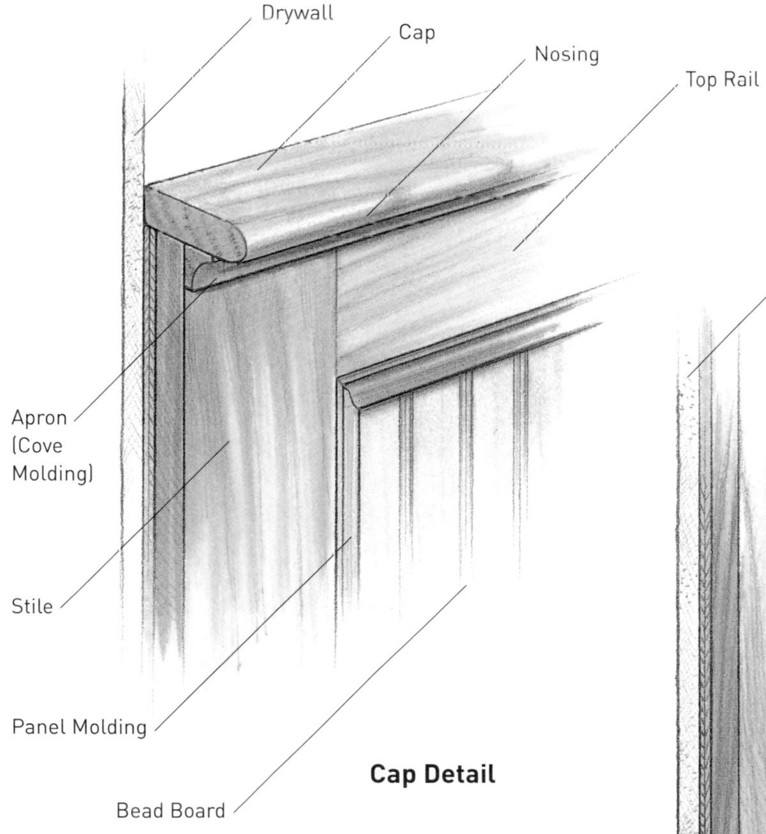

Drywall
Cap
Nosing
Top Rail
Apron (Cove Molding)
Stile
Panel Molding
Bead Board

Cap Detail

Base Detail

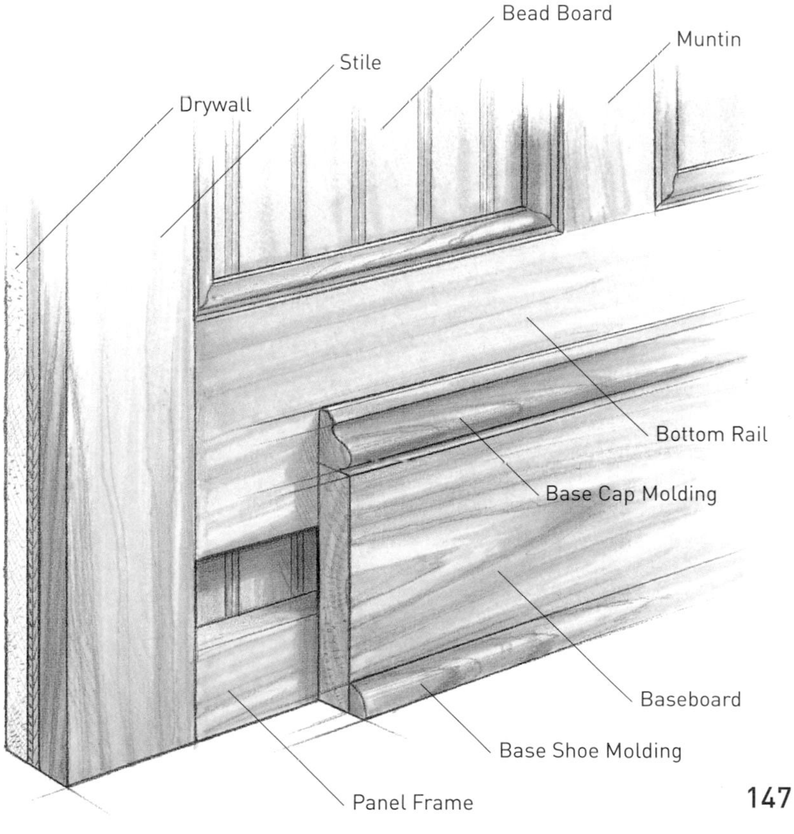

Bead Board
Muntin
Stile
Drywall
Bottom Rail
Base Cap Molding
Baseboard
Base Shoe Molding
Panel Frame

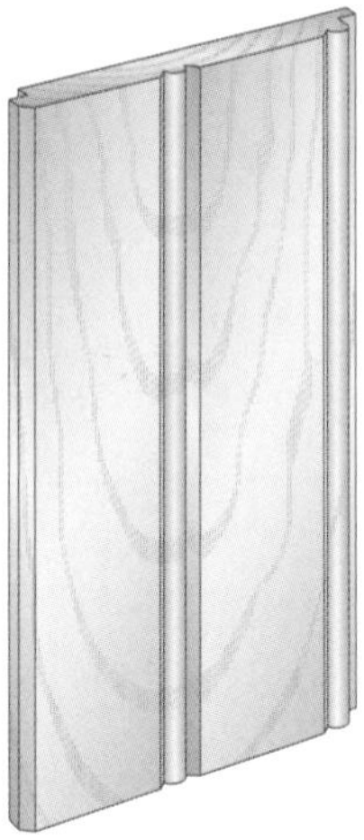

½" x 4¼"

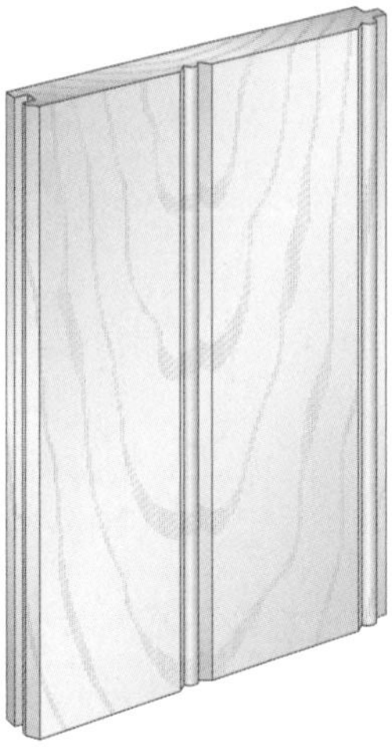

9⁄16" x 5⅛"

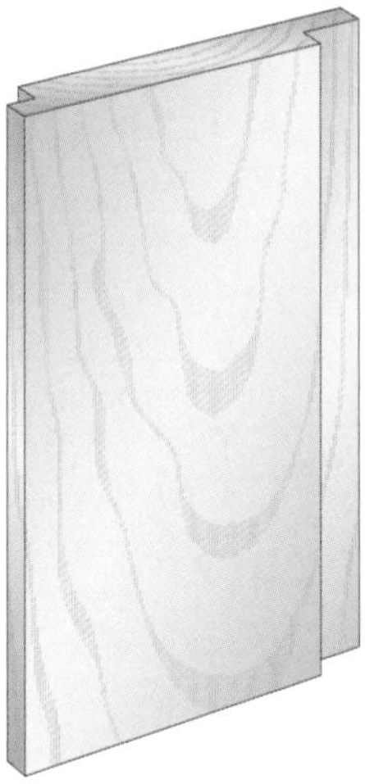

¾" x up to 8⅞"

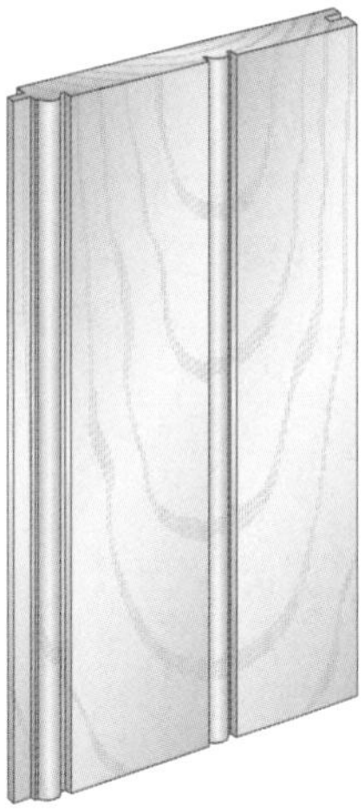

½" x 4¼"

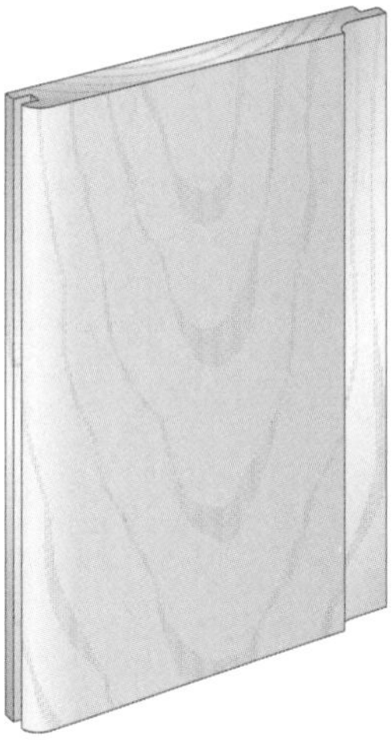

⅝" x 5¼"

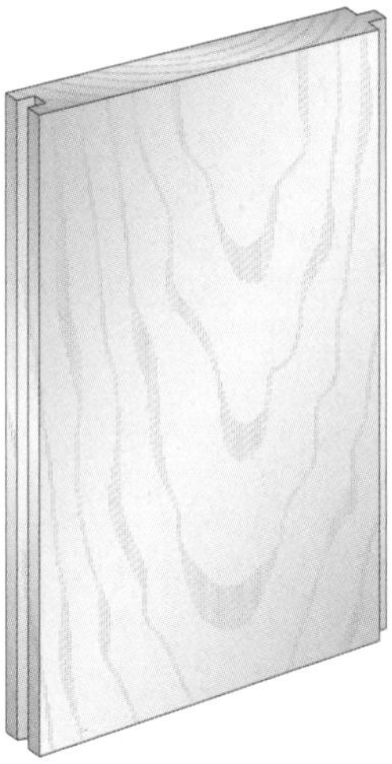

¾" x up to 9"

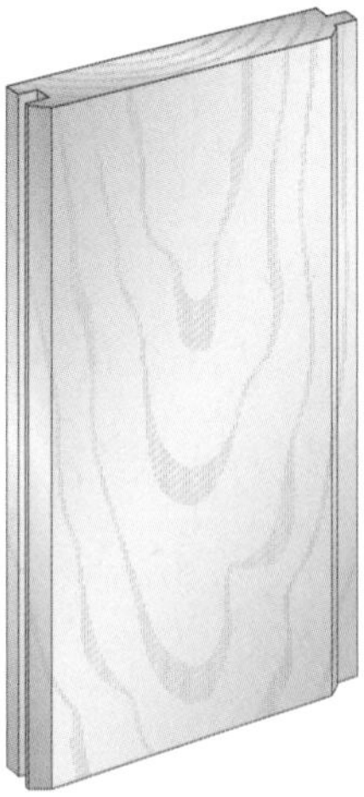

¾" x up to 9"

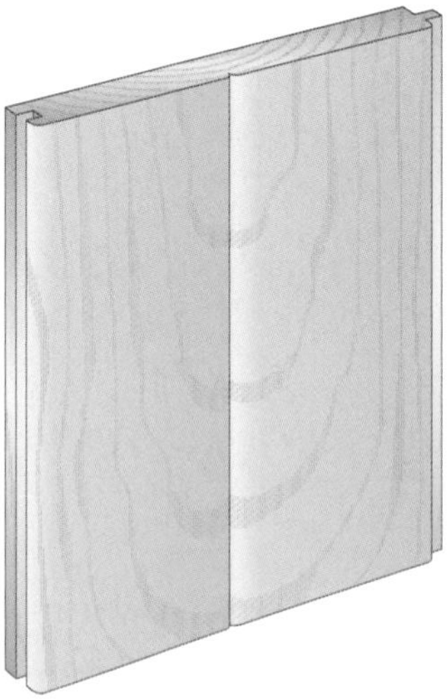

¾" x 6½"

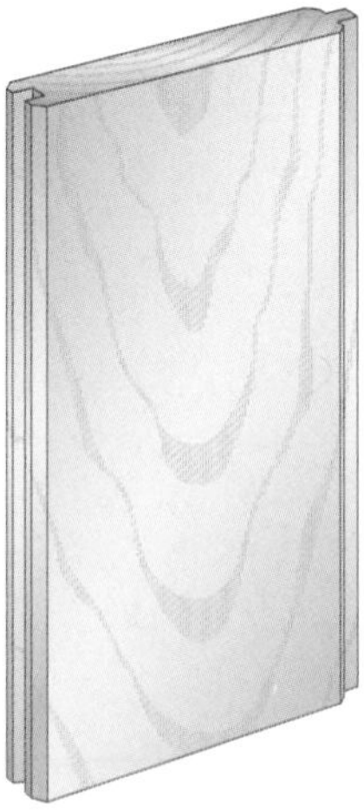

¾" x up to 9"

Above Three-quarter-height wainscoting provides a handsome textural and color contrast to the painted wall above it.

Mission-Style Wainscoting

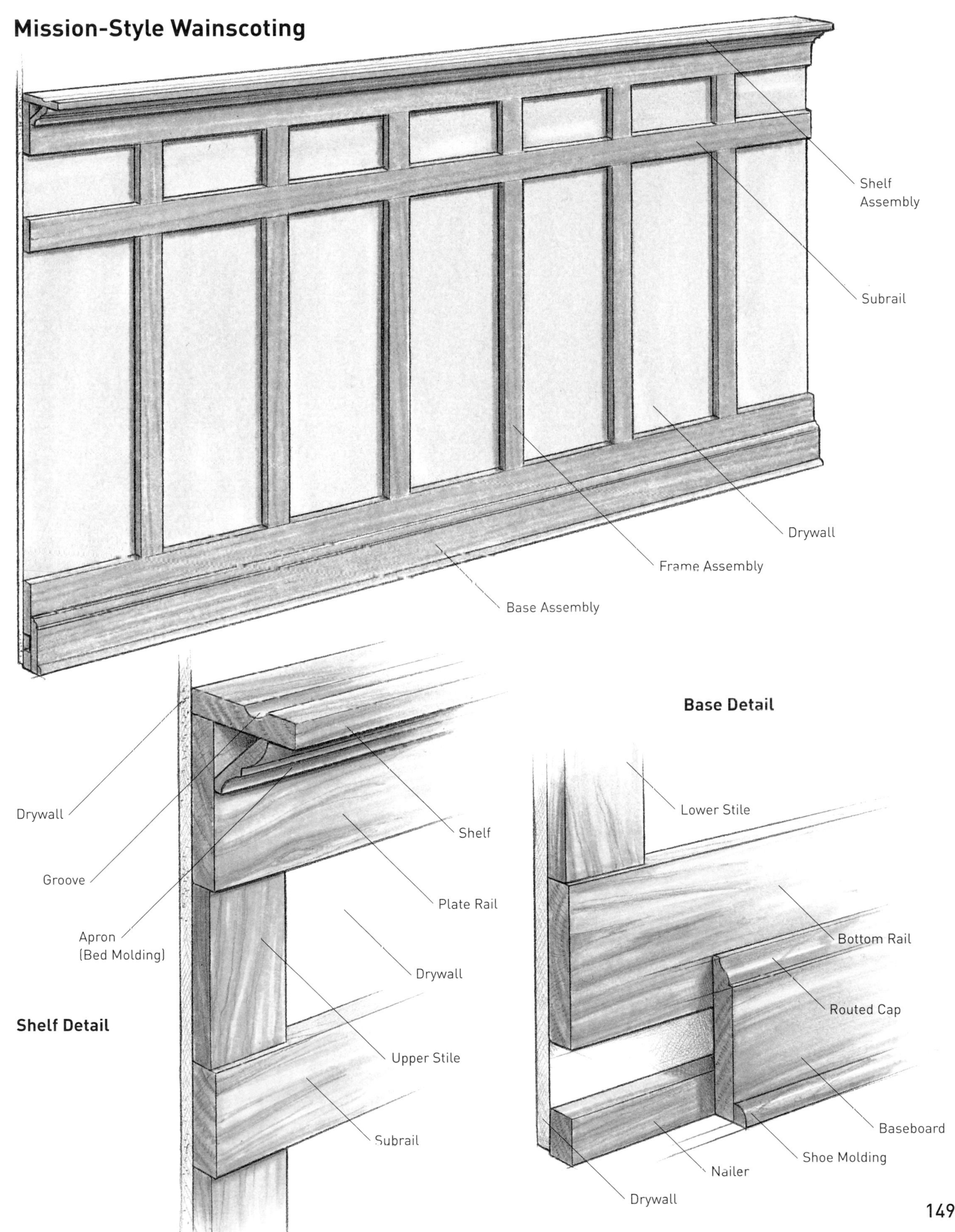

1

Smart Tip **Wainscoting Materials**

You can use many different materials for the main wainscot sections and the framing components. Your choice depends on several factors, including the style and treatment of other moldings in the house and whether the materials are available locally at a reasonable price.

Oak is a traditional choice, but buying wide ¾-inch-thick boards for framing components can be costly. You can use pine or other softwoods, or medium-density fiberboard (MDF) if you plan to paint the walls. Many professionals like working with MDF because it has no grain, which means it won't warp and twist the way wood can. It also won't shrink or swell noticeably with seasonal changes.

1 Plate rails enable a homeowner to display items that add color and character to a room.

2 Traditional tongue-and-groove wainscoting is dressed up with a handsome chair rail that adds architectural interest.

3 The wainscoting and deep chair rail tie in with this airy built-in cabinet and unifies the trim throughout the room.

2

3

Wall Frames

Wall-frame trimwork divides walls into large, aesthetically pleasing units. It makes a stronger statement than you can make with paint or wallpaper alone. You can design and install a wall-frame treatment just below a chair rail, or both above and below it. The frames above the rail maintain the same width and the same spacing from other elements on the wall as those below.

1

Frame Sizes

It's important to space frames evenly. Carefully measure each wall in the room, making allowances for doorways, windows, and other openings. Estimate how many ideally sized wall-frame intervals will fit into each run. In a room with either an 8- or 9-foot ceiling, the recommended chair-rail height is 32, 36, or 60 inches.

Smart Tip **Frames and Electrical Outlets**

If the vertical side of a wall frame falls on an electrical outlet, either move the outlet or install an outlet box extension and a spacer frame into which you can butt the side of the wall frame. When it comes time for installation, hold the wall frame in position, mark where it intersects the outlet, cut that section out, and install the frame as usual. Switches will present you with an obstacle only if the chair rail is at 60 inches. In this case, consider moving the switch. As with any area in which you lack experience, call an electrician if you're not familiar with moving switch boxes and other electrical work.

The side sections of the wall frame butt the outlet's spacer frame.

2

3

1 Graceful pilasters dress up the wall frames that sit above and below the chair rail.

2 The wall frames in the bay provide symmetry, lining up with the window casings.

3 A wide interval of wall frame is flanked by narrow intervals to add architectural interest.

Picture Molding

The picture rail was made to hang framed pictures without damaging plaster walls. Instead of driving a nail for each picture frame, supporting hooks are hung on the strip of molding. When installed below cornices, a picture rail doubles as a frieze molding, creating an upper horizontal band of the wall surface. That band is often treated differently from the main wall surface—for example, with wallpaper or a complementary paint color. Picture rails, such as those shown here, typically have a rounded top edge; frieze moldings are flat moldings with decorative relief carving or a classical profile.

1

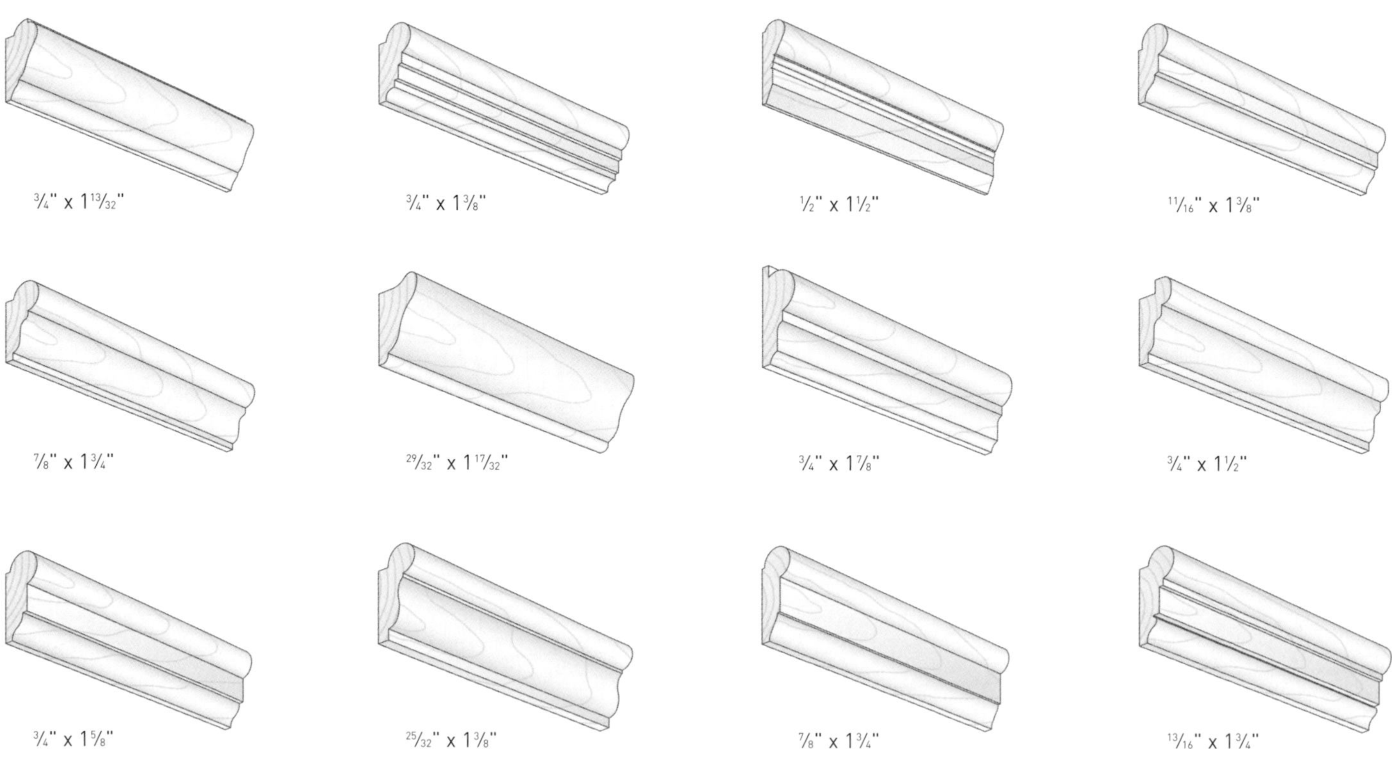

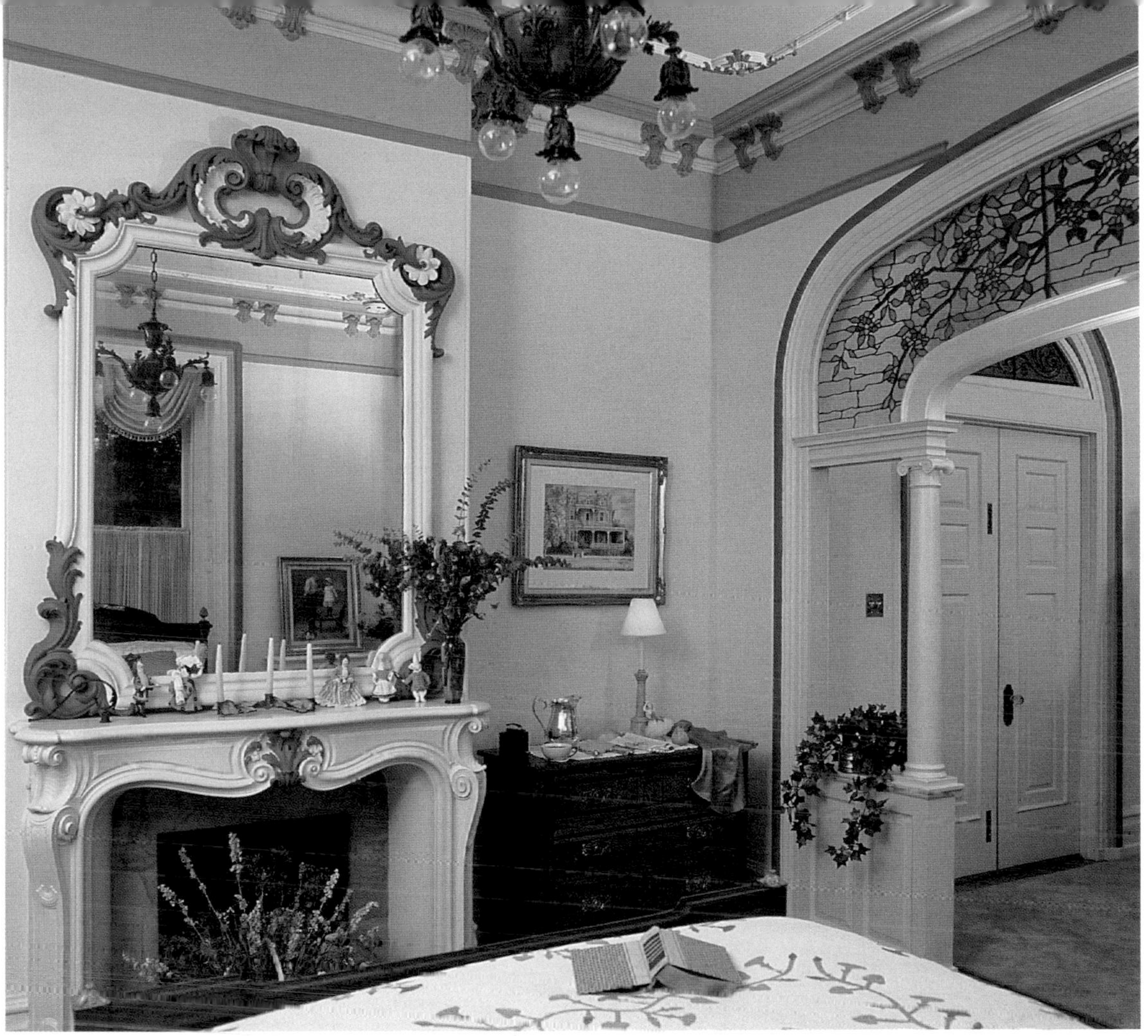

2

1 The frieze trim adds a formal, almost neoclassical tone to complement the furnishings.

2 Painting the space between the cornice and picture rail a bold color draws the eye upward.

5/8" x 1 1/4"

13/16" x 1 5/8"

27/32" x 1 9/16"

19/32" x 1 1/2"

11/16" x 1 3/4"

11/16" x 1 3/4"

3/4" x 1 3/4"

3/4" x 1 3/4"

11/16" x 1 3/4"

3/4" x 2 1/4"

13/16" x 2"

13/16" x 1 9/16"

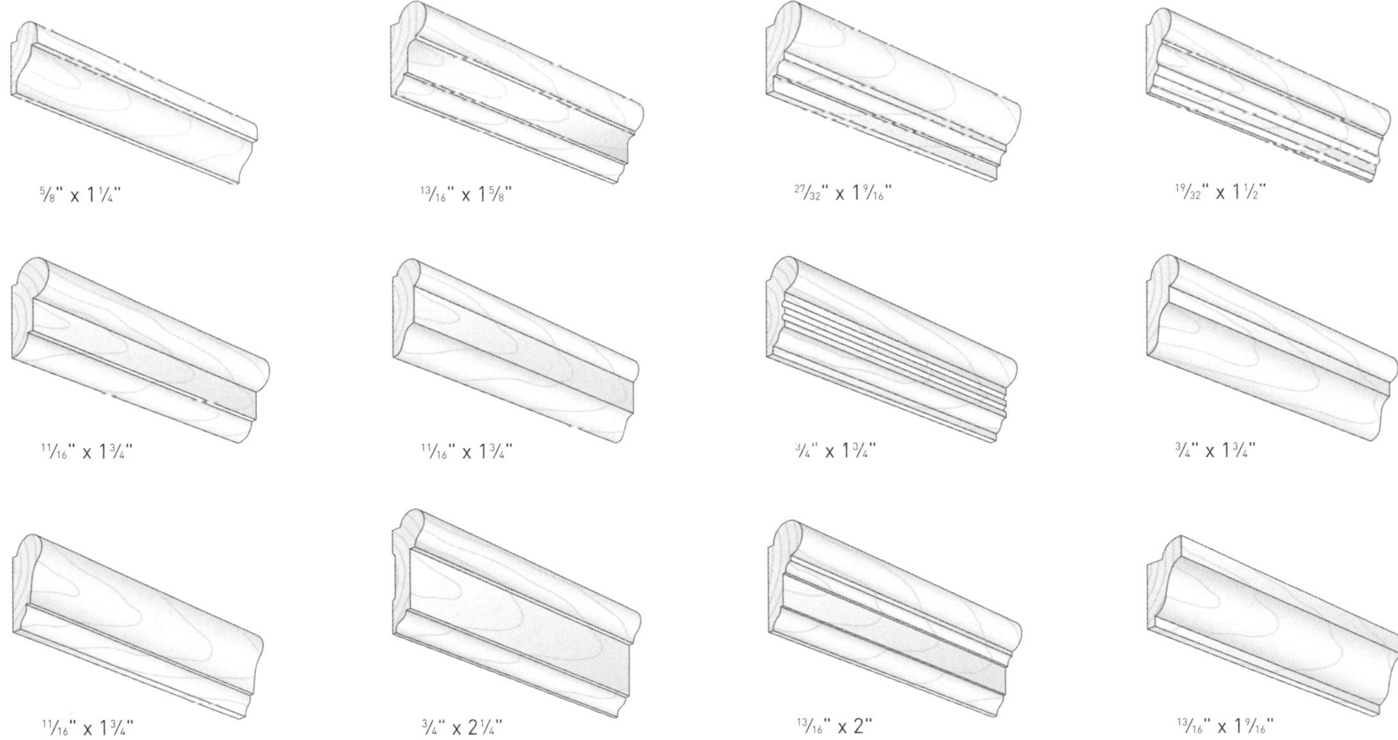

Window Seats

It's not surprising that window seats are popular. In cramped rooms, a window seat provides not only economical seating but much-needed storage space. In larger, less personal areas, a window seat can be a semi-private nook from which sitters can focus their attention on either the activity in the room or what's happening outside of its window. Typically, window seats are built into wall alcoves or recesses made by bay windows, but other applications can be just as effective.

1

2

1 This cozy and cushioned bedroom window seat provides a private nook in this otherwise open space.

2 This low, pillowed seat adds charm and strikes a nice balance with the imposing scale of this ceiling-high window.

3 Ganged windows are ideal for window seats. They provide an expansive view from the seat and add a great deal of light to a room.

3

Window Seat with Standard Cabinets

The best cabinets to use for a window seat are the short wall units designed for installation over a refrigerator. At 15 inches tall and 24 inches deep, these cabinets are good building blocks for using as is, or as a base that will have a few inches added here or there.

If your window seat will go into an existing alcove, the cabinets should fit fairly well, but you can always hide gaps at the sides by using filler boards. Home centers carry stock cabinets (the cheapest option), or you can order semi-custom options (more expensive but with better selection) from a cabinet showroom. In either case, try to match the cabinet door styles and finishes to any other cabinetry in the room.

Finish off the seat by adding baseboard and other trim to hide the window seat base, and apply caulk or small trim to cover any large gaps along the seat or filler boards.

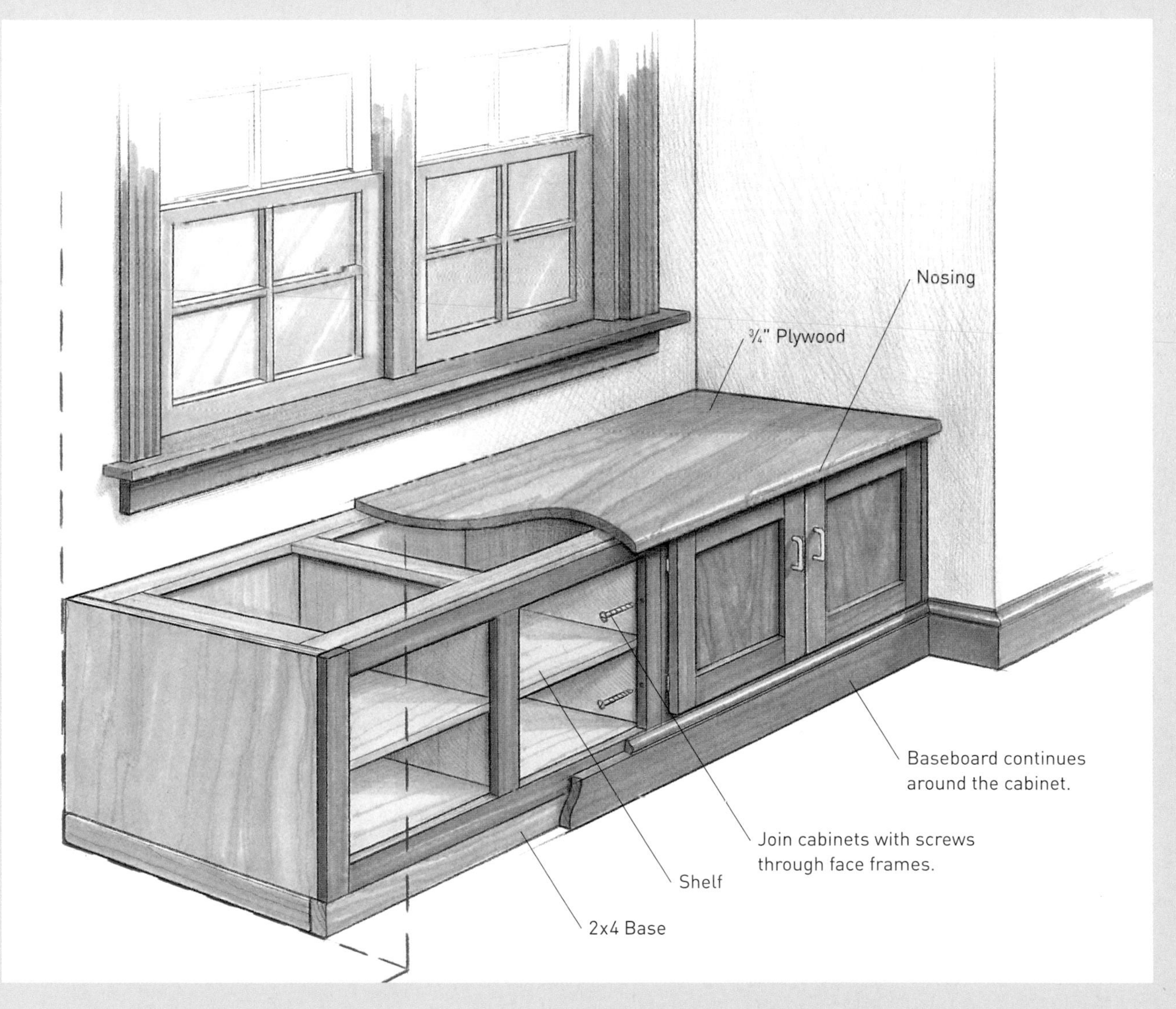

Shelving

A home's decor and furnishings may reveal a lot about the owner's taste, but it's the decorative items that tell the personal stories. People display their favorite pieces on shelves not only because they like to view them but also because they want their homes to reflect their lives and experiences, and they want to share their prized mementos with guests.

Decorative shelves may hold conversation pieces and can themselves be worthy of comment and admiration. An attractive, well-built, and well-placed shelf is an instant focal point that adds architectural detail and, of course, a personal touch. Decorative shelves are great decorating tools because they go almost anywhere—above doors, in corners, over cabinets, or along stairwells.

Types of Shelving

Bracketed shelves are the most common—a flat shelf surface supported by right-angle brackets. Ornate versions are available through millwork companies.

Cleated shelves are supported on the sides and back by one-by cleats secured to the wall. They are a good option for rounded corner shelves.

Bracketed Shelf

1-By Cleat
1x10 with Routed Edge
Bracket
Bullnose Strip

Cleated Shelves

1

2

1 A grooved plate-rail shelf tops this wainscoting and displays a personal collection and other items.

2 Small shelves that hold curios become part of this ornate fireplace mantel.

Suspended shelves hang from cables, chains, or all-thread (threaded rods) and have a distinctly contemporary look. They can hang freely from the ceiling.

Cantilevered shelves have no visible supports, thus appearing to defy gravity. In reality, the shelf surface may be secured to the wall.

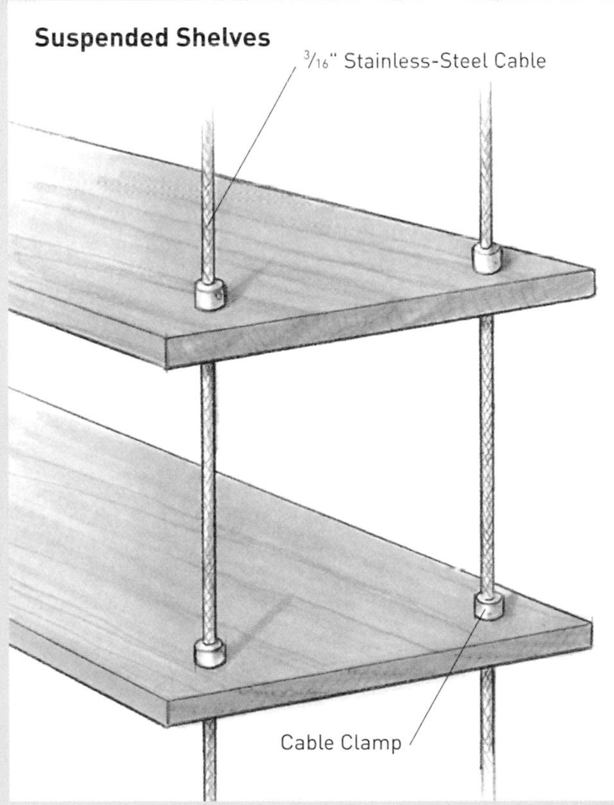

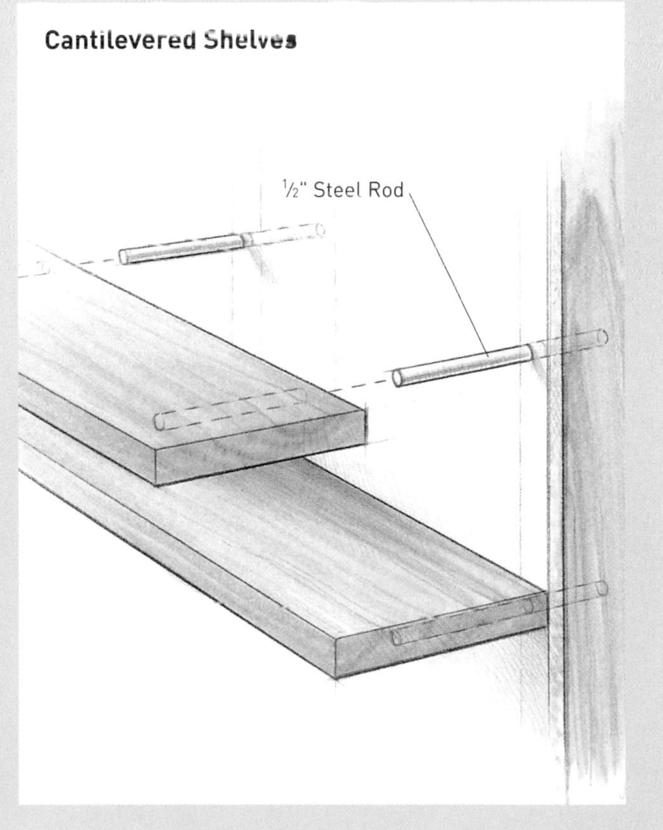

3

1 Individual built-in wall units are unified by the use of crown molding and the cabinets below.

2 Framing the fireplace mantle, these built-in shelves and cabinets are perfectly integrated with their surroundings.

3 A lighted wall niche adds drama to this room. Keep the display simple for the best effect.

4 The bookshelves extend over a pass-through, maintaining a consistent look without taking away from the open space.

1

2

THE GREEK
The Rockefellers
Hurry Sundown
O JERUSALEM!
THE THORN BIRDS
DUNE
the caine mutiny
THE HUMAN FACTOR
536 PUZZLES & CURIOUS PROBLEMS
Blind Ambition
COUPLES
THIRTEEN DAYS
A SECOND-HAND LIFE
CHARLES JACKSON
LAKE WOBEGON DAYS
WORLD ATLAS

4

Mantels

The term "mantel" refers to the entire decorative surround and not just the shelf. In historic homes, the quality of a mantel indicated the homeowner's status, and its form was a showpiece for the architect's personal art and the handiwork of many local craftsmen. Today, it remains as the social and aesthetic focus of any room it occupies. But what has changed is the amount of options one has when designing or installing a mantel. Using these options in replacing an old mantel or embellishing a bland brick surround not only transforms the appearance of your fireplace, it can change the architecture of the entire room.

Mantel Anatomy

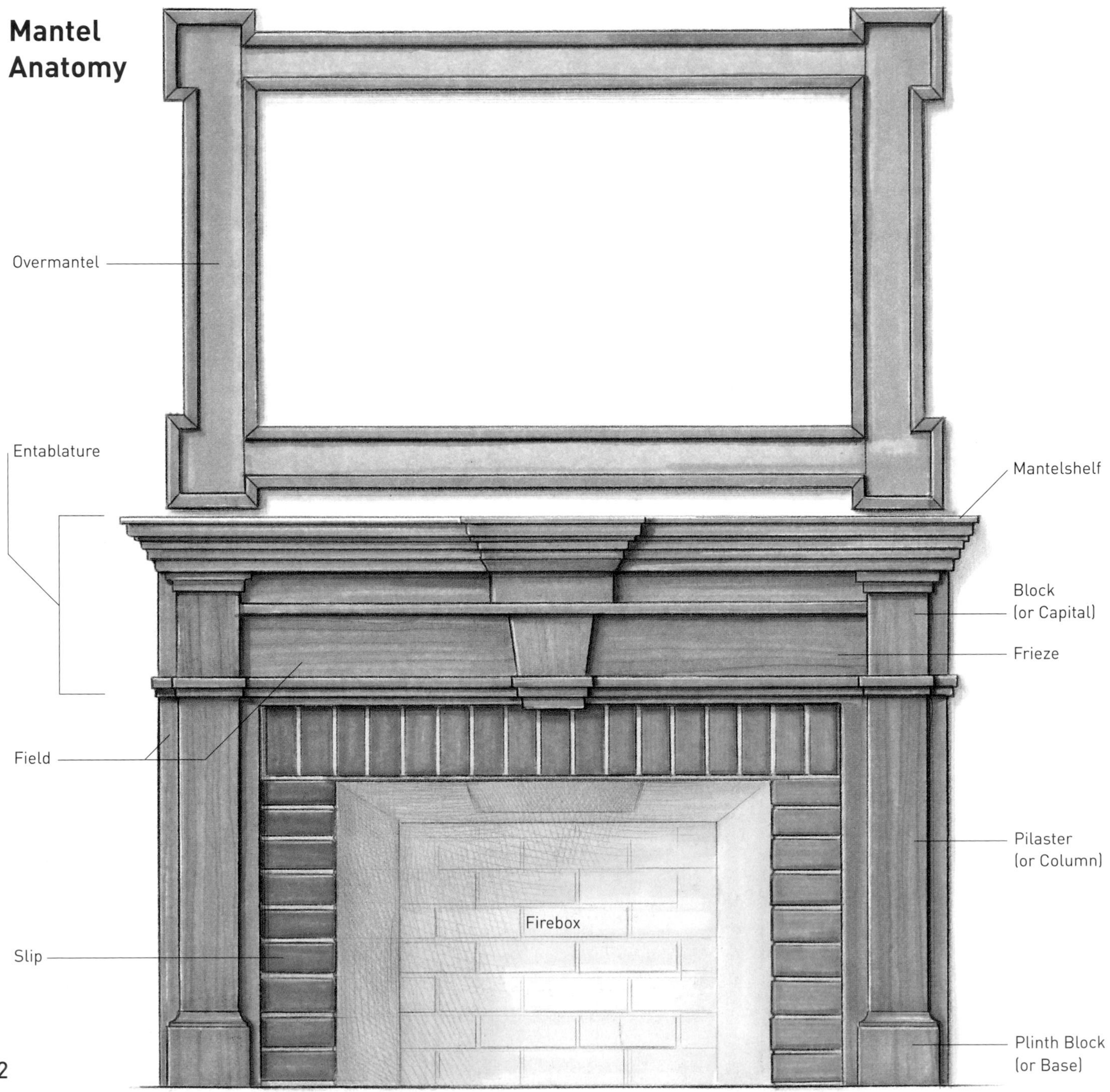

1

2

1 The natural finish of the bookshelves, cabinets, and mantel tie all aspects of the room together beautifully.

2 Victorian-style homes often contain elaborate overmantels, such as the one shown here.

3 The wood-and-marble mantel is capped by an ornate shelf, complete with dentil detailing.

3

3

1

2

1 The wood-and-tile mantel echoes the florid furnishings and area rug.

2 A massive mantel becomes the impressive focal point in this living room.

3 This smaller mantel makes up for its size with intricate detailing.

Mantel Molding

The illustration below shows a basic four-piece mantel made with ¼-inch MDF, which is a good choice for a mantel you'll be painting. The shelf is made from two layers of MDF laminated together with glue and screws. If you prefer a natural-grain finish, use finish-grade plywood with a hardwood veneer and cover all of the exposed edges with molding.

You can add molding that won't come in contact with the wall or fireplace opening while the mantel is still on your bench. Install other molding to hide gaps after you have mounted the mantel to the wall. However, you might choose to hide the mounting fasteners behind some molding, and therefore would leave off the appropriate pieces until later.

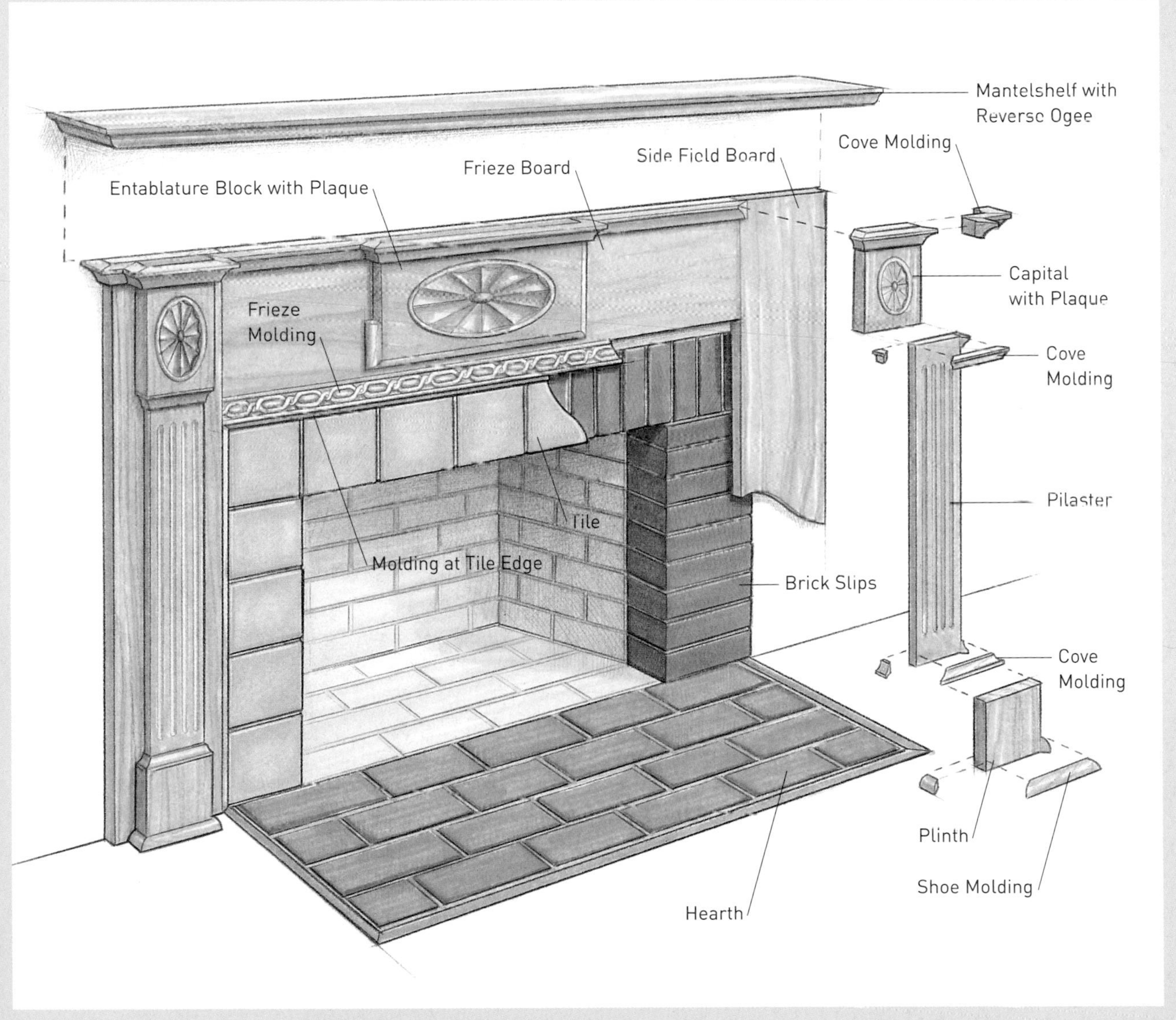

Chapter 7

Pillars and Pilasters

Pillars and pilasters are among the most important and enduring details of ancient architecture. They still remain highly popular interior elements, appearing in everything from door surrounds to room dividers to table bases to decorative shelves to mantels. Pillars and pilasters lend a classic touch to most interiors.

Even in a modern home, pillars provide the feelings of strength, durability, and timeless design.

The pillar, or column, is found all over the world, but no one has done more with it than the ancient Greeks and, later, the Romans. So successful were the early designs that they are still followed in precise detail by column makers today.

As a design element, a pillar defines a point in space. A single column can serve as an obstacle or part of an implied barrier; it can also become a tall decorative item, like a sculpture to be viewed from all sides. Two or more columns placed near each other suggests a spatial boundary, delineating interior areas or creating a threshold through which one can freely pass. An extension of this idea is the colonnade, a series of spaced columns that creates a permeable and architecturally dynamic wall plane. Whether alone or in groups, columns are especially effective in open floor plans.

In the average home, pilasters have many more uses than columns. By definition, a pilaster is a flat, square-edged pier or column that is attached to a wall. Because it projects from the wall a distance equal to a third of its width (or less), a pilaster has the appearance of a full, square column that is embedded into the wall with only its front portion left exposed. Pilasters were favored by ancient and Italian Renaissance builders. Like columns, they follow classical orders in design, but accurate replication today is less common than with column construction.

Pillars and Pilasters

As a rule, classical pillars have always been round. But the basic form has assumed many shapes and styles throughout the years. Today, column manufacturers offer a standard range of classically inspired columns and perhaps a few alternative styles, such as octagonal or spiral shapes. Finding something unusual might require a thorough search, but it is well worth the effort.

Most columns are made in three pieces—base, shaft, and capital—and often with different materials used for each piece. This makes the column less expensive, and it allows you to mix and match parts of your own choosing.

The benefits of pilasters are numerous. With strong vertical lines, projecting faces, and a structural appearance, a pilaster is a highly visible ornament yet it takes up very little space. These qualities make pilasters ideal for adding definition to wall openings and passageways. Pilasters can also divide spaces along a continuous wall plane. In many cases, pilasters offer relative subtlety in an application where a column would be obtrusive or seem excessive. Pilasters have an inherent "built-in" quality that makes them an appropriate decoration for many situations, adding a sense of craftsmanship to a home.

1 Pillars provide a formal demarcation between rooms without closing off the open space of this spacious home.

2 The fluted pilaster next to the fireplace visually supports the mantel and is echoed by another pilaster sitting atop the wainscoting.

3 These natural-finish square pillars reflect the Craftsman period and add drama to the grand oversized modern fireplace.

3

1

2

3

4

1 Pilasters and/or columns add drama to a fireplace mantel and are usually narrower than the vertical field boards.

2 This unconventional tree-like column adds architectural interest and echoes the wood ceiling, floor, and cabinets.

3 Pairs of square pillars with fluted faces sit on top of podiums to create an elegant passageway through the home.

4 Craftsman-period post-and-beam construction relies on the column as both structure and ornament.

Classical Orders

A basic column includes three parts: the base, the shaft, and the capital. The appearance and style of each of these parts indicates the column's order. Three orders come from the Greeks: **Doric, Ionic,** and **Corinthian.** Two come from the Romans: **Tuscan** and **Composite.**

Doric. The oldest and simplest in form, Doric columns are the only ones without a base. Their shafts have shallow flutes, or grooves, that meet at sharp edges. Doric capitals are plain, with one rounded or ogee-shaped section topped by a square-edged plinth.

Ionic. These have a rounded base and a capital with distinctive scrolls, called volutes. Their shafts are fluted with deep, round-bottomed grooves, each separated by a flat edge along the perimeter of the shaft.

Corinthian. The most ornamental of the Greek orders, Corinthian columns have a traditional rounded base and fluted shaft, like Ionic columns, but a highly ornate capital made up of rows of flaring acanthus leaves and pairs of volutes meeting at the top corners.

Tuscan. They are a variation of the Doric column, but with a rounded base and usually a band of half-round molding beneath the capital.

Composite. They are a mix of styles. They combine forms of the Corinthian order with Ionic elements.

1

1 The strong-looking column is in proportion to the load it's carrying.

2 The square wood columns are complemented by the graceful ceiling arch.

3 The tapered pilaster works beautifully with the wall frames.

4 The column and wall pilaster reinforce the vertical theme in the room.

2

3

4

Creating Flute Patterns

You can mill flutes into a knot-free 1x8 using a fixed-base or a plunge router. Of the two, the plunge router provides the most flexibility, allowing you to create flutes that stop short of the end of the board.

Clamp the board to a solid work table so that it will not shift. A round-nose core-box bit is a good bit to use. Use a shallow setting on the first cut, deeper settings to remove material, and a final shallow setting to clean surfaces in the flute.

Neoclassical Fluted Pattern. The hallmark of this style is a pilaster surface that is more fluted than flat. It is highly decorative, bordering on ornate, and requires a lot of setup time for the router work. Each time you cut another flute you need to reset your guides.

Victorian Fluted Pattern. This style is much easier to make. You need to set up to rout the center flute, of course. But after that one is done, you need to make only one more setup because the margin in from the edge is the same on both of the other flutes.

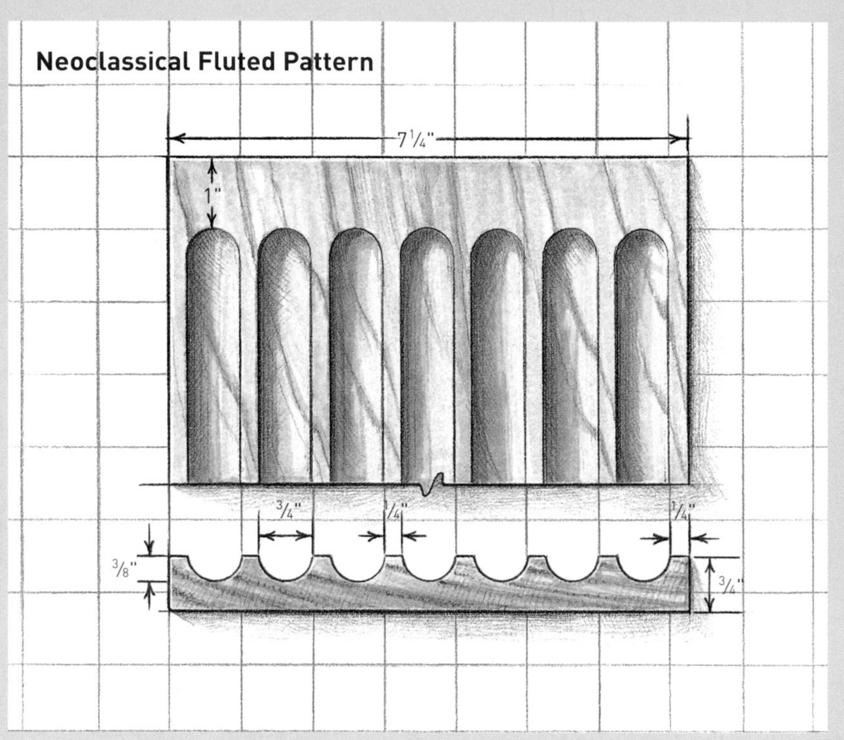

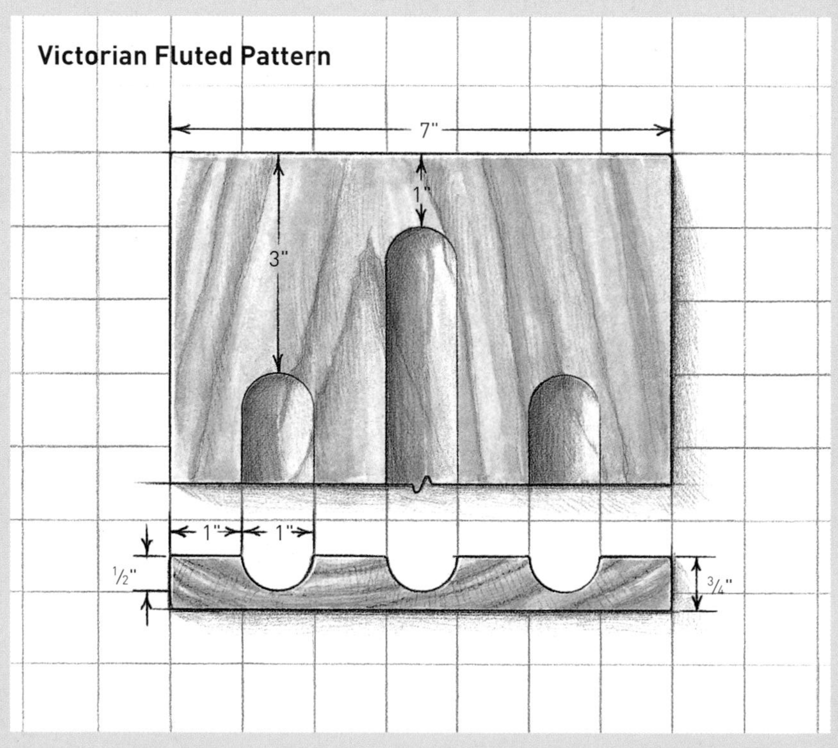

1 Ornate Corinthian columns reinforce the classical theme.

2 A pair of Doric columns creates a cozy alcove.

3 Marble columns convey a sense of strength and stability.

4 A contemporary colonnade borrows from a classical design.

1

2

3

1 Pairs of columns separate the dining room from the living room while maintaining the open feel to the rooms.

2 Simple, unadorned freestanding columns blend in handsomely in this contemporary space.

3 The spiral design of the columns creates a kinetic effect in a room full of hard lines.

Building a Room Divider

To ensure that everything will fit properly, select the columns and all the trimwork before framing the pedestals. Build the pedestal frames with 2x6 lumber, and attach them to the side walls of the opening. For slimmer pedestals, you can rip the 2x6s down to match the width of the side walls. Sheath the pedestal frames with plywood; then add rails and stiles to create recessed panels. Install a shelf and molding to cap the pedestals, notching one end of the shelf to fit around the wall and create horns that extend beyond the trim.

Install one-by jambs under the header and beside the opening, making sure the columns will fit between the pedestal shelves and the header jamb. Install columns so their bases align with the inside faces of the pedestals and the shelf ends overhang the bases.

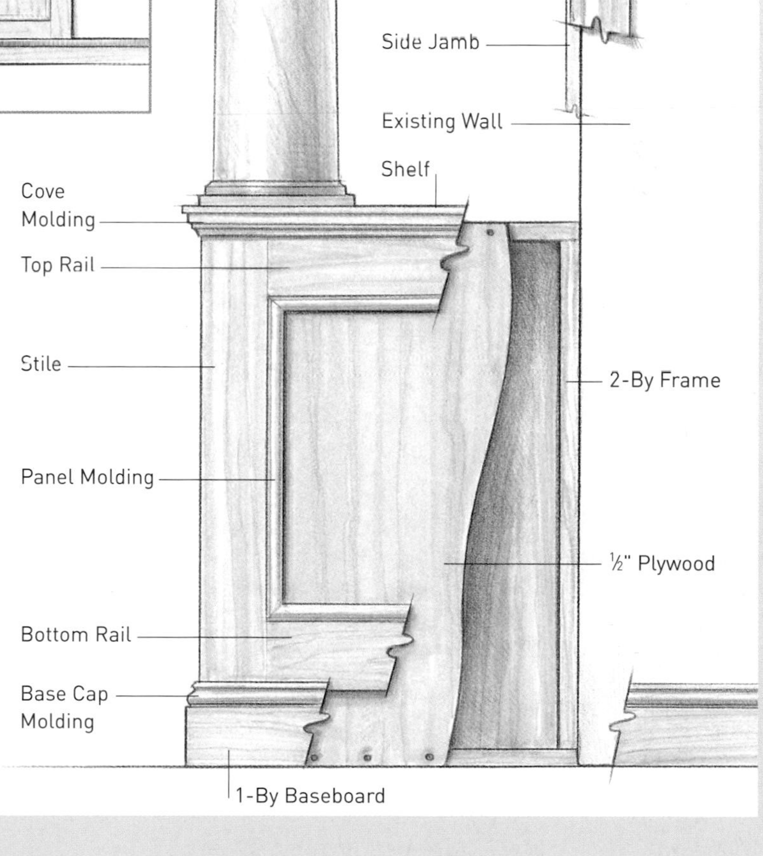

Design Tip **Faux Finishes**

Enhance and customize the look of pillars and pilasters with the creative use of paint and finishes. Try marbleizing wood columns to make them look like the real thing. Other faux finish effects include aging, patinating, or adding painted on flutes or horizontal lines to imitate segmented construction.

Draw attention to columns or pillars by using an assortment of paint colors to accentuate the various details of bases, capitals, and flutes. Oppositely, to help columns and pilasters blend into the room, use a neoclassic color scheme—painting the walls, wainscoting, and columns the same color—to lend a sculptural quality to the room.

1

2

3

1 Doric columns create a threshold through which one can freely pass.

2 The column-and-pedestal treatment is a popular room divider.

3 Natural-finish pilasters draw the eye upward to the beamed ceiling.

4 A pair of pillars delineates the space between sitting room and dining room.

Chapter 8

Stair Treatments

The importance of the staircase to interior design is matched only by its practical service. Ascending at dramatic angles from floor to floor, traditional staircases proudly display fine materials and elegant, useful designs. When considered in parts, a staircase is full of architectural details, each contributing to the visual impact of the whole.

While the balance between beauty and function has shifted toward the practical through the years, even the most ordinary modern staircases can be made over with a variety of upgrades and additions. The basic structure of most staircases (especially modern versions) allows for major decorative changes without rebuilding.

A notable characteristic of staircase design is that the finished product reveals very little about its basic construction. Identifying the standard parts and learning about how your staircase is built are the first steps to redecorating.

Each step of a staircase has two parts: the tread is the horizontal part that you walk on, and the riser is the vertical part between the treads. Where steps run along a wall, many staircases have a decorative skirtboard, which serves the same purpose as a baseboard. Staircase railing parts are known collectively as the balustrade, which includes the newels (or newel posts), the balusters, and the railing. Newels are the primary supports for the railing, while the balusters provide secondary support and create a barrier.

Each one of these staircase elements can be replaced or upgraded to provide period charm or a unique custom look to your home.

Natural-finish newels and treads contrast handsomely with the painted risers and balusters.

Stair Treatments

The fundamental design of the staircase has changed little through the years, but its architectural stardom has seen some ups and downs. Stairs in modest Colonial homes were concealed behind a door in the fireplace wall. Late-Colonial and Georgian builders brought the staircase out into plain view in the central hallway, which led to more embellished decoration and a greater architectural significance for the staircase. Staircases in modern homes seem to follow the whim of the architect or the confines of the floor plan more than the tide of fashion.

The staircase is one of the most closely regulated elements of a house, and any changes that you make to yours must conform to the local building code. Everything from the steps to the stairwell width to the size and strength of the railing must meet strict specifications, and with good reason. Most of the time, stairs are climbed unconsciously—or blindly, when arms are full of laundry—and any irregularity can cause a fall. This is a hazard when entertaining guests who are unfamiliar with your home. Most cosmetic changes won't require a permit, but it's a good idea to start your planning process by getting a copy of the staircase code from the local building department.

1 The ornate circular balustrade and window fretwork add distinctive detail to this second-floor landing.

2 Decorative box newels set the tone for this stair landing, which serves as a cozy art gallery.

3 The grand winding staircase is made grander when combined with the arched passageways and columns.

1

2

3

1

2

1 The columns and wainscoting add a classical feel to this staircase.

2 Natural-finish fretwork and painted chair rail echo the stair railing and balusters.

3 The dark hardwood newels and railing provide a charming contrast to the lighter coffered ceiling.

Anatomy of a Staircase

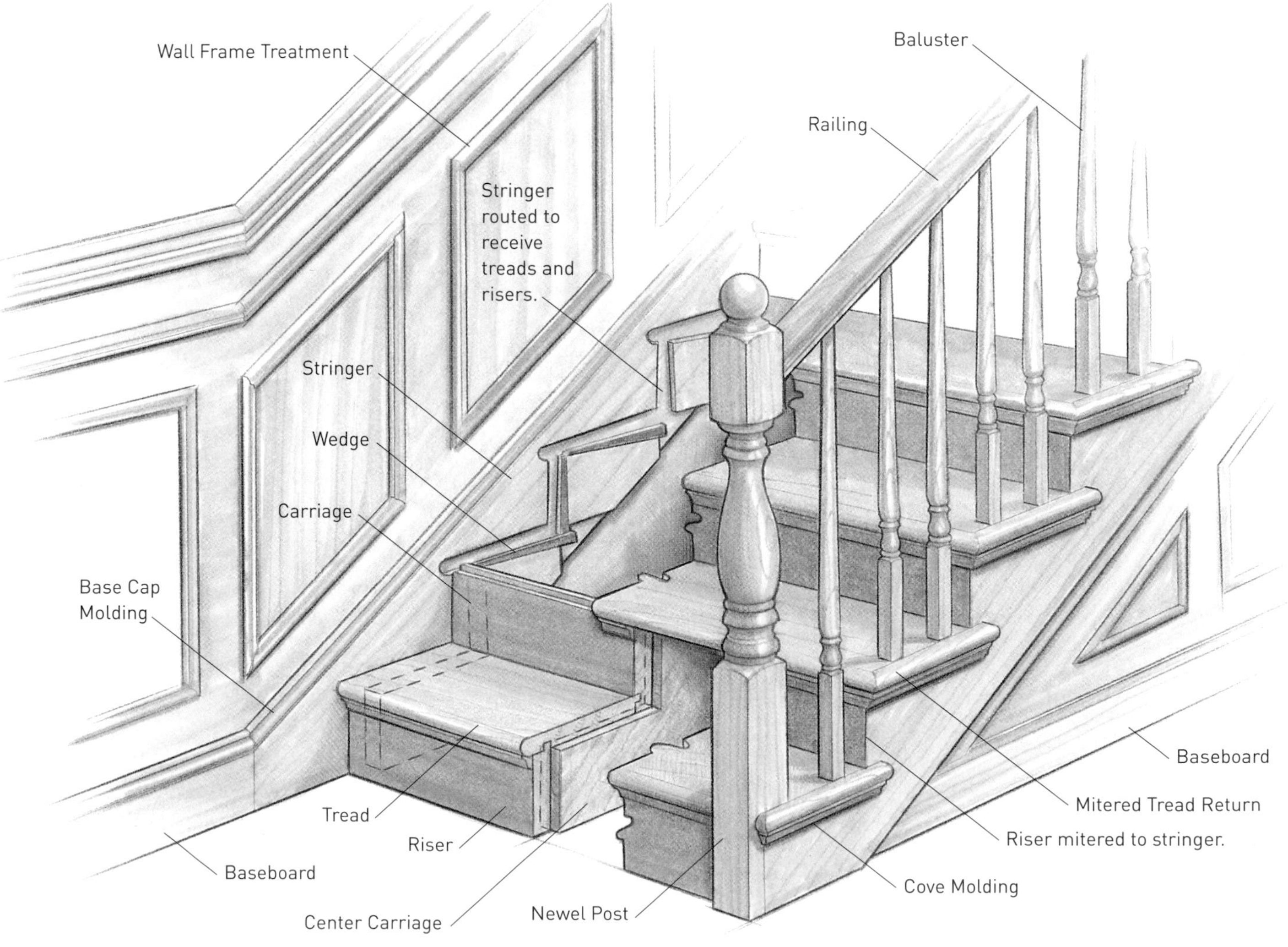

Wall Frame Treatment
Baluster
Railing
Stringer routed to receive treads and risers.
Stringer
Wedge
Carriage
Base Cap Molding
Baseboard
Mitered Tread Return
Riser mitered to stringer.
Tread
Riser
Baseboard
Cove Molding
Center Carriage
Newel Post

3

Design Tip **Staircase Makeovers**

An easy method for adding a finished look to risers is to cover them with ¼-inch-thick pieces of hardwood veneer plywood or, if you want to paint them, paint-grade plywood. To add new treads and riser panels, carefully pry up the old treads. Measure and cut each riser panel individually; test-fit each; and finish as desired. Now install with glue and finishing nails. Measure for each tread, and cut it to length. Secure the treads to the stringers with adhesive and finishing nails driven through pilot holes. If desired, add scotia molding underneath the tread overhangs.

2

1

1 Custom balusters and newels add visual drama to this staircase.

2 Wall-frame treatments provide architectural interest.

3 Curvilinear railings and carpeted stairs draw the eye upward.

4 The custom-made newel and wall mural create a by-the-sea mood.

5 The rectangular balustrade echoes the post-and-beam ceiling.

4

5

1

2

1 Grand light fixtures were once incorporated into the design of newels.

2 The staircase and wall-frame treatment creates a space to display art.

3 Handy built-in shelves complement the natural-finish staircase.

4 The log-like newels and railing set a truly rustic tone.

5 The dark stained newels echo the furniture and picture frame.

3

4

5

Newel Posts

Newels appear in an endless variety of styles, but they are most commonly made of wood and are categorized as either "solid" or "box" type. Solid newels are just that—solid pieces of wood that are milled or turned on a lathe for a decorative profile. Box newels are hollow wood boxes topped with a molded wood cap and sometimes a finial ornament. They may have embellishments such as flutes, or chamfered corners. Some newel designs combine a box-style base with a turned solid post.

2

1

3

Smart Tip **Finding Stair Parts**

Stair parts manufacturers carry a larger selection of supplies than the typical home center or lumberyard. Other sources include millwork companies and architectural products dealers. You can also find some parts, such as newels and various accessories, at salvage yards and antique shops. Quality salvage items can be expensive; they are valued as antique artifacts that display a craftsmanship and use of materials rarely found in modern products. If you're doing any kind of decorating or remodeling, it's worth taking a trip to a local salvage dealer.

4

5

1 Newels come in a variety of styles to fit any decor or theme.

2 A series of staircase newels is topped by distinctive finials.

3 The carved newel and light fixture set a grand tone to the room.

4 The dark stained railings and finials provide a striking contrast to the painted newels and balusters.

5 Iron or steel balusters and newel finials pair up beautifully with the natural finish on the railings and treads.

Railings and Balusters

Together, railings and balusters provide architectural definition to a staircase, in addition to their obvious functional roles. From a design standpoint, the two parts are related to the extent that the baluster's top end must conform to the hole or groove in the underside of the railing. Likewise, the bottom end of the baluster must fit with the tread or curb design. But beyond that, baluster and railings come in a wide variety of materials and shapes.

1

2

Most railings are made of hardwood, but iron and steel are also common. Balusters are most often made of wood, but other materials can be used. The main balustrade elements (newels, railings, and balusters) are sold by stair-parts manufacturers both separately and as sets.

3

1 A circular railing and spiral-shaped balusters offer visual drama to the room.

2 There is little that limits the decorative possibilities of a baluster. Here a Craftsman-style baluster provides a period look.

3 Most balusters are made of hardwood, such as oak, maple, cherry, or mahogany, but iron and steel are also common.

Design Tip **Spiral Stairs**

Spiral staircases have a romantic history, but in modern homes, building codes prohibit the use of spiral staircases as the only means of access between full stories. However, they can serve as secondary staircases between main levels or provide access to lofts and other private places. Factory-built spiral stairs are available in a variety of wood and metal designs, including complete, one-piece units and do-it-yourself assembly kits.

A spiral staircase provides function and offers architectural drama in this contemporary space.

Stair Accents

In addition to upgrading its essential parts, you can enhance the appearance of a staircase with a number of applied features that can be added without altering the basic staircase parts. Skirtboards can be added to unfinished basement or attic staircases and to carpeted stairs that have gaps between the rough tread and the wall. They are usually made of particleboard with a hardwood veneer. A good way to embellish the ends of treads on the open side of a staircase is to install tread brackets. Stair seats are built-in features that were born out of the custom of placing furniture, such as a bench or settle, against the wall next to the bottom of a staircase. Adding a window seat on a stair landing turns wasted space into an inviting destination. A novel variation of the paneling treatment involves using trim to create a "shadow railing" on the staircase wall. A shadow railing is projecting trimwork that mirrors the lines of the balustrade railing.

2

1

3

4

1 A painted-on "runner" adds warmth and eye appeal to this simple wooden staircase.

2 Iron or steel balusters and finials pair well with natural-finish treads and newels.

3 Tread brackets and a stair bench create colorful counterpoints to the blue walls.

4 Tread brackets are easy to install and are popular accents in Georgian and later Colonial homes.

MICHELANGELO

Chapter 9

Cornice and Ceiling Treatments

As the largest unused surface in any room, the ceiling is an ideal place for architectural detail and trimwork. Ceiling treatments add depth, dimension, and character to any room. Cornice molding provides a decorative transition between the walls and ceilings. As a dominant horizontal component, cornice molding tends to set the tone for the rest of the room.

Some specialized molding suppliers offer large, complex, and expensive cornice moldings that include details such as dentil blocks and other intricate features. But even if you stick to local sources and reasonable prices, your design doesn't have to be limited to stock types.

To create larger and more complex trim, or to match an existing pattern, you can combine several different sizes and patterns into one built-up shape. Cornices can be used to dress up windows as well as ceilings.

Trimwork can do more for ceilings than it does for walls because ceiling decoration is so unexpected. Plain ceilings provide an empty canvas for decorative lines of molding, and here there really aren't any rules of form or application. A molding treatment can highlight a central feature, such as a chandelier, by radiating outward from the center in progressively larger bands. The finest historic interiors often used plaster ribbing to add ceiling detail, but you can accomplish a similar effect with moldings installed in the manner of wall frames. Paint the frames to create a contrasting color scheme, or decorate the inside with wallpaper or stenciling.

Cornice molding around the ceiling echoes the picture rail below it, adding a formal tone to this modern space.

Cornices

Cornices have adorned interiors since the advent of the plastered ceiling. By concealing and dressing up the joint where walls meet ceilings, these moldings do more than any other to eliminate boxiness in an untrimmed room.

The term "cornice" describes large, one-piece molding installed along the top of a wall or above a window. The same treatment made from multiple pieces of trim is called a built-up cornice.

Traditionally, cornices reflected the type and intended use of the rooms they decorated. Reception rooms and primary bedrooms typically had ornate cornice treatments, while kitchens and other functional areas had much plainer detailing. Through the years cornices have become much smaller, but most still bear the shapes of their Greco-Roman origins.

Generally, the larger the molding and the more elaborate the detailing, the harder it is to install, especially if the material is wood. Built-up cornices, because they consist of simpler, smaller pieces, provide the opportunity to copy elaborate single-piece designs.

1 The natural-finish cornice picks up the wood cabinets and table in this kitchen.

2 This projecting cornice hides dramatic strip lighting.

1

2

Design Tip **Cornices and Ceiling Height**

As with all trim, the size and scale of the molding should be appropriate for the room. Lower ceilings (8 feet or less) have a harder time supporting large, elaborate cornices than 10- or 12-foot ceilings. As with coffers, a deep cornice placed on a low ceiling will make the room feel cramped. But when installed on a high ceiling, a cornice stands out without overwhelming the space.

1 The built-up, painted cornice provides a handsome contrast between this wall and ceiling.

2 The high cornice echoes the formal theme of the elaborate chandelier and china cabinet.

3 As a horizontal element, a cornice connects components of a design.

4 A cornice design complements the decorative beams in this room.

5 The wallpaper border adds heft, color, and eye-appeal to the thin crown molding.

1

2

4

5

Crown Molding

In architectural nomenclature, crown generally refers to the types of single-piece molding that are installed at an angle to the adjoining surfaces. As its name indicates, crown molding serves as an ornamental capping to walls, cabinets, and built-ins; it is also useful as a decorative support for horizontal elements, such as a fireplace mantelshelf. (A variety of crown molding profiles are shown below, opposite, and on page 204.)

Crown molding can be difficult to install yourself unless you are skilled at the basic cuts involved. Some polymer crown moldings are available with decorative corner blocks that eliminate difficult corner cuts. (See "Using Decorative Corner Blocks," page 205.) In any case, caulking and painting the molding instead of staining allows you to hide small gaps and other imperfections.

Above Crown molding ties in the passageway, built-in bookshelves, and the fireplace to create a unified space.

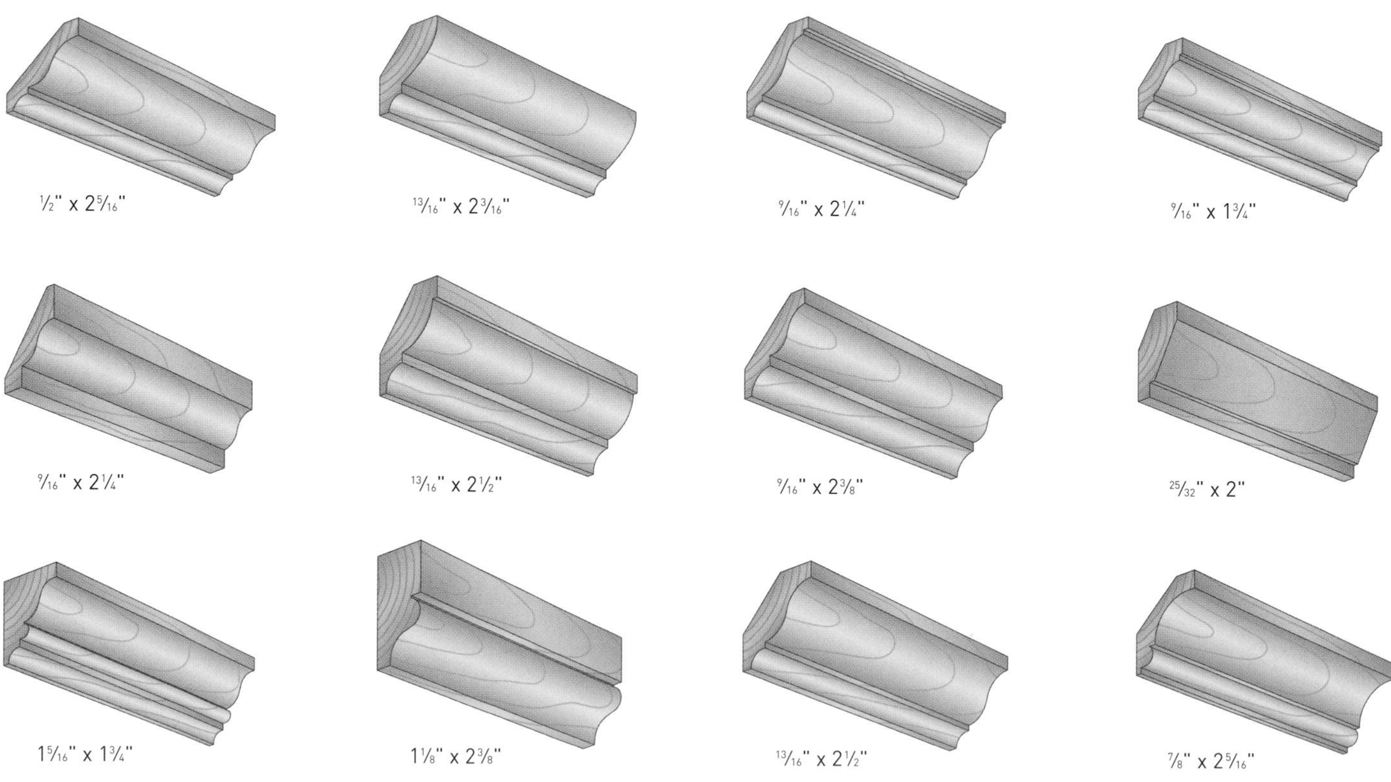

Installing Crown Molding

Installing crown molding often requires more than one method. Along walls that are perpendicular to the ceiling joists, nail the crown to the wall studs and ceiling joists. On walls parallel with the joists, there's usually no joist where you need it. One solution is to install triangular nailing blocks before running the molding; fasten the blocks to the studs or top plates; then fasten the molding to the blocks.

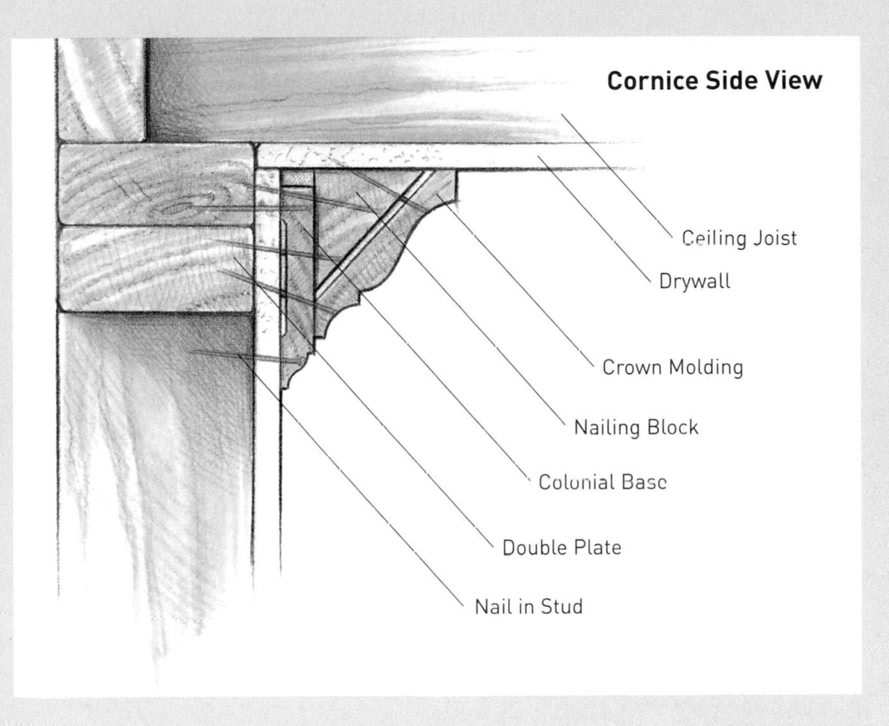

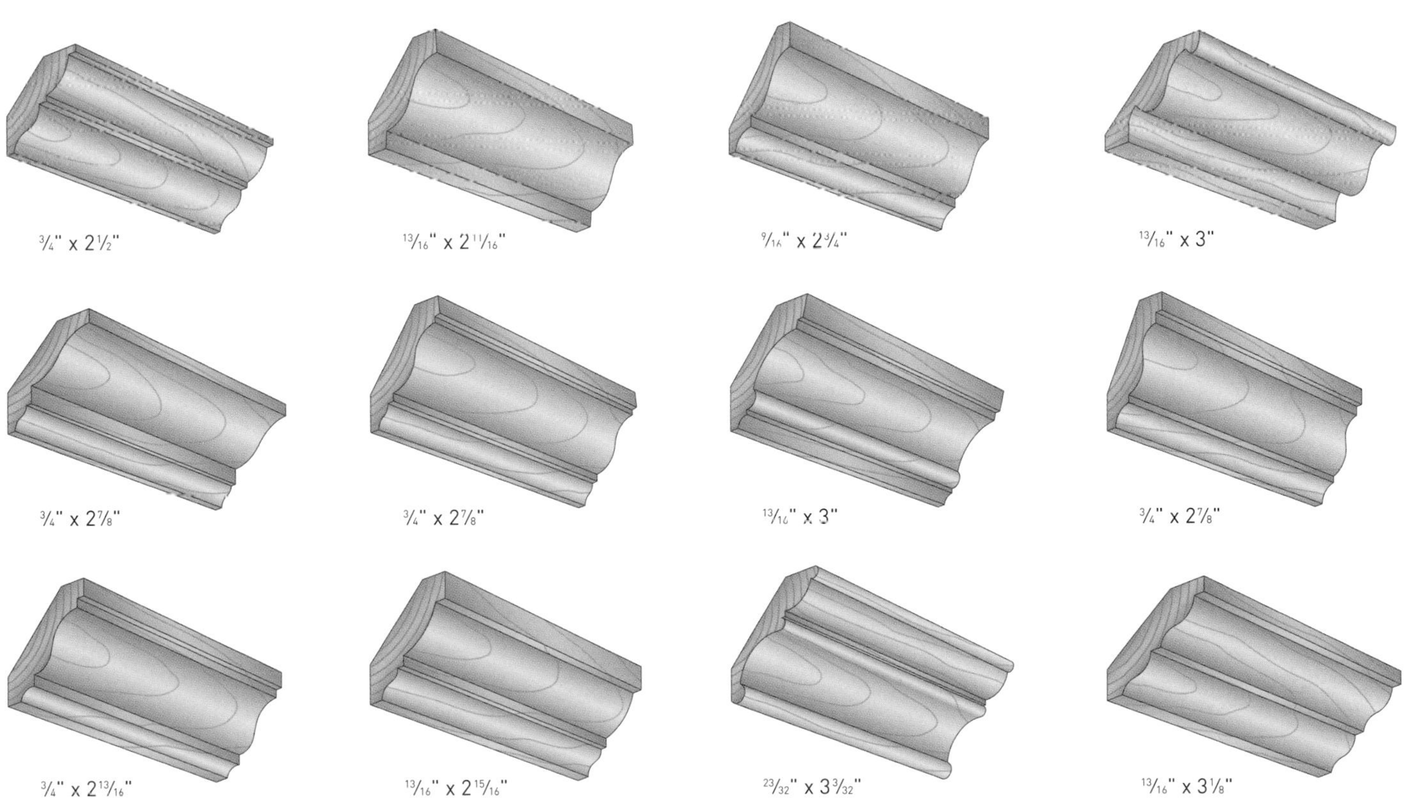

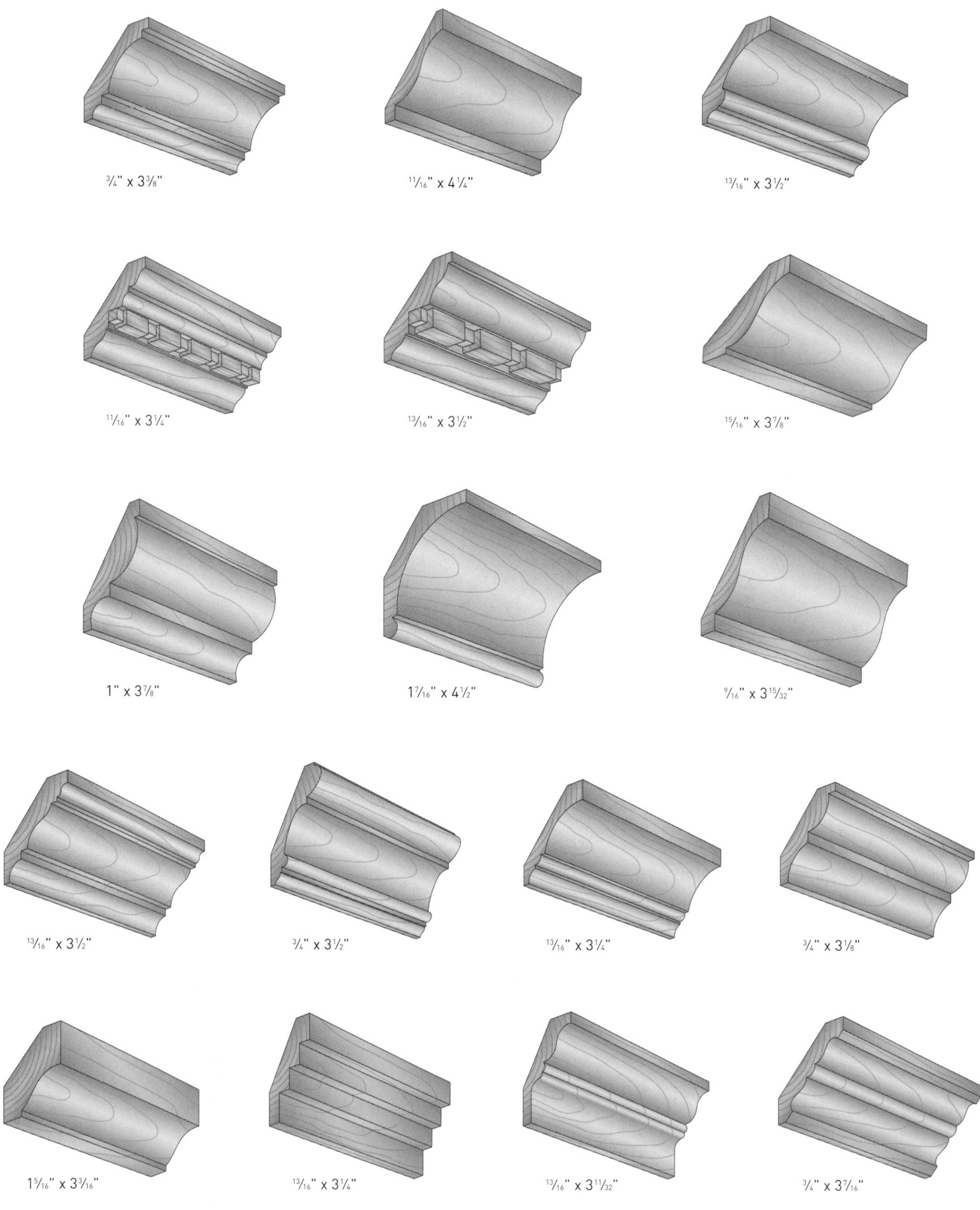
3/4" x 3 3/8"
11/16" x 4 1/4"
13/16" x 3 1/2"
11/16" x 3 1/4"
13/16" x 3 1/2"
15/16" x 3 7/8"
1" x 3 7/8"
1 7/16" x 4 1/2"
9/16" x 3 15/32"
13/16" x 3 1/2"
3/4" x 3 1/2"
13/16" x 3 1/4"
3/4" x 3 1/8"
1 5/16" x 3 3/16"
13/16" x 3 1/4"
13/16" x 3 11/32"
3/4" x 3 7/16"

Design Tip **Using Decorative Corner Blocks**

Coping and mitering can be difficult, especially in older homes where framing may not be square. An attractive alternative is to use corner blocks like these. The moldings and blocks are polyurethane foam, but wood corner blocks are also available. The system also uses blocks, instead of scarf joints, between pieces in long runs of molding. Be sure to plan where your blocks will fall, and space them evenly along the wall.

Molded fittings can be used to cover corners where you would have to cope a wood joint.

Decorative fittings that complement the molding can also serve at corners instead of compound miter joints.

1 This large-scale cornice treatment gracefully follows the turns of the living room walls and the bay window.

2 Painted cornice molding turns inside and outside corners, giving a built-in feel to cabinets and appliances.

1

2

Cove and Bed Molding

A simple trim, similar to crown molding and usually with a concave profile, is called cove molding. As you can see from the illustrations on this page, cove comes in a wide range of profiles and depths, and like crown molding, can be painted or stained and varnished. Cove molding can be combined with picture molding to create a distinctive look.

While cove and crown molding add a traditional look to a room, bed molding (opposite page) is ideal for those who prefer a more modern, understated look.

Both types of molding are often used in built-up assemblies. Depending on the individual profile, cove and bed molding are installed at an angle similar to crown molding, or they fit snugly in the right angle created by two adjoining surfaces.

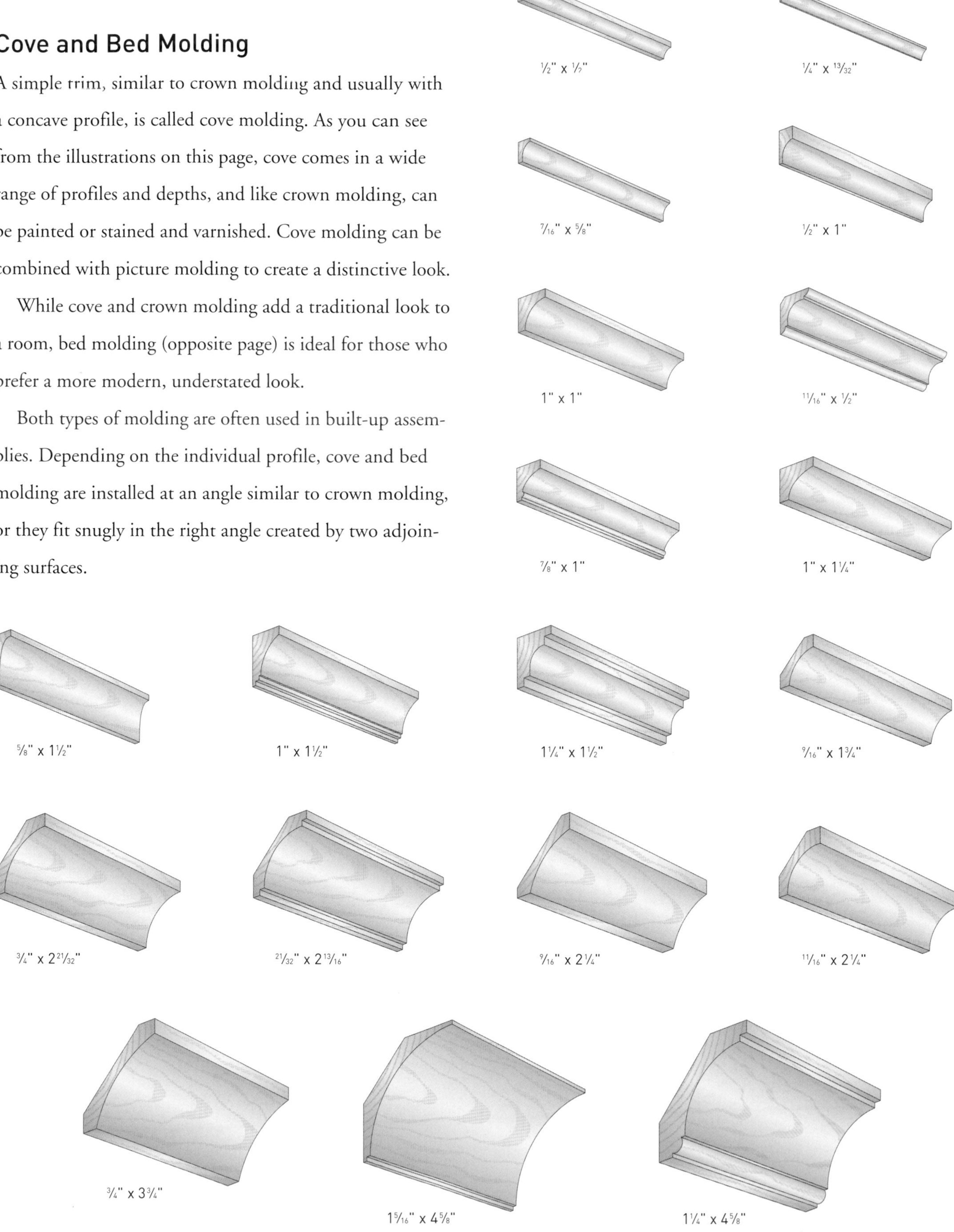

Design Tip **Salvage Molding**

If you want vintage molding from the past rather than a modern reproduction, try visitng an architectural salvage warehouse. Most sizable cities have at least one or two salvage dealers—look in the phone book under "Salvage," "Antiques," and "Demolition Contractors."

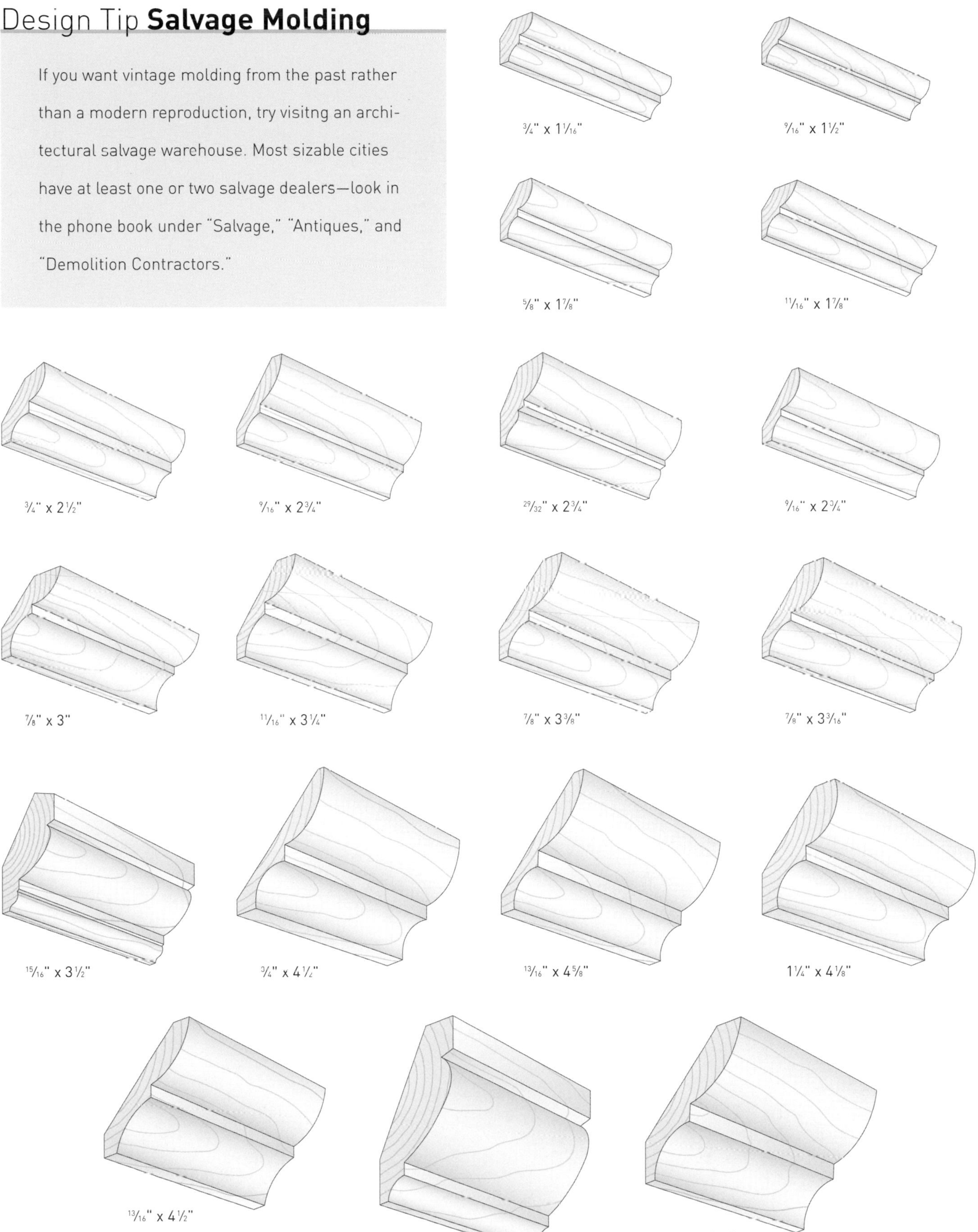

Built-Up Cornices

To create larger and more complex trim you can combine several different sizes and patterns into one built-up shape, as shown below. A simple way to dress up a cornice is to nail a crown molding on top of an inverted Colonial base molding. Some suppliers create elaborate assemblies that they ship in sections. (See samples of elaborate built-up assemblies on page 211.)

Built-ups are installed the same way as one-piece cornices. The job takes longer because you need to repeat the sequences of cutting joints at corners with each layer of the different components.

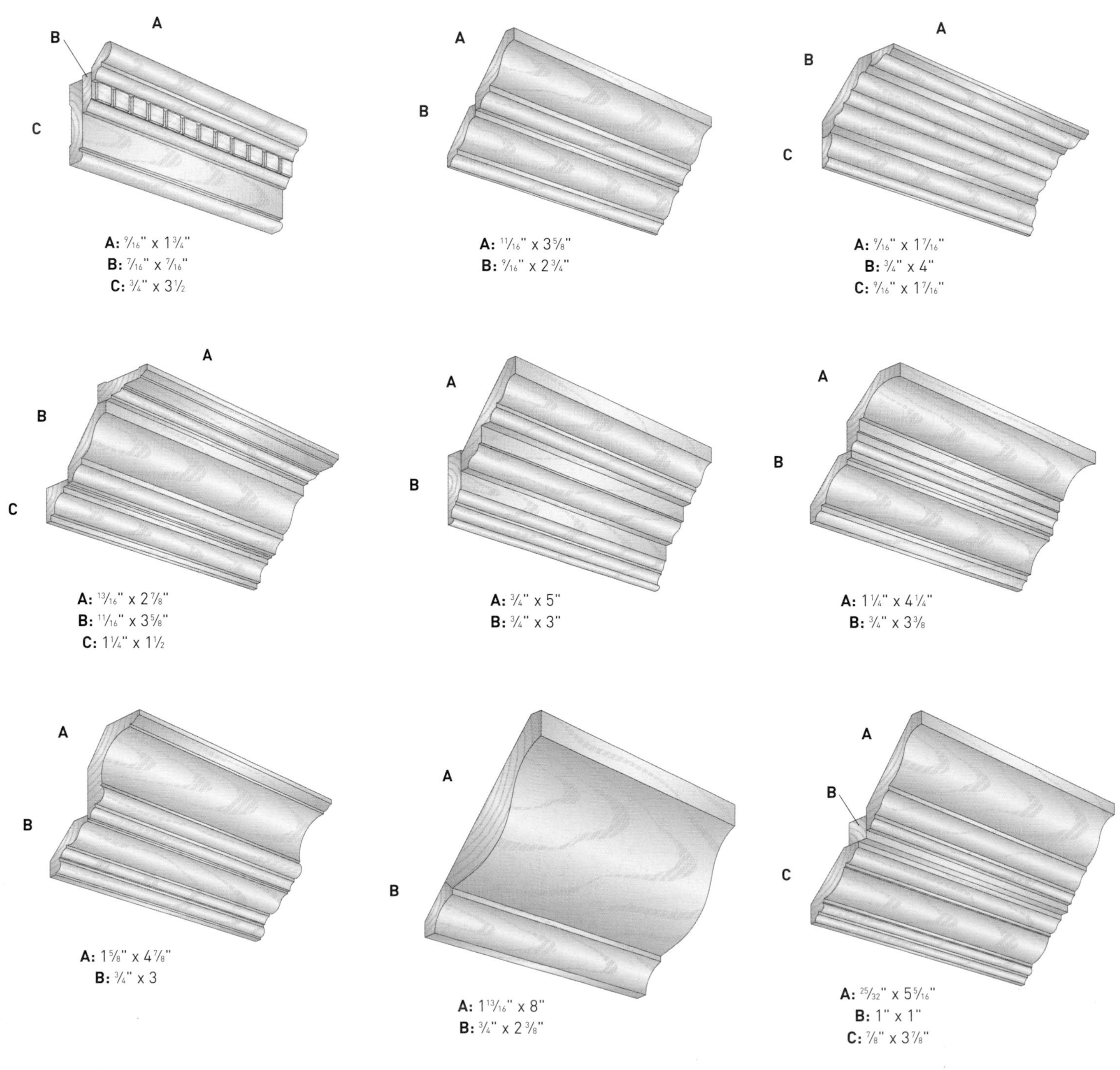

1 The built-up cornice echoes the wainscoting below it and complements the furnishings.

2 Combining several types of molding—from crown to frieze to rosette—creates a classical look.

3 Crown, bed, and cove moldings are often used to create built-up cornices.

Design Tip **Decorative Caps**

Using crown molding to create decorative caps is an area of trimwork in which you have a lot of design leeway. In rooms with a standard ceiling height, you may want to stick to a modest design. For example, you could install a bullnose cap and a 1x4 over the crosshead, cap it with a 1x3, and add a piece of 2½-inch crown molding. (See the illustration at right.) In rooms with higher ceilings, of course, you can use larger stock boards, such as a 1x6 or 1x8.

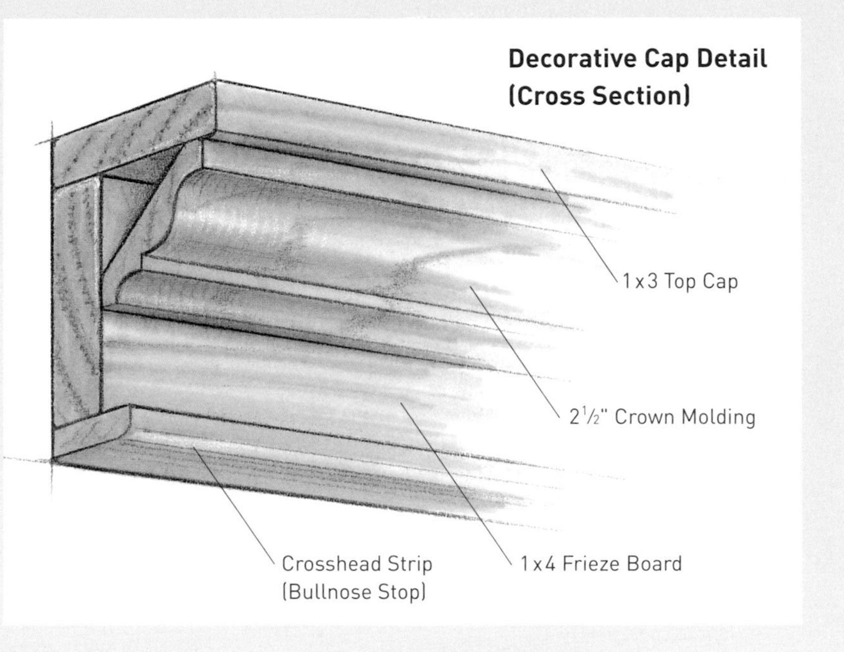

1 Crown molding adds even more eye appeal to the decorative header of four windows.

2 The dentil cornice and elaborately carved armoire add romance to this room.

Built-Up Cornice Assemblies

Dimensions shown are width and height (measured level and plumb) for overall size.

7" x 6 29/32"

4 23/32" x 6 7/8"

6 1/4" x 7 9/32"

6 27/32" x 7"

6 1/4" x 6 31/32"

3 1/2" x 6 7/32"

5 7/8" x 7 1/32"

6 5/16" x 7 9/32"

6 13/32" x 7 1/2"

Ceiling Treatments

Beamed and coffered ceilings, two of the most popular ceiling treatments, have been in style since medieval times, when most of the beams were real and coffers were created by cross-beaming between the main structural members. Decorative beams add a heavy, structural look, but this is merely an illusion. While some applied beams are actual solid timbers, most are constructed of simple hollow boxes adorned and bolstered with trim molding.

By definition, a coffered ceiling is any of a variety of treatments consisting of a projecting grid framework that creates a series of uniform recessed panels. Coffered ceilings create a formal atmosphere, but they are not without warmth. In general, they tend to feel more decorative than beams and appear less structural and more ornamental.

Structural ceilings take advantage of the inherent aesthetic quality of house framing. Roof structures, ceiling joists, and floor frames can be quite beautiful when uncovered. Soffits and recesses are built-in features that add depth and interest to a ceiling. Recessed ceiling ornaments like domes and applied accents like medallions can be used as focal points over a dining room table.

1

3

4

1 A coffered ceiling with eye appeal should be in scale with the room it occupies.

2 The magic of wallpaper tricks the eye and creates the look of a coffered ceiling without wood.

3 Cornice, coffers, and a stone fireplace combine to make a grand architectural statement in this room.

4 Decorative beams add beauty and function to this kitchen. The pot hanger is attached to ceiling joists, not the beams.

Decorative Beam Construction

Most decorative beams are not solid but rather hollow, C-shaped channels made with three finish boards and applied molding. It's this construction that gives them the common name "box beam." Box beams are made today pretty much as they have been for hundreds of years. A bottom face board is joined at its edges by two side boards to create the basic box.

Basic Construction. The box frames are typically built in a workshop, then installed and trimmed on the ceiling. Installing the boxes is easy: first, a two-by lumber cleat is fastened to the ceiling joists following the beam layout. The box frames are fitted over the cleats and secured with glue and finishing nails. Molding is then added as embellishment to the boxes and to hide any gaps. Where beams run parallel with ceiling joists, the beam layout must follow the joist spacing, or you can install blocking between the joists to support the cleats. Beams running perpendicular to joists have no such layout limitations.

End Treatments. There are a number of possibilities for treating the ends of the beams. They can meet walls at a wide trim board installed along the room's perimeter, or their ends can rest on brackets or corbels mounted to walls. The typical treatment for walls parallel with the beams is to add half-beams that appear to be partially covered by the wall. The same effect can be created at perpendicular walls, with a relatively larger beam that appears to support the ends of the regular beams. A third option is to incorporate a partial-beam detail into a built-up cornice treatment.

Traditional Box Beam

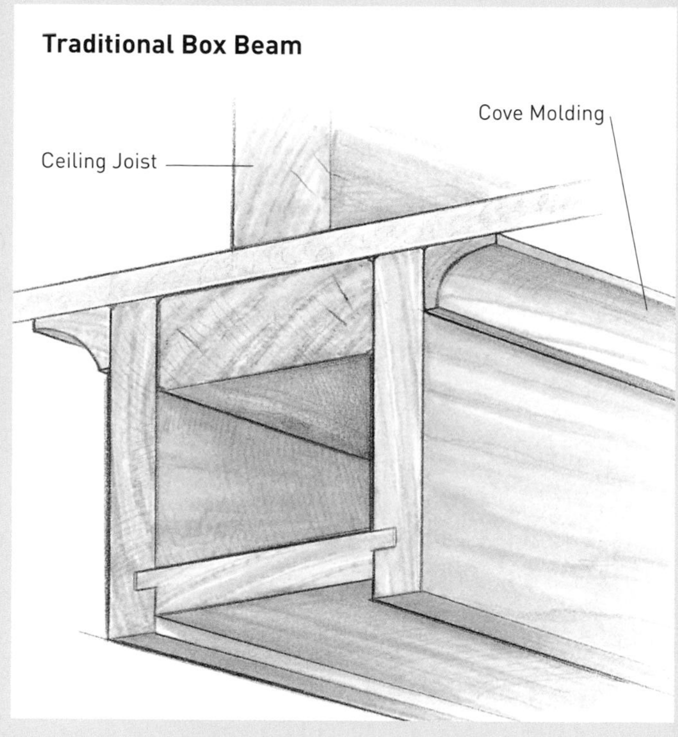

Butted Box Beam

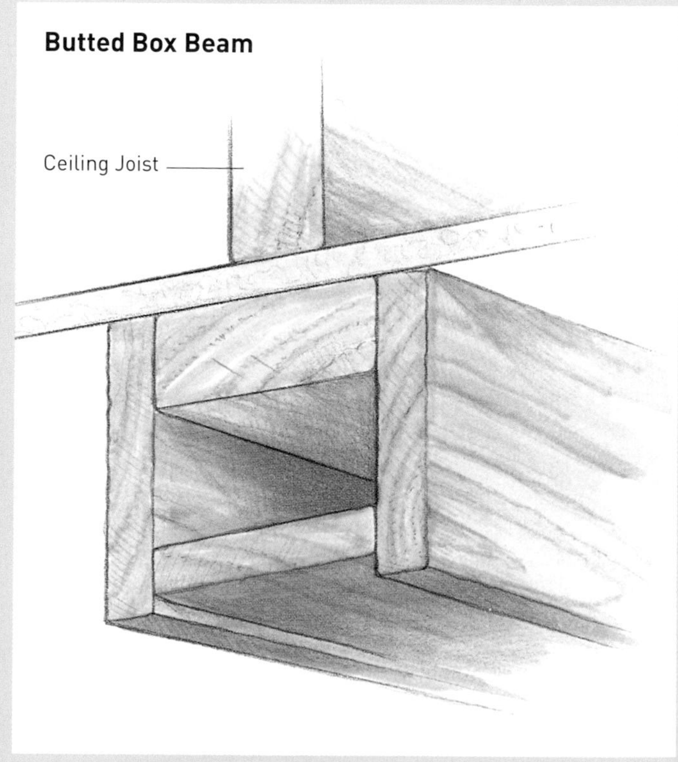

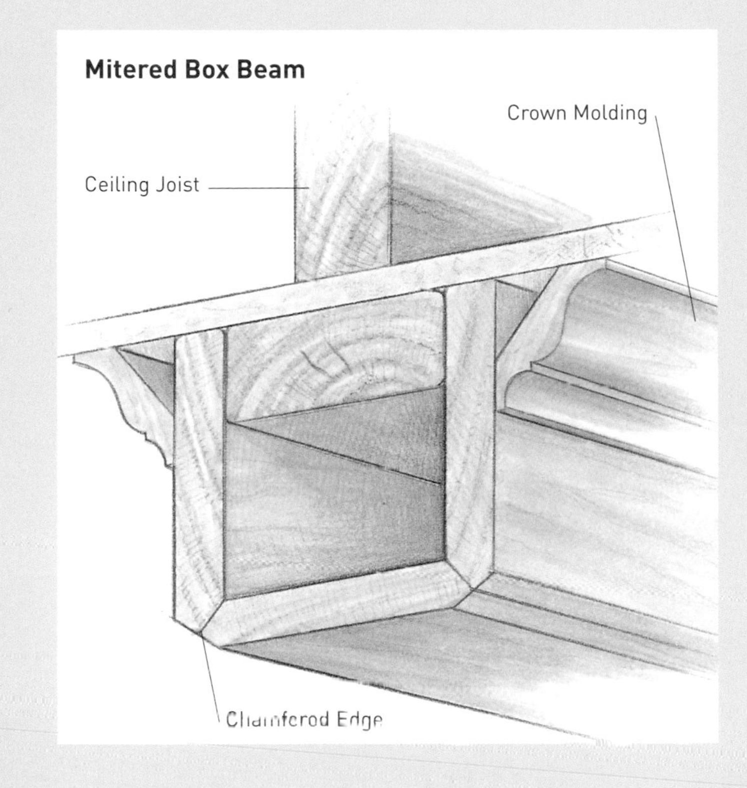

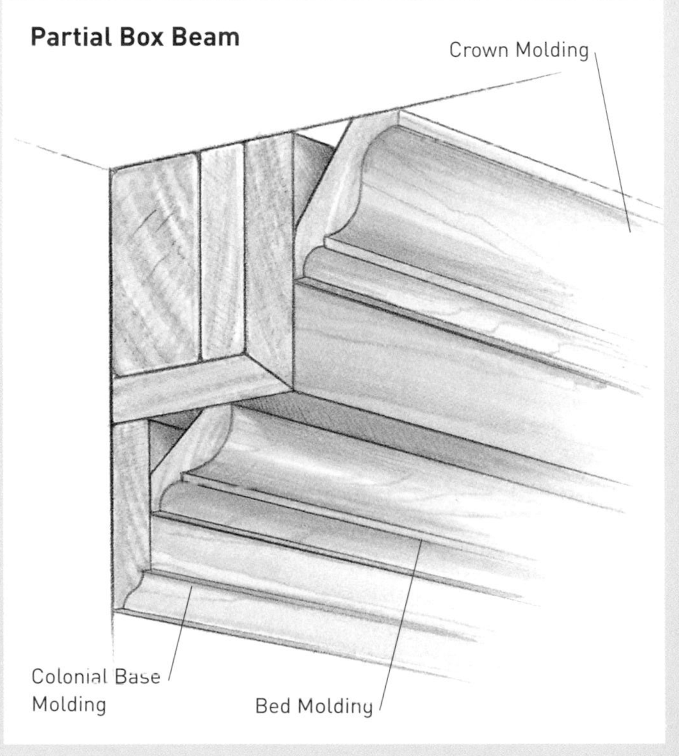

1 A monochromatic scheme softens the impact of the beams.

2 Decorative beams work best in large rooms where their boldness is in scale with the rest of the room.

1

2

Building a Framed Recess

Building a framed-in recess is a fairly complicated project, but the result is a striking ceiling treatment rarely found in any but high-end custom homes. The project illustrated here works only on ceilings below an accessible attic space. To build the recess, add temporary supports under the joists at both sides of the planned opening. From the attic, install double joists to frame the sides of the recess (or add a sister joist to each existing joist that will serve as a side). Cut off the intermediate joists, and support them with headers at the ends of the recess. Add joists and nailers to create a ceiling for the recess. For a deeper recess, build up the depth of the original joists by adding a two-by frame, then install the recess joists and nailers. From below the ceiling, cut out the recess opening and wrap the insides of the frame with drywall. Add corner bead to the outside corners, and tape and finish the drywall.

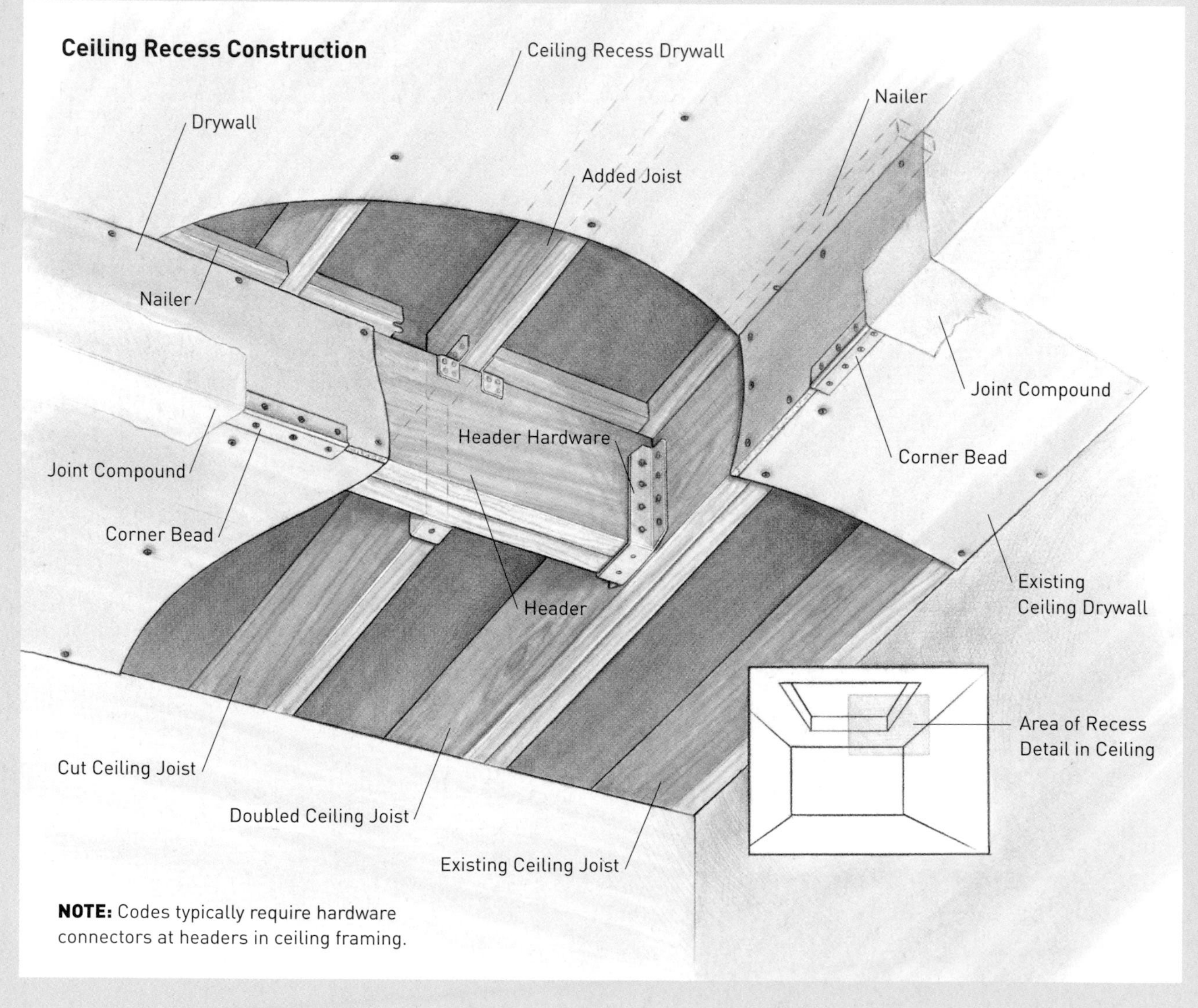

1

2

1 The ceiling's recessed, geometric forms appeal to the human eye.

2 Backlighted ceiling trim makes a strong statement.

3 Handpainted recessed panels turn the ceiling into an art exhibit.

3

Corbels and Medallions

Many of the best—and easiest—techniques used today to make plain ceilings more interesting are similar to traditional methods. In a modern home, where a ceiling often consists of a spray texture and a drab coat of paint, even the most basic accent can add a great deal of style.

Corbels and medallions are two popular options used by homeowners to dress up a ceiling. The original function of corbels was to support a structure. Often carved with rich details, corbels (found in wood, stone, and iron) add architectural interest to cornice and decorative beams. As you can see opposite, corbels come in a wide variety of styles. Medallions are classic ceiling accents and were used extensively by decorators from the early eighteenth century to the beginning of the twentieth century.

1

Smart Tip **Steel Soffits**

For soffits, light-gauge steel framing is better than wood; it's lighter and straighter than wood and requires fewer and shorter screws for installation. It is also fireproof—an important consideration when light fixtures are involved. Steel studs, tracks, and angles are available at most home centers in standard $1\frac{5}{8}$, $2\frac{1}{2}$, and $3\frac{5}{8}$-inch widths.

2

1 The graceful corbel seems to hold up an ornate cornice beam complete with goldleaf freize molding.

2 A pair of corbels adds to the charm of the cornice while ornate molding dresses up the decorative cross beam.

Corbel Designs

3½" x 3½" x 13"

4" x 6" x 9"

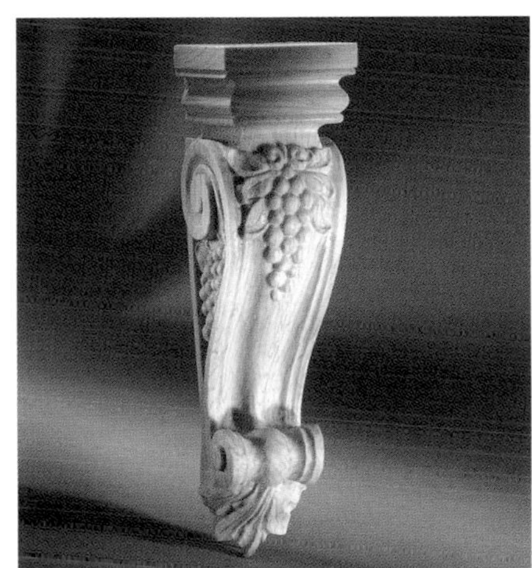

3½" x 3½" x 13"

9" x 3½" x 12"

4" x 6" x 9"

9" x 3½" x 12"

2¾" x 3" x 6"

4" x 6" x 9"

1

2

1 A trio of corbels adds architectural interest to a simple kitchen shelf holding decorative dinnerware.

2 Corbel-like elements in the shape of human faces sit atop fluted pilasters, creating a classical tone.

Ceiling Medallions

With their rich detailing and ornate, deep-relief patterns, medallions were especially favored by the Victorians, who put them in the principal rooms of the house. Traditionally, the size and level of detail of a medallion reflected the importance of the room as well as the status of the household. Medallions, often featured above hanging light fixtures in a highly complementary arrangement, work well with crown molding. Also, early plaster medallions are now being replicated in lightweight synthetic materials. They are available in simple classic designs, floral patterns, and traditional styles. As with cornice, make sure the size and style of the medallions doesn't overwhelm the room.

Architectural products dealers carry medallions in a wide range of sizes and styles. To install, mark the desired location on the ceiling; run a bead of adhesive over the medallion's back side; then tack it in place with a few nails. To add a light fixture to a medallion that is not predrilled, cut a center hole, using a handsaw or jigsaw.

Part 3

Trimwork in Today's Home

Chapter 10

Trimwork Room by Room

Just as each room in your home serves a specific purpose, the trimwork throughout the house should provide a particular decorative function. In the most general terms, elaborate trimwork designs are usually reserved for "public" rooms, such as entries and formal living rooms. More private spaces tend to receive less-elaborate trimwork designs.

If you live in a house built in the last 50 years, there is a good chance that most of the interior decoration is due to the layout of the rooms, furniture, and applied materials, such as window treatments, wallpaper, and paint. The same is true for older homes, but many well-designed older houses also contain elaborate molding treatments that add beauty and character that applied treatments cannot match.

Trimwork transforms a room. It can turn a sterile nondescript room into an inviting, cozy space. Some trimwork designs can harken back to an earlier time, allowing you to add Victorian-, Colonial-, or Craftsman-style touches to your home. Others help define the purpose of a room—an elaborate mantel may signal the center of the home and the place where the family tends to gather together, for example.

Some trimwork can correct a room's flaws. The addition of trimwork often makes a room appear larger and wider. Long horizontal lines can make you feel as though a room is longer or wider than it really is. Likewise, long vertical lines can make a low ceiling appear higher than it actually is.

A distinctive mantel, wainscoting, and flanking built-in display cases add an air of formality to this living room.

Entries and Stairs

Designers of grand homes, especially those built in the early part of the twentieth century and before, knew the importance of first impressions. Entries and foyers were large spaces that set the design theme for the rest of the house. In many homes, the main staircase originated in or near the entry, so it also received special treatment in terms of design.

Add distinction to the entry area of your home by replacing simple door and window casings with more elaborate molding profiles. In large areas, separate the entry from living space by installing columns on podiums.

Dress up staircases by adding distinctive newel posts, decorative balusters, and a complementary railing.

1

2

1 Simple columns serve to separate the entry from the rest of the living room.

2 A curving railing follows the contour of this graceful staircase.

3 Large, open areas require distinctive trimwork to make them more intimate.

3

1

2

3

1 The elaborate casing around the passage signals the transition from entry to formal living room.

2 Pillars are mostly decorative, but as shown here, they should appear to be supporting an overhead structure.

3 Plain molding and wainscoting provide a simple, inviting entry to this informal home.

4

5

6

4 When installing elaborate trimwork on many surfaces, select complementary designs as shown here.

5 Tasteful door casings and a double balustrade that ends in a flourish add distinction to this entry area.

6 A mud room provides another opportunity to use trimwork to make your home more inviting.

Living Rooms

Many homes contain two living rooms. The formal living room, which is usually near the front door, is used on special occasions and to entertain guests. The family does most of its actual living in a family room located somewhere else in the house. Both should receive distinctive trimwork treatments that reflect the way in which the rooms are used.

Homes with one living room present a challenge when it comes to selecting trimwork. The design should have an air of formality, reflecting the status of the room. At the same time, the profiles and designs selected should be warm and inviting, and in keeping with the overall design of the house.

1 The trimwork over the mantel ties elements of the room together and hides the rest of the chimney.

2 Window cornices add a design detail that is often found in formal living rooms of older homes.

3 Distinctive pillars mounted on half-walls create an opening that ushers visitors into an informal living room.

4 Stay true to the design of your house by selecting embellishments that fit with the building's architectural style.

1

2

3

4

1 The wall space between the wainscoting and the cornice in this room serves as a personal gallery to display family treasures.

2 Built-in shelves, a distinctive mantel, a decorative cornice, and wall panels draw the eye to that end of the room.

3 Decorative wall panels, wainscoting, and a projecting cornice help make this high-ceiling room more intimate.

1

2

3

Dining Rooms

In some homes, the dining room may be the most formal room in the house. One reason for this is that many families only use the dining room on special occasions. In the past, the dining room was the main area to entertain visitors and often received elaborate trimwork treatments.

Wainscoting, wall panels, deep crown molding, and chair rails are some of the trimwork types often found in dining rooms. Many dining rooms contain a hanging light fixture, presenting the perfect opportunity to embellish the ceiling with a medallion, decorative beams where appropriate, coffers, or some other treatment that will add decoration to the ceiling. Cornice molding that hides strip lighting will create a dramatic effect in rooms with high ceilings.

1

2

1 The wall panels in this dining room provide an appropriate backdrop for the period-style furniture and chandelier.

2 The window and door casings, wainscoting, and mantel trimwork are in keeping with the design of this Colonial-style room.

3 An elaborate mantel and built-up cornice give this dining room a formal feel.

3

Bedrooms

Master bedrooms generally receive more elaborate trimwork than the other bedrooms in the house. Large master suites often use molding and trim pieces to tie together sleeping and dressing areas. Master bathrooms often contain the same appointments as the sleeping area, unifying the overall design.

Other bedrooms generally contain simpler trimwork. One technique is to use the same molding in the bedrooms as is found in the hallway near the bedrooms. This is a good way to unify the overall design while giving family members the chance to decorate bedrooms according to personal taste.

1

2

1 A cornice painted a dark color serves to lower the ceiling in this child's bedroom, making the space more intimate.

2 Trimwork details embellish this large master suite, but they also serve to separate activity areas.

3 Attractive crown molding and a special ceiling treatment add distinction to this inviting bedroom.

4 If you are lucky enough to have a fireplace in your bedroom, use trimwork to enhance the focal point further.

3

4

Kitchens and Baths

Kitchens have undergone a drastic design change in recent years. Once considered utilitarian rooms, they are now used as gathering spaces for family and friends. And they should be treated as such when considering trimwork. Some cabinet manufacturers provide decorative corbels and crown moldings with their cabinets. Many kitchen designers are placing the cooking center in an alcove and surrounding it with distinctive trimwork. Range hoods, built-in appliances, and backsplashes present the opportunity for eye-catching trimwork.

Bathrooms have also undergone a change, becoming more luxurious than the bathrooms of the past. Use trimwork in the forms of rich cornices and wainscoting to complement natural-stone surfaces and the distinctive cabinetry found in many baths.

1

1 The finish on these stylized pillars mimics the finish on the cabinetry and other woodwork in this kitchen.

2 Bead-board wainscoting complements the simple cabinetry in this Country-style bathroom.

2

1

2

3

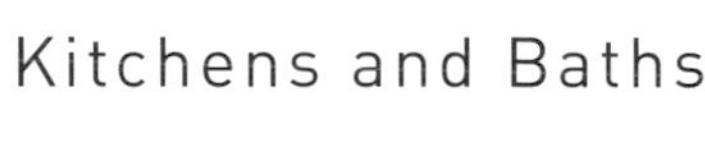

4

5

1 Decorative corbels are part of the design around a cooking center.

2 Three-quarter-height wainscoting is a focal point in this kitchen.

3 Fluted columns add a classic touch to this master bath.

4 Select trimwork based on the design of the room.

5 Crown molding provides the finishing touch to these cabinets.

1 The wide shelf on this wainscoting serves both practical and purely decorative functions.

2 Kitchens are becoming gathering places; select trimwork to make them more inviting.

3 Let the style and color of the kitchen cabinetry guide you when selecting molding for the rest of the room.

4 Window casing and glass shelves create a focal point out of what would otherwise be wasted space.

4

Resource Guide

The following list of manufacturers and associations is meant to be a general guide to additional industry and product-related sources. It is not intended as a listing of products and manufacturers represented by the photographs in this book.

ABI Mouldings
5050 Skyline Way NE
Calgary, Alberta
T2E 6V1 Canada
1-866-730-1850
www.abimouldings.com
Manufactures medium-density fiberboard and wood moldings. The Web site offers product and design information.

Bailey Hardwoods, Inc.
628 Kimble Ct.
Springfield, IL 62703
1-800-800-1913
www.baileyhardwoods.com
Manufactures custom moldings to match existing decorative moldings in older homes. Visit the company's Web site for more information or to obtain a quote.

Bendix Moulding, Inc.
37 Ramland Rd., S.
Orangeburg, NY 10962
800-526-0240
www.bendixmouldings.com
Supplies decorative wood molding. The company's Web site includes links to the company's various departments.

Benjamin Moore and Co.
51 Chestnut Ridge Rd.
Montvale, NJ 07645
1-800-344-0400
www.benjaminmoore.com
Manufactures paints, stains, and related finishing products. Visit the company's Web site for color selection information.

CAS Design Center
12201 Currency Circle
Forney, TX 75126
800-662-1221
www.casdesign.com
Manufactures natural and synthetic moldings, columns and pilasters, niches, ceiling domes, and medallions. The company's Web site features product offerings and ordering information.

Classic Details
Southern Rose
P.O. Box 280144
Columbia, SC 29228
www.classicdetails.com
Supplies natural and synthetic moldings, niches, ceiling medallions and domes, stair brackets, carved ornaments, and more. Visit the company's Web site for design ideas as well as FAQs and how-to manuals.

Cumberland Woodcraft Co., Inc.
P.O. Drawer 609
Carlisle, PA 17013
800-367-1884
www.cumberlandwoodcraft.com
Manufactures natural and synthetic moldings, fireplace mantel surround kits, brackets, and ceiling medallions. See the company's Web site for a full product line.

CurveMakers, Inc.
612 W. Hargett St.
Raleigh, NC 27603
919-821-5792
www.curvemakers.com
Supplies a kit to convert standard wall openings into arched openings. Visit the company's Web site to see its project gallery.

Decorative Concepts
11880 West President Dr., Ste. F
Boise, ID 83713
866-328-8033
www.decorativeconcepts.net
Manufactures fireplace mantels and mantel surround kits. Visit the company's Web site for installation tips and to locate a distributor.

The Decorators Supply Corp.
3610 S. Morgan St.
Chicago, IL 60609
773-847-6300
www.decoratorssupply.com
Manufactures plaster and wood moldings, fireplace mantels, niche shells, and ornamental inlays. The company's Web site offers a virtual tour of its factory.

Dixie-Pacific
1700 W. Grand Ave.
Gadsden, AL 35901
800-468-5993
www.dixiepacific.com
Manufactures wooden and synthetic architectural details, columns, posts, and stair parts. Visit the company's Web site for more information about its products.

Flex Trim
www.flextrim.com
Manufactures flexible architectural molding. Visit the company's Web site for measuring and installation tips.

Forester Moulding & Lumber, Inc.
152 Hamilton St.
Leominster, MA 01453
800-649-9734
www.forestermoulding.com
Manufactures hardwood and softwood moldings and other specialty products. Visit the company's Web site for a product catalog and gallery of ideas.

Fypon
960 W. Barre Rd.
Archbold, OH 43502
800-446-3040
www.fypon.com
Manufactures urethane millwork. The company's Web site offers a help center for architects, builders, homeowners, and remodelers.

Jiffy-Trim
P.O. Box 1789
Loomis, CA 95650
1-800-642-8457
www.jiffy-trim.com
Offers a miterless molding system that the company says is equally beneficial to the do-it-yourselfer and seasoned professional.

Melton Classics, Inc.
P.O. Box 465020
Lawrenceville, GA 30042
1-800-963-3060
www.meltonclassics.com
Offers a line of moldings, and architectural columns and details. The company's Web site offers product information and project profiles.

NMC America, Inc.
7000 Central Pkwy., Ste. 1501
Atlanta, GA 30328
770-349-1835
www.nmcdecousa.com
Manufactures ceiling, wall, and floor moldings. Visit the company's Web site for a store locator and product catalog.

Old World Mouldings, Inc.
821 Lincoln Ave.
Bohemia, NY 11716
(631) 563-8660
www.oldworldmouldings.com
Manufactures decorative hardwood moldings. Visit the company's Web site to learn about its customization process.

Ornamental Mouldings
3804 Comanche Rd., P.O. Box 4068
Archdale, NC 27263
800-779-1135
www.ornamentalmouldings.com
Designs and manufactures solid wood architectural moldings and accessories. Visit the company's Web site for molding motifs, decorating ideas, and installation and finishing tips.

Smith+Noble
800-560-0027
www.smithandnoble.com
Manufactures and supplies window treatments, including wood and fabric cornices and shutters. The company's Web site offers a full product line and an interactive design center.

Vintage Wood Works
Hwy 34 S., P.O. Box 39
Quinlan, TX 75474
903-356-2158
www.vintagewoodworks.com
Manufactures traditional solid wood millwork for interiors and exteriors. Visit the company's Web site for product information.

Westfire Manufacturing, Inc.
8751 SW Pamlico Ct.
Tualatin, OR 97062
800-692-6996
www.westfiremfg.com
Supplies wood stair parts and staircase balustrade components. The company's Web site offers a catalog as well as information about stair codes.

Associations

Association of Millwork Distributors (AMD)
10047 Robert Trent Jones Pkwy.
New Port Richey, FL 34655
727-372-3665
www.nsdja.com
Provides leadership, education, and promotion for and of the millwork distribution industry. The organization's Web site offers links to educational materials, membership information, and a discussion board.

National Association of Home Builders (NAHB)
1201 15th St. NW
Washington, DC 20005
800-368-5242
www.nahb.org
Promotes public appreciation for the importance of housing and those who provide it, and works to balance regulatory policy in homebuilding. The organization's Web site offers membership information along with educational services and event information.

National Association of the Remodeling Industry (NARI)
780 Lee St., Ste. 200
Des Plaines, IL 60016
800-611-6274
www.nari.org
Develops programs to expand and unite the remodeling industry. Visit the organization's Web site for membership information and educational literature.

Glossary

Alkyd-based A paint containing synthetic resins. Cleans up with paint thinner or other toxic solvents. Often referred to as oil-based.

Analogous colors Adjacent colors on the color wheel that share an underlying hue.

Backsaw A straight fine-toothed saw often used with a miter box to create clean-edged miter cuts for trim and picture frames.

Baseboard A trim board attached as part of a base treatment to the bottom of a wall where it meets the floor.

Bead A general term referring to a convex, semicircular profile on a molding.

Bench plane A large tool (compared with a block plane) designed to shave wood off the surface of a board.

Bevel An angle other than 90 degrees cut into the thickness of a piece of lumber or other material.

Blocking Small pieces of lumber used to fill a gap in framing or provide a nailing surface. For example, triangular blocking might be used to bridge the gap between the wall and the ceiling and provide a nailing surface for angled crown molding.

Block plane A small single-handled tool that shaves wood from boards.

Casing The general term for any trim that surrounds a door or window.

Caulk A variety of flexible materials used to fill seams and seal connections. The caulk used to fill seams around trim is usually made of siliconized acrylic.

Chair rail A horizontal band of trim installed on a wall between the floor and the ceiling. Usually placed 30 to 36 inches above the floor.

Chamfer A bevel resulting from cutting the corner off of a board.

Color wheel A graphic representation of the full color spectrum used to describe and compare the relationship among different paint colors.

Combing A decorative paint technique in which you remove a certain amount of paint by dragging a comb or similar object across the wet surface.

Compound miter saw A power saw mounted on a pivoting arm and a swiveling base that allows you to make both bevel and miter cuts.

Cope To cut the end of a molding so that its profile will match that of an abutting piece of similar molding.

Coping saw A small handsaw with a thin, flexible blade used for cutting tight curves.

Cornice Any molding or group of moldings used in the corner between a wall and a ceiling.

Countersink To drive a fastener below the surface of a board in order to give the surface a more finished appearance. Also, the name given to the bit used to cut a recess in a board in order to make it possible to sink a screwhead below the board's surface.

Cove A general term referring to a concave semicircular profile on a molding.

Crosscut A cut across the grain of a piece of lumber. A general-purpose crosscut saw has a blade designed for this purpose with about eight teeth per inch.

Dado A wide flat-bottomed groove cut at a right angle to the grain of a piece of wood. Also, the lower area of a wall (below a chair rail) that is wallpapered.

Dead-ending The treatment of a piece of molding at its end; usually a chamfer or a return.

Dentil molding A molding with a pattern that includes alternating blocks and spaces.

Door casing The trim applied to a wall around the edge of a door frame.

Drywall A sheet material made of gypsum and paper used to cover the interior walls of most homes.

Egg-and-dart molding A molding pattern that includes egg-shaped relief carvings.

File A long thin metal tool with a rough surface used to shape material. Often, the term file is reserved for fine-surfaced tools used on metal, and the term rasp is reserved for coarse-surfaced tools used on wood.

Finger joint A joint used to make long lengths of material from shorter lengths. The ends of the short lengths are cut in a fingerlike interlocking pattern and glued together. Less expensive moldings are often made by finger joining short pieces of lumber together.

Hardwood Generally, the wood of large deciduous trees such as maple, oak, and poplar.

Inside corner A corner in which the faces of the walls bend in toward each other at an angle less than 180 degrees.

Jamb The frame around a window or door.

Joint compound A soupy material made primarily of crushed limestone and liquid vinyl used to repair holes and fill joints between panels of gypsum drywall.

Kerf The material a saw blade removes in a single cut, usually about ⅛ of an inch, or the thickness of the blade.

Latex-based Paints that can be thinned and cleaned up with water.

Level Term used to define a surface or line that is perfectly horizontal. Also, the name given to a variety of instruments used to determine whether a surface or line is perfectly horizontal.

Masking Covering a surface when painting near it, usually with masking tape.

Medallion A decorative, usually round relief, carving applied to a wall or ceiling.

Miter An angle cut into the face or thickness of a piece of lumber or other material to form a miter joint.

Miter box A wood, plastic, or metal jig with a saw designed to manually cut wood at various angles.

Molding Decorative strips of wood or plastic used in various kinds of trimwork.

Monochromatic scheme A paint scheme in which the trim, walls, and ceilings in a room are all painted the same color but with different values.

Nail set A blunt-pointed metal tool used to sink nailheads below the surface of wood. The pointed end is held on the nailhead as the other end is struck with a hammer.

Outside corner A corner in which the faces of the walls project out and away from each other in an angle greater than 180 degrees.

Pilaster A vertical relief molding attached to a wall, usually made to resemble the surface of a pillar.

Pillar A column stretching from the floor or other support base to the ceiling or header above a passageway.

Plate joiner A power tool that cuts slots in the edges of two boards so that they can be joined by inserting and gluing a wooden wafer in the slots; also called a biscuit joiner.

Plumb An expression describing a perfectly vertical surface or line. A plumb surface will meet a level surface at 90 degrees to form a right angle.

Power miter saw A circular saw mounted on a pivoting base with angle measurements that is used to cut accurate angle cuts in lumber and other materials.

Predrill To drill a hole in a piece of lumber before nailing or screwing it to a surface to make driving the fastener easier and to prevent the lumber from splitting.

Rabbet A groove cut across the edge of the face of a piece of lumber, generally so that another piece of lumber can be inserted in the groove in order to join the two pieces at a right angle.

Ragging A decorative paint technique that involves adding or removing layers of paint using a rag.

Rail Horizontal trimwork installed on a wall between the cornice and base trim. It may stand alone, as a chair rail, or be part of a larger framework.

Rasp A long, thin metal tool with a rough-toothed surface used to shape wood.

Return A small piece of molding attached to the end of a long run of molding to carry the profile from the front of the molding back to the wall.

Rip A cut made in the direction of the grain on a piece of lumber. A rip saw with a blade designed for this type of cutting has about six teeth per inch.

Roundover bit A router bit used to cut a semicircular profile along the edge of a board.

Router A power tool with a rotating shaft that accepts a variety of specially shaped bits. Designed for many purposes, such as cutting contours on the edges of molding or grooves through the face of a piece of lumber.

Sandpaper Sandy grit on a paper backing used to smooth wood and other materials. Numbers printed on the backing refer to grit size. Higher numbers indicate finer grits, while lower numbers indicate coarser grits that remove more material.

Scarf joint The connection between two pieces of trim joined by overlapping opposing miters in order to disguise the joint.

Sliding T-bevel An adjustable tool, often called a bevel square or bevel gauge, used to capture and transfer angles.

Softwood Generally, the wood of coniferous, needle-bearing trees such as pine, fir, or spruce.

Sponging Adding or removing layers of paint for decorative effect using a sponge.

Stile The outer vertical members forming the framework of a wainscot wall system.

Stipple Tiny ridges in a paint surface left by the nap of a roller.

Stippling A decorative paint technique that involves spraying bits of paint on to a wall with a stiff bristle brush.

Toenailing Attaching the end of a board to the face of another by nailing at a steep angle through the face of the first board into the second.

Wainscoting Any trim structure installed in the area between a baseboard and a chair rail.

Window casing Trim that surrounds the edges of a window frame.

Window stool The horizontal surface installed below the sash of a window, often called a windowsill.

Index

Credits

Molding illustrations by Mario Ferro unless otherwise noted.

Molding designs by Forester Moulding & Lumber, Inc., Ornamental Moulding, Inc., and Bendix Moulding, Inc.

page 1: Jessie Walker **page 2:** Brian Vanden Brink **page 5:** Brian Vanden Brink, architect: John Morris Architects **page 6:** *top* Jessie Walker; *center* Brian Vanden Brink; *bottom* Brian Vanden Brink, architect: Jack Silverio **page 8:** Brian Vanden Brink **page 10:** *top* Jessie Walker; *bottom* Tony Giammarino/Giammarino & Dworkin, architect: William Darwin Prillaman & Assoc. **page 11:** *top* Brian Vanden Brink; *bottom* Mark Lohman **pages 12—13:** Brian Vanden Brink **pages 14—15:** Brian Vanden Brink, architect: John Morris Architects **page 16:** *left* Brian Vanden Brink; *right* www.davidduncanlivingston.com **page 17:** Brian Vanden Brink, architect: John Morris Architects **page 18:** Brian Vanden Brink **page 19:** *top* www.davidduncanlivingston.com **page 21:** *top* Tria Giovan, *bottom left & bottom right* K. Rice/H. Armstrong Roberts **pages 22—23:** *left* Tria Giovan; *right* Brian Vanden Brink **pages 24—26:** Jessie Walker **page 27:** *top* Jessie Walker; *bottom* Jessie Walker, Country Living House of the Year **page 28:** *top* Tria Giovan; *bottom* illustration: Robert LaPointe **page 29:** *top left* Brian Vanden Brink; *top right* www.carolynbates.com; *bottom* Jessie Walker, Country Living House of the Year **page 30:** *left* www.davidduncanlivingston.com; *right* Brian Vanden Brink **page 31:** *top left* Mark Lohman; *top right* Jessie Walker **page 32:** www.davidduncanlivingston.com **page 33:** *top left* Jessie Walker; *top right* Tria Giovan; *bottom* illustration: Robert LaPointe **page 34:** www.davidduncanlivingston.com **page 35:** *top left* Brian Vanden Brink, architect: Steven Foote; *right* Brian Vanden Brink, design: Martin Moore, Coastal Design; *bottom left* www.carolynbates.com **page 36:** *top* illustration: Robert LaPointe; *bottom* www.carolynbates.com, design/builder: George & Buck Hubbard, Hubbard Construction Inc. **page 37:** *top left* Brian Vanden Brink, architect: Lo Yi Chan; *right* Brian Vanden Brink; *bottom left* www.davidduncanlivingston.com **page 38:** *left* Robert La Pointe; *top right* www.davidduncanlivingston.com; *bottom right* www.carolynbates.com, design/builder: George & Buck Hubbard, Hubbard Construction Inc. **page 39:** Tria Giovan **page 40:** Brian Vanden Brink, architect: Tom Catalano **page 41:** *left* Brian Vanden Brink; *right* Brian Vanden Brink, architect: John Morris Architects **page 42:** *top* M. Barrett/H. Armstrong Roberts; *bottom* www.davidduncanlivingston.com **page 43:** *top* M. Barrett/H. Armstrong Roberts; *bottom* Todd Caverly/Brian Vanden Brink photos **page 44:** Mark Lohman **page 45:** Brian Vanden Brink **pages 46—47:** *top left* Brian Vanden Brink, *bottom left* K. Rice/H. Armstrong Roberts; *center* www.davidduncanlivingston.com; *right top & center* Tony Giammarino/Giammarino & Dworkin, architect: George F. Barber; *bottom right* www.davidduncanlivingston.com **pages 48—49:** Mark Lohman **page 50:** www.davidduncanlivingston.com **page 51:** *top* Jessie Walker; *bottom* Lisa Masson **page 52:** courtesy of Fypon **page 53:** *left* www.carolynbates.com, design/builder: Harry, Carolyn & Ken Thurgate, H.R. Thurgate & Son, LLC; *top right* courtesy of Architectural Accents; *bottom right* Rob Melnychuk **page 54:** www.davidduncanlivingston.com **page 55:** *top left* Jessie Walker, Mansion Hill Inn; *bottom left* www.carolynbates.com; *right* Jessie Walker, design: Cynthia Muni **pages 56—57:** *left* Gary David Gold/CH; *center* Rob Melnychuk; *top right* Jessie Walker, design: Prauss Interior Design, LTD.; *bottom right* www.carolynbates.com **pages 58—59:** illustration: Robert LaPointe **page 63:** www.carolynbates.com **page 65:** www.carolynbates.com **page 67:** Tria Giovan **page 68:** *left* Brian Vanden Brink; *right* illustration: Robert LaPointe **page 69:** Jessie Walker, design: Adele Lampert, Page One Interiors **page 71:** www.davidduncanlivingston.com **page 73:** www.davidduncanlivingston.com **pages 74—75:** www.davidduncanlivingston.com **page 76:** courtesy of Fypon **pages 78—79:** John Parsekian/CH **pages 80—81:** John Parsekian **page 82:** *left* Gary David Gold; *right all* John Parsekian **page 83:** *left* John Parsekian; *right all* Gary David Gold **page 84:** *all* John Parsekian/CH **pages 85—86:** *all* Gary David Gold **page 87:** *top all* Gary David Gold; *bottom* John Parsekian/CH **pages 88—89:** *all* John Parsekian/CH **pages 90—91:** Jessie Walker **page 92:** Bill Rothschild **page 94:** *top* Rob Melnychuk; *bottom* Bill Rothschild **page 95:** *top* www.davidduncanlivingston.com; *bottom* Brian Vanden Brink, architect: Steven Foote **page 96:** Brian Vanden Brink, architect: John Gillespie **page 97:** *top left* Brian Vanden Brink, architect: Eric Chase Architects; *top right* www.carolynbates.com, design/builder: George Hubbard, Hubbard Construction Inc.; *bottom* Brian Vanden Brink, design: Drysdale Associates **page 98:** www.davidduncanlivingston.com **page 99:** courtesy of Ornamental Moulding **page 100:** *top* illustration: Robert LaPointe; *bottom right* Gary David Gold **page 102:** Gary David Gold **pages 105—106:** Gary David Gold **pages 107—109:** illustration: Robert LaPointe **page 110:** Brian Vanden Brink, architect: John Morris Architects **page 112:** Mark Samu, architect: Mojo-Stumer A.I.A **page 113:** *top* courtesy of Fypon; *bottom* www.carolynbates.com **page 114:** *top left* Brian Vanden Brink, architect: Siemasko & Verbridge Architects; *top right* Mark Lohman; *bottom* Bill Rothschild **page 115:** *left* Brian Vanden Brink, architect: Jack Silverio; *right* Tria Giovan **page 116:** *left* Bill Rothschild; *top right* Tony Giammarino/Giammarino & Dworkin; *bottom right* www.carolynbates.com, trimwork design/builder: Tom Moore, Tom Moore Builder, Inc. **page 117:** illustration: Robert LaPointe **page 118:** Brian Vanden Brink **page 119:** *top left* Brian Vanden Brink, architect: Dominic Mercadante; *top right* Tria Giovan; *bottom left* Brian Vanden Brink; *bottom right* Brian Vanden Brink, architect: Siemasko & Verbridge Architects **pages 121—122:** illustration: Robert LaPointe **page 124:** illustration: Robert LaPointe **page 126:** *all* courtesy of Ornamental Moulding **page 129:** illustration: Robert LaPointe **page 130:** *top* Jessie Walker; *bottom* John Parsekian **page 133:** *top both* John Parsekian/CH **page 135:** Mark Samu **pages 136—137:** www.davidduncanlivingston.com **page 138:** *left* courtesy of Ornamental Moulding; *right* www.carolynbates.com, architect: William McClay, William McClay Architects **page 139:** Lisa Masson **pages 140—141:** *left* Eric Roth; *center* Mark Lohman; *top right* Tony Giammarino/Giammarino & Dworkin, design: Beth Scherr; *bottom right* www.davidduncanlivingston.com **page 143:** *all* courtesy of Ornamental Moulding **page 145:** *top both* Gary David Gold; *bottom* Tony Giammarino/ Giammarino & Dworkin **page 146:** *top* Brian Vanden Brink **page 147:** illustration: Robert LaPointe **page 148:** Mark Lohman **page 149:** illustration: Robert LaPointe **page 150:** Tria Giovan **page 151:** *left* Mark Samu, design: Deidre Gatta Design; *right*: Tria Giovan **page 152:** *top* Bill Rothschild; *bottom* illustration: Robert LaPointe **page 153:** *all* Gary David Gold **page 154:** www.carolynbates.com, design/builder: Tom Moore, Tom Moore Builder, Inc. **page 155:** *top* Tony Giammarino/Giammarino & Dworkin **page 156:** *left* Brian Vanden Brink, architect: Elliott Elliott Norelius Architects; *top right* Brian Vanden Brink, architect: John Sterling; *bottom right* www.carolynbates.com **pages 157—158:** illustration: Robert LaPointe **page 159:** *top left* www.carolynbates.com, architect: Sandra Vitzthum Architect, LLC; *top right* www.carolynbates.com, architect: Glenn Mead, design/builder: George & Diana Davis; *bottom* illustration: Robert LaPointe **page 160:** *top left* www.carolynbates.com, design/builder: Mark Albee Construction; *top right* Tony Giammarino/Giammarino & Dworkin, builder: Blackwood Construction; *bottom* Rob Melnychuk **page 161:** Jessie Walker **page 162:** illustration: Robert LaPointe **page 163:** *top left* www.carolynbates.com, design/builder: Tom Moore, Tom Moore Builder, Inc.; *top right* Tony Giammarino/Giammarino & Dworkin; *bottom* Bill Rothschild **page 164:** *top left* www.davidduncanlivingston.com; *top right* Tony Giammarino/Giammarino & Dworkin, architect: Charles Aquino; *bottom* Bill Rothschild **page 165:** illustration: Robert LaPointe **page 166:** Mark Samu, architect: Bruce Nagle AIA **page 168:** *top* Bill Rothschild; *bottom* Jessie Walker **page 169:** Brian Vanden Brink, architect: Winton Scott **page 170:** *top left* Brian Vanden Brink; *top right* Brian Vanden Brink, builder: South Mountain Company; *bottom* Brian Vanden Brink, architect: Dominic Mercadante **page 171:** Brian Vanden Brink, architect: Jack Silverio **page 172:** Tony Giammarino/Giammarino & Dworkin, design: Scott & Christine Hoppe **page 173:** *top left* www.carolynbates.com, Italian Victorian Historic Home; *top right & bottom* www.davidduncanlivingston.com **page 174:** illustration: Robert LaPointe **page 175:** *top both* www.carolynbates.com; *bottom left* www.davidduncanlivingston.com; *bottom right* Mark Lohman **page 176:** *top left* www.davidduncanlivingston.com; *right* Brian Vanden Brink; *bottom left* Jessie Walker, design: Gavin Mullin **page 177:** illustration: Robert LaPointe **pages 178—179:** *left* www.carolynbates.com, design: Milford Cushman, The Cushman Design Group, Inc.; *center* Eric Roth; *top right* Jessie Walker, design/architect: George Niedecken; *bottom left* Jessie Walker, architect: James Goldberg Architects **pages 180—181:** www.carolynbates.com **page 182:** *left* Tony Giammarino/Giammarino & Dworkin, design: Home Masons; *right* Tony Giammarino/Giammarino & Dworkin **page 183:** Mark Samu, architect: Bruce Nagle AIA **page 184:** *top left* Tony Giammarino/Giammarino & Dworkin, design: Janice Hall; *top right* Tony Giammarino/Giammarino & Dworkin, design: Carol Germana; *bottom* illustration: Robert LaPointe **page 185:** Brian Vanden Brink, architect: Elliott Elliott Norelius Architects **page 186:** *left* www.davidduncanlivingston; *right* Eric Roth **page 187:** *top left* A. Teufen/H. Armstrong Roberts; *right* Brian Vanden Brink, architect: Jack Silverio; *bottom left* Mark Lohman **page 188:** *top* Eric Roth; *bottom* Mark Lohman **page 189:** *top both* www.davidduncanlivingston; *bottom* www.carolynbates.com, architect: Sandra Vitzthum Architect, LLC **page 190:** *left & top right* Brian Vanden Brink, architect: John Gillespie; *bottom right* www.carolynbates.com, Italian Victorian Historic House **page 191:** *left* www.davidduncanlivingston; *right* Mark Samu **pages 192—193:** *far left* Brian Vanden Brink, architect: Pohlemus Savery DaSilva Architects; *center left* www.davidduncanlivingston.com; *center right* Mark Samu; *far right* Jessie Walker, architect: Gary Frank **page 194:** *left* Brian Vanden Brink; *top right* Mark Samu; *bottom right* Jessie Walker **page 195:** Jessie Walker **pages 196—197:** www.davidduncanlivingston.com **pages 198—199:** *left* Mark Lohman; *right* Brian Vanden Brink **page 200:** *top & bottom* Mark Lohman **page 201:** *top* Bill Rothschild; *bottom left* Tony Giammarino/Giammarino & Dworkin, design: Sue Ellen Gregory Interior Design; *bottom right* K. Rice/H. Armstrong Roberts **page 202:** Mark Lohman **page 203:** illustration: Robert LaPointe **page 205:** *top both* Gary David Gold; *bottom left* Jessie Walker, design: Marilyn Davis; *bottom right* Bill Rothschild **page 209:** *top left* Jessie Walker; *top right* Eric Roth; *bottom* Tony Giammarino/Giammarino & Dworkin, architect: William Darwin Prillaman & Assoc. **page 210:** *top* illustration: Robert LaPointe; *bottom both* Bill Rothschild **page 211:** *all* courtesy of Ornamental Moulding **page 212:** www.davidduncanlivingston.com **page 213:** *top left & right* Brian Vanden Brink; *bottom right* Tony Giammarino/Giammarino & Dworkin **page 215:** *left* illustration: Robert LaPointe; *top right* Tony Giammarino/Giammarino & Dworkin, architect/builder: Hamilton Mitchell & King, Inc.; *bottom right* www.davidduncanlivingston.com **page 216:** illustration: Robert LaPointe **page 217:** *top left* Mark Lohman; *top right* www.carolynbates.com, design/builder: Tom Moore, Tom Moore Builder, Inc.; *bottom* Brian Vanden Brink **page 218:** *both* Eric Roth **page 219:** *all* courtesy of Ornamental Moulding **page 220:** *both* Bill Rothschild **page 221:** *all* courtesy of Fypon **pages 222—223:** Bill Rothschild **pages 224—225:** www.davidduncanlivingston.com **page 226:** *top* www.davidduncanlivingston.com; *bottom* Jessie Walker, design: Barbara Metzler **page 227:** www.carolynbates.com, design: Milford Cushman, The Cushman Design Group, Inc. **pages 228—229:** *top left* www.carolynbates.com, design: The Snyder Companies; *bottom left* Jessie Walker, design: Adele Lampert, Page One Interiors; *center* Rob Melnychuk; *top right* www.davidduncanlivingston.com; *bottom right* www.carolynbates.com, architect: Sandra Vitzthum Architect, LLC, design/builder: Pat Pritchett, Vermont Vernacular Design **page 230:** Brian Vanden Brink, design: Custom Electronics **page 231:** *top left* www.davidduncanlivingston.com; *top right* www.carolynbates.com, design/builder: Tom Moore, Tom Moore Builder, Inc.; *bottom* Jessie Walker **pages 232—233:** *top left* www.carolynbates.com, design: Robyn W. Fairclough; *bottom left & right* Bill Rothschild **page 234:** *top* Mark Lohman; *bottom* Jessie Walker **page 235:** Mark Samu, design: Sherrill Canet Design **page 236:** *top* www.carolynbates.com, design: The Snyder Companies; *bottom* Brian Vanden Brink **page 237:** *top* Tony Giammarino/Giammarino & Dworkin, design: Sue Ellen Gregory Interior Design; *bottom* Bill Rothschild **pages 238—239:** *left* Brian Vanden Brink; *right* Mark Samu **page 240:** *top left* Jessie Walker; *top right* Tria Giovan; *bottom* Mark Samu, design: Lee Najman **page 241:** *top* Rob Melnychuk; *bottom* Brian Vanden Brink **page 242:** *top left* Mark Samu, courtesy of Hearst Magazines; *top right* Tony Giammarino/Giammarino & Dworkin, design: Marge Thomas; *bottom* Brian Vanden Brink **page 243:** Todd Caverly/ Brian Vanden Brink photos **page 244:** Brian Vanden Brink **page 245:** *top* Brian Vanden Brink, design: Martin Moore, Coastal Design; *bottom* www.carolynbates.com, design/builder: George & Buck Hubbard, Hubbard Construction, Inc. **page 246:** *top* www.davidduncanlivingston.com; *bottom* www.carolynbates.com, architect: William McClay, William McClay Architects **page 247:** Tria Giovan **page 248:** Tony Giammarino/Giammarino & Dworkin **page 249:** Tony Giammarino/Giammarino & Dworkin, design: Scott & Christopher Hoppe **page 250:** Brian Vanden Brink **page 251:** Tony Giammarino/ Giammarino & Dworkin